Christian Ethics Introduced

Christian Ethics Introduced

Religious Convictions in Secular Times

Hans O. Tiefel

☙PICKWICK *Publications* · Eugene, Oregon

CHRISTIAN ETHICS INTRODUCED
Religious Convictions in Secular Times

Copyright © 2024 Hans O. Tiefel. All rights reserved. Except for brief quotations in critical publications or reviews, no part of this book may be reproduced in any manner without prior written permission from the publisher. Write: Permissions, Wipf and Stock Publishers, 199 W. 8th Ave., Suite 3, Eugene, OR 97401.

Pickwick Publications
An Imprint of Wipf and Stock Publishers
199 W. 8th Ave., Suite 3
Eugene, OR 97401

www.wipfandstock.com

PAPERBACK ISBN: 978-1-6667-6548-9
HARDCOVER ISBN: 978-1-6667-6549-6
EBOOK ISBN: 978-1-6667-6550-2

Cataloguing-in-Publication data:

Names: Tiefel, Hans Otto, 1935–, author.

Title: Christian ethics introduced : religious convictions in secular times / Hans O. Tiefel.

Description: Eugene, OR : Pickwick Publications, 2024 | Includes bibliographical references.

Identifiers: ISBN 978-1-6667-6548-9 (paperback) | ISBN 978-1-6667-6549-6 (hardcover) | ISBN 978-1-6667-6550-2 (ebook)

Subjects: LCSH: Christian ethics.

Classification: BJ1261 .T52 2024 (print) | BJ1261 .T52 (ebook)

03/05/24

I dedicate this book to my friend Jake (John P.) Mascotte,
who has been my conversation partner about
the themes of this book for decades.
And we are still on talking terms!

Contents

Preface | ix

1. What Is Christian Ethics? | 1
2. The Biblical God and Triangular Ethics | 22
3. Christian Ethics and American Secularism | 47
4. The Social Contract | 68
5. Love and Faith | 86
6. Christian Worship and Ethics | 116
7. Human Rights | 141
8. Abortion in America | 176
9. Judgment | 209

Bibliography | 239

Preface

THIS PREFACE OFFERS SEVERAL introductions, the first of which briefly introduces the author. Subsequent paragraphs name and describe ethical concepts helpful throughout this book. To name them here: the goodness of the ordinary; the meanings of ethics and metaethics; the importance of language analysis for ethics; implications of relating "American" to "Christian"; and last, how or when moral issues begin.

THE AUTHOR

I was raised in secular cultures, in both Germany and the USA, where religion was considered to be outdated and irrelevant. Religious belief—so the popular assumption—was left behind when magic and miracles lost credibility. If there was a sense of loss, it reflected a wistful admission that something reassuring was gone, and gone for good. No one in my family or in our neighborhood was a church-goer. Churches continued to offer worship service, though not in the church building but in modest side chapels. I do not recall any expressions of hostility to Christian faith or church goers. It was simply a matter of time having left religion to the past.

I was greatly surprised, therefore, when attending a worship service simply to "find out about religion" while serving in the US Army as a young man that I was converted to the Christian faith. The experience that changed me was the awareness of being loved, surprised by love, filled by love. It was not a response to the sermon or a result of having made a decision to believe. Rather it was the awareness of being loved, so profound as to change the direction of my life! The meaning of that event was explained to me as "being born again." And the love experienced was ascribed to God's Spirit. A new vocabulary for me! When my Army enlistment ended, it was clear that whatever God intended for me would require an education. The GI Bill and savings as well as construction work in the summers paid for four years of college. After that, fellowships aided a theological education at Yale Divinity School and a PhD in religious ethics at Yale. And I still was unsure about a professional future. What eventually persuaded me was that my impatience disqualified me for pastoral responsibilities but might be forgivable in academics. My academic profession focused on Christian ethics, mostly in applied contexts such as in environmental responsibilities, in issues of warfare and in moral aspects of death and dying.

THE GOODNESS OF THE ORDINARY

Having survived the hardship years of the Second World War in Germany, the subsequent return to normal was slow. And childhood memories linger. The end of the war meant no longer having to get up in the middle of the night to shelter in the cellar. That bleak room was reinforced with logs to support the ceiling from collapsing from airborne bombings. Three houses down the street a neighbor's house had a direct hit leaving only a large pit. No one survived. Bread was eventually no longer rationed. Children were no longer sent South by rail to escape bombing raids in the industrial North. Round reinforced bomb shelters offered new peacetime uses. And the awareness grew that we had been saved through it all, saved literally. Yet surviving modern urban warfare in the 1940s and writing about it may not offer a reliable precedent. A future world war will expose countless persons to improved and more deadly weapons. The current logic that human safety lies in mutually assured destruction may be the best argument against the assurance that humans are rational beings. May the current decades of ordinary times continue far into our future.

KEY TERMS FOR THE STUDY OF CHRISTIAN ETHICS

Every academic field of inquiry creates its own specialized terms. Learning to understand and use such key terms is the price for entering a field of study. The two terms introduced here are *ethics* and *metaethics*. Ethics, the word by itself, ordinarily means normative ethics. Normative ethics provides direction and guidance about how to respond to moral/ethical issues. The capacity to detect a moral problem when it occurs is assumed here. Lacking such ability would suggest moral blindness or indifference and indicates the lack of moral sense—a troubling human deficiency. The inclusive assumption here is that humans, by nature or upbringing, can and should function morally. The ability to discern moral right from wrong tends to be included in definitions of personhood.

Metaethics adds a Greek prefix, *meta*, to *ethics*. That addition means *beyond, after, along with*. For example, a meta-text would be a text about a text. It would be self-referring. In the context of ethics, meta-ethics means reflections about the nature and functions of ethics. Christian ethics creates both a new meta-perspective as well as transformed or new responsibilities. Christian ethics constitutes the affirmation of personal faith in the life, teachings, death and resurrection of Jesus. Such faith focuses primarily on probing and practicing the love of God and humans manifested in the person and teachings of Jesus. Christians understand Christian ethics not only as being compatible with biblical traditional ethics (the dual commandments to love God and neighbor) but as fulfilling the spirit of ancient traditional laws. Christian ethics, moreover, not only affirms the spirit of ancient biblical ethics in looking to Jesus as a model of faith and ethics but relies on God/Jesus as sources of strength for fulfilling the demands of the new law taught by Jesus.

Metaethics is primarily a philosophical term. The word "ethics" by itself is also used in philosophy and usually means normative ethics. In Christian contexts, as here, metaethics is replaced by *theological ethics*. *Theological ethics* can function inclusively or widely as a worldview and, again as metaethics, it can analyze and evaluate key ethics terms probing in depth. Theological ethics begins with assuming key confessional affirmations, as a creed. Creedal affirmations then become reference points with which to interpret life theologically and morally. Christian ethics can function inclusively in that it can reason morally in decision-making as well as metaethically when it analyzes biblical assumptions or cultural practices, affirmations, values.

A key goal in theological ethics—and in any philosophy or faith—is the importance of being able to make sense of human life in a wide range of contexts (metaethics). A view of life ought to be substantial enough to provide insights into inevitable moral complexities. A metaethics or a theological ethics should be able to create coherent visions of reality. The intent is to transform complex realities into a coherent, interconnected, and manageable perspective. The Christian faith may be said to create a version of metaethics when it seeks to make human life meaningful by relating everything to the biblical God. When successful, there is something satisfactory in making sense of life as a whole. At best, everything should have a name, an identity and a place in the grand scheme of things. The attraction of metaethics/metaphysics may lie in trying to make sense of most things with common or shared denominators. More modest versions of metaethics may simply attempt to make sense of life, coherently, low-key and ad hoc. Given the complexities of modern life, the quest for coherence may remain a work in progress. Besides, the biblical moral command is not to understand the ways of God but to imitate them, as in love of God and neighbor. Such love need not insist on the ability to understand the complexities of modern life. It only needs to love God back and take its bearings from the character of God—as expressed in the consistent patterns of God's actions in creating and blessing humankind. Ordinarily, being moral need not require being smart, even if smart has its advantages.

IN PRAISE OF NAMING

Metaethics can have amazingly creative effects. It names, identifies, probes reality. Any or all reality! One thinks of early discoverers of continents: Their very words of naming bestowed identity and ownership. Naming included claiming. Legal justice relies on naming. Law judges create both the guilty and the innocent by declaration. Human couples marry and their vows in the right context transform them into husband and wife. Parents name their newborns and thereby give them the family name and family membership. We do such and more simply with naming. Creating a livable culture, establishing a meaningful world we call ours, distinguishing moral right from immoral wrong—all of which presuppose metaethics—proceed and rely on naming, identifying and relating. In short, we create our coherent and understandable world with naming. Naming has its limits, however. It may not last forever but yields to new ways of seeing and understanding. Reading old laws may amuse. Rereading our old letters may surprise and take us aback: "is that what I actually thought?!" One of the advantages or disadvantages of being married and having children is that those closest to us remember what we said and hold us to it. Yet even our best old certainties may fade or fade out. Creating a livable culture, establishing a meaningful world we call ours, distinguishing moral right from immoral wrong—all of which presuppose metaethics (a coherent worldview) proceed and rely on identifying and naming. That is how we create our coherent and understandable world. But beware of letting anyone read your old letters.

Naming can create our reality. That would be noticeable in close human relationships. In the right contexts, clergy naming will officially transform bachelors into husbands and newborns into family members. With judgments decreed in court proceedings, judges may decree citizens into lawbreakers. Or, in my case, create citizens out of aliens. Since "meta-" means "beyond," beyond ethics here, naming identifies, orders and provides a *handle* or connection with what is being named. To remain unnamed as a human being may result in dehumanization. Thus, in contexts of human slavery, some slaves were recorded as numbers rather than with personal names.

An example of the importance of naming: The inability to make sense of our world with naming can be alarming. An example of such an experience is the not uncommon experience of reality confusion when awakening in a strange place: lacking familiar reference points can elicit panic. When—in a flash—such strange place transforms into reassuring familiarity, one can breathe freely again. Theological ethics proceeds similarly in naming and thereby identifying and perhaps in claiming what is being named.

The Christian hymn, "This is my Father's world," is a form of Christian naming. This hymn is the equivalent of an early explorer naming a continent after his homeland. Except that this hymn lays claim to the whole world. Moreover, this world—read: *our* world—acknowledges the goodness and reliability of our world. The first verse of that hymn celebrates that assurance with, "I rest me in the thought." In contrast, human experience remaining without familiar reference points remains chaotic and alienating. We create names, stories, and relationships with which to ban the chaos of reality devoid of meaning. Christians have reasons for considering this world as our world and for deeming it to be good. God created the world as a blessed home for humankind. The first chapter of the biblical Genesis celebrates biblical metaethics when it declares—no less than *seven times*—that God judged God's creation to be good! The value judgment that human life is good because it is created and blessed by our good God is so direct and plain—to Christians—that it borders on a truism. Humankind is created purposefully in the image of the biblical God. That bestows status on humankind and on their claims to this world. We are not strangers to *our* God.

METAETHICS AND VERIFICATION?

One meaning of the claim that humans are rational is the quest for understanding everything. That includes the meaning of human life. Yet there may be no sure-fire verification of metaethical convictions. Some reassurance might result after having lived one's conviction for a lifetime. But that also could end ambiguously. So, if asked, we may well invoke human rational limits or offer reassurance of the dignity of the quest for the meaning of life.

The previous paragraph gives voice to the skeptic. It makes the search for existential meaning a solely human quest. In contrast, the biblical story begins with God and offers the conviction that not only did God create humankind but made humans in God's image. This "likeness" with God remains indefinite without further identification. But at least the "image of God" assures Christians that God has designs on and for us. Identifications of the "image" abound. Assuming that the biblical similarity refers to shared character, likeness may manifest itself in the human ability to love the neighbor and to respond to God's love and invitation. Since Jesus includes love of enemies (Luke 6:27), that may reduce the crowd of willing imitators. Christians may well be tested by a text that makes the divine character the model for imitation. The reader may well be tempted by such imitation requirements to postpone its advent to a resurrected life. Those who claim redemption already in and for this life may invoke the enabling presence of God to initiate an enabling resemblance here and now. At least for those of us who affirm the Christian Story, God is not a stranger to us.

NORMATIVE ETHICS

Normative ethics contrasted with metaethics insists on right or moral conduct. This ethics is prescriptive, directing human conduct, distinguishing moral right from wrong and insisting on what is right. The most obvious reason for the need of normative ethics is the fact that humans are not reliably, predictably or consistently moral. That holds for both the religious and the secular. Christian worship services begin with a confession of sins. To be sure, Augustine declared that loving God assured a natural spontaneity to do good, in which those who love God may do as they please. Perhaps Augustine may have had saints in mind. Ordinary mortals, however, secular or Christian, may not only see and respond to important facts differently but begin with different assumptions, motives and eyes.

Distinguishing between metaethics and normative ethics may be more problematic in practice than understanding the relevant definitions. Metaethics (what is or exists) and normative ethics (what should be done) are useful distinctions. Describing the facts of an issue and agreeing on what they are normally precede resolving disagreement. Agreeing on the facts and on their meaning precedes any resolution. Moreover, consensus in describing an issue or contested claim does not assure agreement in resolving the problem. The claim that facts speak for themselves, simply is not reliably true. Humans make facts speak. But it sounds better when the facts speak for themselves and the human interpretive contribution is obscured.

"Interesting" facts may be said to speak in more ways than one. But the actual speaking remains a human contribution.

Metaethics and normative ethics seem easy enough to distinguish definitionally. But when applied to resolving moral issues their definitional clarity may become opaque. For example, human slavery was generally practiced and deemed morally acceptable for centuries. But there came a time when the practice became morally questionable. At that point, the claim that metaethics was merely descriptive broke down. It became no longer possible to restrict the word "slavery" to its factual or descriptive meanings without moral or ethical overtones or coloration. The word "slavery" itself took on odious connotations—as it should have from its origin. Human slavery became no longer immune from the charge of dehumanizing persons into property. Slavery, the practice and the meaning of the word, underwent transformation. Now the word "slavery" functions as immoral for everyone. The word "slavery" became both descriptive and normative in the sense that slavery was evil and should cease.

Reality to be accessible to human understanding requires naming. Humans name reality and, in the right contexts, establish what the thing named is or shall be. Through naming clergy will officially transform bachelors into husbands and newborns into family members. With judgments decreed in court proceedings judges may change citizens into lawbreakers or aliens into citizens. Since "meta-" means "beyond," beyond ethics here, naming identifies, orders and provides a "handle" or connection with what is being named. To remain unnamed *as a human being* may result in dehumanization. As noted, human slaves could be recorded as numbers rather than personal names.

Metaethics creates, discovers and names and thereby provides bearings and makes it possible to create coherence out of chaos. The Christian hymn, "This is my Father's world," acknowledges the coherence, reliability and goodness of our world. The first verse of that hymn celebrates that assurance with, "I rest me in the thought." A world that belongs to our Father is a good and reassuring world. Christians have reasons for calling this world *our* world and for deeming it good. God created the world as a blessed home for humankind. The first chapter of Genesis celebrates biblical metaethics when it declares *seven times* that God judged God's creation to be good! Secular metaethics, by definition, lacks such personal interpretations of the origin and nature of this world. It ascribes the coherence and malleability of our world to human creative discovery. Our meaningful world reflects human ingenuity and persistence.

LANGUAGE ANALYSIS AND ASSUMPTIONS

Attention to words is a responsibility of ethics. Philosophical ethics analyzes the wording of moral/ethical terms to recognize the leading or misleading quality of words. No doubt, those who sell and advertise have long been aware that words do more than communicate and inform. Political speech writers and other wordsmiths will remain in demand. And understanding them may well require the skill of those sophisticated in demythologizing public speech and to distill "what was really said."

Language analysis reveals the importance of words. Understanding each other and making sense of the world requires a shared language. Study abroad—where English is not spoken—has been recommended for a liberal education. Naming, at least initially, is how we teach our children to speak, to learn and to find their way. As adults we do much the same, but with more sophistication. Since change in human perception and in learning tends to be gradual, we may only recognize change in ourselves when we reread old letters, newspapers or the like. Re-reading letters from years past can surprise those who wrote the letters. We may well disown our own earlier affirmations.

"Word analysis" or probing key terms at length is not unlike chemical analysis: one looks for what becomes visible only in closer perspective. Analysis may yield what was not apparent at first sight. One linguistic caution insists on being aware of the context of a word or a text. It may make a world of difference who said or wrote it. When it was said or written counts. Who and to whom it was addressed may matter. Was the speaker also the author? A friend? Were the words spoken in an official or in a private setting?

Language, while learned and acquired individually, is a social or communal invention and may teach us more than we may realize. Over time, our culture may mold us into its own image. Humans seem carried and moved by cultural tides that sweep us along. We speak the language of our times. When time hurries along, we may hasten to keep pace. But even when we intend to resist the flow, who can resist the tide? Thus, an American's self-understanding may well be individualistic. But such expressions are widely shared, social and prove to be inclusive. We may discover when traveling beyond our national surroundings that we stand out, do not blend in naturally, and are easily recognized and identified as American.

BEING AMERICAN AND BEING CHRISTIAN

American Christians may be said to have two identities—American and Christian. Both identities are precious. Or, to use Christian terms, both constitute great blessings. Given the poverty in our world, being born and being raised cannot be taken for granted. In the poorest nations poverty and hardship threaten survival. Becoming American citizens is the hope of countless refugees and was the intent of my parents in leaving Germany for the United States. Indeed, "the land of opportunity" is not a misnomer. However, becoming Christian was unforeseen and unintended. Secular cultures consider religious faith as a thing of the past.

The previous sentence may mislead. It implies that the key question about God asks whether God exists. The fact of experiencing the presence and love of God makes the question of God's existence moot. The actual questions focus on the implications of having met God. It seems as if God were standing in the door of one's life waiting to be invited in. An encounter is not an argument. But it does create implications. For one, it may question the direction of one's life. And whatever the direction, the singular "I" adjusts to the plural "we."

Trying to describe God's character—referring to coherent patterns of God acting over time –may well be misconceived. The creature describing the Creator? Yet children feel free to describe their parents. Especially when expressing gratitude and loyalty. And perhaps even complaints may prove to be manageable in a parent/child relationship. Surely mutual love will prove strong enough to sustain the relationship throughout both good and hard times.

Christian ethics relies on God's character and directions for its own bearings. The basic commandments are to love God and neighbor (1 John 4:7–21; 1 Cor 13:1–13). Christians are invited to share that pattern. Redemption, being forgiven and restored, cannot be self-created. The religious term for such restoration is *grace*—the term refers to generosity and to being forgiven. Persons experiencing the love of God may emphasize forgiveness of (their) sins. And indeed, Christian worship ordinarily begins with repentance and praying for forgiveness, for good reasons. What may well be missing and odd, however, is the *joy of being forgiven*. Perhaps relief and the need to start over set the tone and mute the relief over being able to face God again.

Being American and being Christian does not remain a simple addition. Being Christian must transform being American. The biblical God is not a tribal or national deity. Every human being is God's creation, has standing as God's child and is protectable with human rights. Human rights are secular in origin. But their protective qualities should be affirmed and welcome into Christian ethics. We hold such truth to be universal and self-evident—as a secular parallel to the Christian conviction that all humans are created in the image of God, kin to God, as it were.

A PARENTAL ANALOGY

Faith in God is a traditional Christian confession of faith. That confession implies that humans are not lords, that they belong to God in some important sense, that their individual liberty is constrained. To be sure, Christians pledge to serve God when they are old enough to know what they are doing. Nevertheless, being related to God is not only redemptive and restoring, it also obligates. Christians become responsible to God and to each other. They may not always do as they would. Of course, that holds true for being married as well. And adding children will limit one's liberty further. Surely it is true that Christians are and remain bound to God in ways similar to the bonds between husband and wife or between parents and children. Christians address God as "Our Father" (of late as "Mother" as well). Moreover, that bond or relationship lasts for a lifetime. Parents remain responsible for their children. And they use possessive pronouns: "my son," "my daughter," "my child." One hopes that God, too, uses possessive pronouns when speaking or thinking of us. These familial relationships last or should last for a lifetime, and will undergo change from close supervision to a child's maturing independence. What sustains these relationships for a lifetime is mutual love, respect, help in need. A father or a mother will celebrate a child's successes, worry when a child is ill, offer care and support when needed—as grown children will do for parents. Christians become personal when thinking or speaking of God. We speak to and with God and call it prayer. We implore and thank God and call it worship. We marvel at God's ways and call that providence. And, of course, we become impatient with God and grumble. And we incline to call that justified.

WHERE DOES ETHICS AND MORALITY ACTUALLY BEGIN?

As a prologue to Christian ethics, it may be helpful to consider where ethics, including Christian ethics, actually begins. Dictionaries describe ethics as conduct that observes and follows certain rules and principles. That can be true, but that is not where morality or ethics begin. Morality begins with the awareness that there is a problem. Ethics, whether secular or religious, actually begins with the experience that something is not right.

A visual analogy may help. On entering a room, one may notice that a picture on the wall tilts. It is not hanging straight! And it is not going to self-correct. It remains noticeable and annoying. Someone should set it straight! The similarity with morality lies in noticing that something is not right but is askew morally. Humans are blessed and burdened with a moral sense. Moral "perception" uses a visual analogy. One "sees" a moral issue. Not noticing a genuine moral problem may imply poor moral vision. Or, if noticed, no one speaks up, perhaps to avoid offending. In fact, drawing attention to a moral problem requires resolve, not to say courage. Of course, such analogy turns conscience into a moral organ of perception and judging. But conscience is not as reliable as is actually seeing. Moreover, moral wrongs require explanations and justifications. Setting a picture straight does not. The analogy remains too simple. Yet moral perceptions seem similar to seeing.

1

What Is Christian Ethics?

CHRISTIAN ETHICS MAY BE conceived as the study and practice of moral (specific) and ethical (general) meanings and implications of Christian faith. Christian faith, in turn, is a relationship with God revealed and offered in the teachings, life, death and resurrection of Jesus. The inclination to conceive of Christian faith as affirming a coherent set of theological truths or beliefs can mislead in regard to Christian faith. That faith is a personal relationship with the living God. Human personal relationships focus on connections with persons that are acknowledged, relied upon, counted on, celebrated or grieved, but as long as life lasts, they are open-ended. That is, they continue and demand mutual care and respect. And, when genuine and deep, they sustain us. Even if we are hard-pressed to describe or fully understand these personal relationships. Marriage, a pledged lifelong commitment, binds persons to each other, even if the partners would be unsure about describing just what their life together means over the span of decades. Christian faith is a lifelong commitment as well, initiated and sustained by the God who creates us in God's image and insists on sharing our lives for better or worse.

That God would be personal when it comes to relationships with human beings is good news. After all, that was the point of creating human beings in the divine image. We use family metaphors when it comes to speak about or celebrate God. It is our personal relationships—our conversations, gratitude, expression of needs, complaints, petitions, invocations, celebrations, confessions that describe and express our God-relationship.

The inclusive relationships of persons of faith with God is love: God's love for us and our love for God. For biblical believers there is the additional affirmation that a resurrection and judgment will resume and continue what God began by creating, loving and redeeming humankind.

Christians confess themselves to be loved and redeemed by God. They identify the story of Jesus, his life, teachings, ministry, death and resurrection as God's good news for humankind. They worship in Jesus' name and understand themselves to be called to live a life that witnesses to God, honors, and testifies to God's friendship for them and for all.

But why should they or anyone else study Christian ethics? What follows serves as initial answers. The most important reason for studying Christian ethics in the USA is that American Christians are Americans. That is a good thing in the sense that we belong to a people and a land that is our home. Countless refugees and would-be immigrants seek admission and asylum. In fact, my parents and I were among them in the late 1940s. Ours is a good and promising land, endeavoring to protect and promising opportunities for all.

Whether born here or becoming citizens by choice, US culture, language, laws, traditions, values—whatever makes us all into Americans—penetrates and permeates our identity. That is normal and right in that belonging forms our core and makes us into who we are. However, that also includes the risk that we assume our American ways and values to be both normal and normative. We do not readily recognize our own assumptions regarding what is good and right. Rather we tend to take them to be self-evident. No wonder academic advisors encourage a year abroad that exposes students to new perspectives. Such exposure makes us all aware that our native *take* on everything is not universal and might in fact be questionable.

The naturalizing process in which we are not just citizens but see, think, speak, and act American poses a special risk for Christians. The USA is now modern and deeply secular. We enjoy religious rights, yet the advocacy of religious social and political values—according to the rules of public expectations—should remain private and personal. To be sure, our money affirms that we trust in God. And every major political speech ends with "may God bless America." These remain mere pious flourishes! Ceremonious decorations! For decades US policy has put its faith and confidence in nuclear deterrence with nary a thought about God. The invocation of national blessings to conclude important political speech uses God for a cameo appearance. God will never have played a role in the policy parts of the speech. In politics, Christianity plays a supportive role, more supportive than critical or reforming.

Biblical traditions and faith communities, in contrast, believe in a real, that is, in a living God with critical and reforming features. This God is public and Lord of everything. This God cannot be confined to the private heart. This God holds all nations accountable. That explains why American Christians can and should find themselves with divided loyalties. In a secular nation, biblical faith cannot avoid countercultural dissonance and dissent.

The natural inclination is of course not only to avoid such conflict but to prevent even noticing it. The slogan "For God and country" can enable a patriotic blending of different loyalties. Loving both God and country may indeed be the right Christian dedication. But only in the best of all possible worlds would that be possible without cost. The phrase can reflect a certain glibness and naivete that takes for granted that our country is right, just, and great. As is! No ifs and buts. Love it or leave it!

The inclination to avoid dissonance is pronounced in public issues. Christian worship will include confession of sins. Indeed, the Lord's prayer makes awareness of sin unavoidable. The tempting solution is to conceive of the concept of sin only in personal relationships and conduct, never in political, economic, or social justice issues. That "respects" public opinion in restricting religion to personal dimensions. A merely personal version of a fallen humanity prevents the possibilities that in fact communities, nations, governments can and do sin. Not merely that they can be wrong, as in "mistakes were made," but oppressive, unjust, and deadly. "Sin," the word, has more or less disappeared except in religious settings.[1] And inventing a secular equivalent proves more elusive than expected.

Loving our country or our laws and policies must not be blind, as in see no evil . . . Christian ethics witnesses to a God who does not just judge us individually but holds us accountable as a people. Christian faith and politics therefore prove inseparable. But the analysis and evaluation of actual political priorities and decisions requires thought, judgment, and care. And if done soundly, it may not be gratefully received.

Studying Christian ethics, is necessary to learn that we are to love and obey God more than our own ways, priorities, and authorities. That takes effort, poses risks, and goes against the grain. Religious ethicists will find Paul's Letter to the Romans to be perceptive: "Do not be conformed to this world, but be transformed by the renewing of your minds, so that you may discern what is the will of God—what is good and acceptable and perfect"

---

1. Indeed, "sin" might be banned from ethics as alien: "Members of religious groups often fail to recognize that 'sin' is a theological concept, not an ethical one. ('Sin' is theologically defined)." Paul and Elder, *Understanding the Foundations*, 10. Israel's ancient prophets apparently had not heard that sin is not an ethical term (HT).

(Rom 12:2). If Paul had exercised such critical discernment in the following chapter, how differently his advice there might have turned out!

Why study Christian ethics? To become aware that American ways and God's ways may differ. And while Christians may love both, loving God first and last outranks patriotism. In fact, witnessing to God's loving justice may be the best way to keep patriotism from degenerating into chauvinism.

Another reason for studying Christian ethics is simply a more inclusive version of the problems associated with the above uncritical Americanism. In the modern Western world we all, whether religious or secular, inherit many of our own beliefs from the eighteenth-century European Enlightenment. Perhaps the most familiar is the Preamble to our Declaration of Independence: "We hold these truths to be self-evident, that all men are created equal, that they are endowed by their Creator with certain unalienable Rights, that among these are Life, Liberty and the pursuit of Happiness."

We incline to support this Declaration and to acknowledge its affirmations and its universal relevance. Yet Christians may claim it too quickly or too easily. These truths are hardly self-evident, since slaves and women had to wait centuries for equal rights. And certain minorities are still waiting. The very concepts of human rights are modern and offer no explicit biblical roots. (I shall consider human rights from a Christian perspective subsequently.) The cited Creator is something of a mystery, lacking a historical identity. Does this Creator have an active role that extends beyond an original creation? Unless the pursuit is the happiness of others rather than oneself, the biblically attested God would be excluded from sponsorship of the pursuit of happiness. Israel is called to be a blessing to the nations (Gen 12:3). Its hope lies in witnessing to God in justice and love. Only Jewish stand-up comics might speculate what Israel's ancient prophets would say about the pursuit of happiness. And Jesus was not ambivalent either: "If any want to become my followers, let them deny themselves and take up their cross and follow me" (Matt 16:24). Why study Christian ethics? To take our bearings individually and communally from the firm ground—or the Rock, as Christian hymns have it—rather than the shifting sands of secular self-evident truths.

To conclude these initial responses to the question of why one should study Christian ethics, for Christians such discipline may serve in discerning their tasks of loving God and neighbor in a secular culture. For others than Christians, such study may be instructive in analyzing and evaluating our own cultural assumptions and of how religious convictions can or should retain their integrity in the context of a secular but tolerant culture. Augustine claimed, "Love God and do as you please." The author of the Gospel according to Mark offers a more discerning and demanding guide: "you

What Is Christian Ethics?

shall love the LORD your God with all your heart, and with all your soul, and with all your mind, and with all your strength" (Mark 12:30).

PURPOSES OF CHRISTIAN ETHICS

Ethics, whether secular or religious, should serve human beings by nurturing respect, limiting harm, and making life more livable. It should make our shared lives less chaotic, more secure, better and more just. Ethics provides backup and authority for law as well as evaluating and criticizing positive (existing) laws. Ethics can offer leverage for judging whether the law serves or detracts from human flourishing. Ethics begins with parenting the young and can guide human lives in all its dimensions, even where the law never reaches. Ethics can go beyond law in offering just and promising bearings toward where we should be headed. Ethics may guide us through conflicting and confusing arguments and laws. The very ability to be moral or practice ethics is a humanizing feature, generally recognized, acknowledged and praised by liberals.

Religious or Christian ethics has the additional calling of serving and loving God in the process. Given the character of the biblical God who creates humans in the divine image, who loves, forgives, redeems and commands love of neighbor—given this God—Christian ethics has the added task of finding fitting patterns of understanding and responding to God in all relationships. A more personal way of saying the same thing, Christian ethics (and Christians) exist in relation to the living God. Whatever Christian ethicists come up with, they do so in the eyes of God. In a sense, ethics becomes an extension of worship serving and loving God. And lest that sounds too demanding, the biblical God forgives even theological sins. Some biblical texts even imply a divine sense of humor.

KEY TERMS: MORALITY, NORMS, AND METAETHICS

The following paragraphs introduce ethics vocabulary. While we all know generally what the words *morality* and *ethics* mean, it may be helpful to provide a working description less formal than dictionary definitions. These two terms are often used interchangeably. But the academic study of ethics distinguishes three distinct aspects in the general field of ethics. These are *morality, normative ethics,* and *metaethics.*

Here *morality* means specific problems, decisions and actions expressing what we owe one another. *Normative ethics,* or simply *ethics,* is a step removed from actual moral problems. Whether prior to, during or after specific decisions about what to do, one searches for norms or guides for what we owe each other. What we owe one another is normatively and generally spelled out with ethical rules, the general guidelines for ethics. *Metaethics* takes a farther step back from both the immediate problem as well as from guiding rule(s), for wider and more inclusive perspectives. Here our views of life, our beliefs and convictions shed light on the moral problem or issue and on normative rules.

Metaethics is a concept (a *concept* is the idea or meaning of a word) that is not immediately action guiding. The Greek "meta" means after, beyond, behind. One might add the term *above*, since more inclusive, and higher considerations are involved. Metaethics is the perspective that seeks insight into a grand picture of everything. In regard to humankind, for example, it asks who we are as citizens, as rational beings, as believers, as skeptics, as human beings. Metaethical concepts mentioned in this text would be the state of nature, intuited self-evident natural rights, humans as rational and social, God to whom humans are answerable.

Since the three terms—morality, normative ethics (rules), and metaethics—keep reappearing throughout this book, a visual analogy may help to understand them better. The website Google Earth adopted an image of our planet taken from outer space to initiate searches for specific earthly locations. The planet image responds to requests and turns to North America. Then it zooms in: the USA, a cluster of states, a city, a neighborhood, my street, my house, my mailbox. Amazing! And it seems surprisingly satisfying to know how our place—and in a sense we as well—fits geographically into the larger scheme of things.

The analogy for the three key ethical terms, morality, ethics rules, and metaethics, also offers nearer/farther perspectives. In the reverse sequence from Google Earth, here is what distinguishes these key terms. Morality considers moral questions in specific contexts or settings. One is as close to a moral problem as one can get. It is ours to deal with, to analyze, to resolve. Of course, most moral situations do not even raise an eyebrow. We know the applicable rule and respond accordingly. The situation only becomes interesting when there is a problem, when there is more than one relevant rule or when the one we assumed to cover the case does not fit. At that point the situation becomes an *issue*, a matter of disagreement, a problem to be resolved, a reflective moral task.

An example of a moral problem: In a year in which my wife and I still struggled to do our own tax returns, Turbo Tax was a help. Mostly. But some instructions, though written in English, remained incomprehensible. We were willing to tell the truth about our deductions, if only we knew what the instructions meant and called for. We disagreed, filled in the lines with answers to questions that we thought were asked, signed the form about being truthful, mailed the return within the deadline, and later were summoned for an audit by the IRS.

Would they summon us if we had done it correctly and honestly? What was an issue between my wife and me now became a moral problem between the IRS and us (as well as a legal and financial issue). Truth-telling, so clear and right in principle, became opaque and a matter of interpretation. And so it goes with other perfectly good rules. When it comes to resolving specific issues, unanticipated problems and new rules pop up. Such as the rule to follow directions. PS: My wife and I agreed that a tax preparer was less expensive than a marriage counselor. PPS: The invitation to the IRS review ended well for all concerned.

ETHICS RULES, AKA NORMATIVE ETHICS

Rules are akin to signposts offering general direction. Here we have some distance from an actual case because the ordinary solution, as "just tell the truth," no longer works or fits. The search is on for rules that do fit. Ethical rules, both general and specific, function as major tools for guiding moral reflection and decision. We all know the rules even though they function under different labels, as ethical principles, codes, norms, commandments. They serve similar roles, but may differ in context, standing and social or legal status.

Normative ethics, as the rule always to tell the truth, are inclusive in the sense that they apply to everyone. Not making exceptions for oneself or for someone else is part of what it means to take an ethical or moral point of view. Rules are general also in the sense that they apply to a large range of human actions. Rules derive their authority from being useful and necessary. Thus truth-telling is the cure for fake news, for misleading recommendations, for politicized national emergencies.

Commandments, religious versions of rules, originate in contexts of faith and differ from secular guides in that their origin and authority is believed to derive from God. Yet their wording and interpretation are human tasks. Religious authors may be inspired but do not take dictation from God. Even Ancient Israel's prophets, who today may be called countercultural, still reflect their times while denouncing its injustices.

The bite of normative rules, secular or religious, lies not in their general status—where we all affirm them—but in their challengeable applications. Coming up with better or more persuasive rules is a treasured skill in law, in politics, in diplomacy, and in child-raising. That also implies that the choice or invocation of rules is not self-evident or beyond question. We, humans, invent, select, cite, argue and contest the rules. We may even follow them.

METAETHICS

The initial Google Earth grand vision is literally of the whole world. The metaphorical meaning of worldview predates the outer space visual and literal use of these words. In German it is even one word, reaches beyond morality and ethics rules to a larger perspective, to a view or a philosophy of life. The negative version of metaethics, used for a view disavowed, is *ideology*. Religious versions of metaethics are named creeds. The clause "we hold these truths to be self-evident" is a patriotic metaethical declaration and assurance. Enough for clarifying each of the three basic classifications of ethics—morality, normative ethics, and metaethics.

ANALYZING WORDS

Paying careful attention to words holds true for word usage generally. Words can lead and mislead—qualities one discovers by close scrutiny of words. Such probing is designated as *word and concept analysis*. Analyzing a text calls for probing what is there, though perhaps not apparent at first sight. Considering the word or phrase in context—of time and place, of author/speaker, of intended reader or hearer—that and more may help to understand the text in depth.

We give meaning and value to the world through our choice of words. Contrary to the claim that facts speak for themselves, we make facts speak. Our naming of facts makes facts speak, interprets them, colors them, implies or leads to outcomes. Linguists, lawyers, analytic philosophers are thought to master the use, meaning and choice of key terms. Ethicists as well, whether religious or philosophical, cannot do without paying attention to the choice of words. Of course, poets should have been named first. But we relegate them to esthetics rather than ethics (here the verb leads).

Again, words can lead and mislead. Not only directly by describing what is going on, but in the sense of leading to implications and outcomes, as in evoking the hearer's or reader's responses to the text. In the examples of truth-telling in this chapter, the options of not telling the truth abound. "To cheat" condemns unequivocally. So does the legal "perjury." "Stretching the truth" seems kinder, softer, more excusable. "Dishonesty" may fit somewhere in between. There are white lies and lies in shades of black; lies to oneself as well as deceiving others. Interestingly, coming up with optional wording for truth-telling is not as easy or as pressing as seeking stand-ins for lies. Truth-telling inspires fewer euphemisms since the term needs no or less justification.

A model for analyzing key words and their concepts has venerable status as the Socratic method. Analyzing the words of others may not always be prudent or elicit gratitude, as Socrates noticed. Conceptual and linguistic analyzing involves hard work and risk of getting it wrong. As with the practice of any skill, one need not like it to benefit from it. Though it can be a solitary quest, it works better in small groups. That holds not only for joined effort but for critical corrections. Analyzing words offers the antithesis to the lecture or monologue, requires sustained effort and attention and may lack guaranteed or welcome results.

Analyzing words and concepts can surprise and frustrate. When successful, one may wonder why insight took so long, was so hard, yet seems so self-evident in retrospect. Also, one does not know when one is done. The back of the book lacks a list of analytic insights. Verifying one's analysis relies largely on consensus among participants or readers. Justification lies in understanding more after than before. One should have a better grasp. One stops when running out of energy and inspiration. Nevertheless, *analyzing words and concepts is the one indispensable skill in ethics.* That assumes that one respects the written word and devotes attention and effort to it.

One reason why analyzing the wording of ethical issues proves to be difficult is that such topics usually come already named, labeled, stamped and framed in a value laden context. The flag of contestants has already been planted on this territory. Both, issues and words, arise in pre-established or processed form. Like processed food, we are actually getting more than we thought or expected when it comes to ethical controversy. Disguised as facts, moral meaning is already built-into the data and the choice of words. Getting an analytic and critical grip on what one actually faces requires objective, sustained and deep probing. Only after we have analytically and critically made sense of what we face, can we respond to it fittingly. The sequence only looks deceptively easy: understanding what we face tends not to be self-evident, may require analysis and effort and precedes dealing or responding to it.

The deceptive aspect reveals itself as soon as we take a closer look at the text at hand. To count as an issue means that people disagree about the matter at hand. That, in turn, occurs when there is more than one way to see and respond to whatever we are trying to resolve morally. Each side, and there likely are more than two sides if it's important, has selected what it deems to be relevant facts. Even if all agree to what the facts are, their ascribed meaning to given facts may well differ. Probably more important than the role of facts are the words with which each side presents its version of the issue. The wrong choice of words may surprise and frustrate its authors. The Trojan Horse comes to mind: If you do not examine words carefully, it makes you vulnerable, serves the opposition and may defeat you.

A brief example from a medical ethics controversy: Physician assisted suicide is the practice of providing a competent patient with a prescription for medication for the patient to use with the primary intention of ending his or her own life. But the word "suicide" has conjured up negative moral and legal implications we associate with "taking one's own life." "Suicide" is the Trojan Horse that can defeat liberal reformers in their legal reform efforts of gaining voter and legislative support for "aid in dying" or "death with dignity." Avoiding leading language in this context insist on replacing the word "suicide" with more suitable or less offensive words. "Physician-assisted dying," "aid in dying," "assisted dying" all point away from the facts that such self-chosen and self-induced ending creates a choice where there was none. Nor does it hint that such a choice might be morally ambiguous. To be pro-choice about ending a human life requires caution in the choice of terms. That remains especially the case for physicians whose professional calling normally serves human life. As an afterthought, persons of faith who affirm "aid in dying" will find it difficult to justify such aid with cautious leading wording. The biblical God is a Master Linguist and has long experience in recognizing leading language.

Enough said to make at least a provisional case that analyzing moral issues is distinct from, prior to, and is as or more important than resolving the issue. In plainer words, the ethics-of-what-is going-on precedes the ethics-of-what-to-do. Seeing, understanding, analyzing a situation precedes and decisively directs reacting to it. The caution here is that nothing—including facts and words—speaks for itself. We, humans, make the world speak.

WHAT FOLLOWS IS A CLOSER LOOK AT WHY WE NEED RULES

The best thing about rules may be that they are so important that we cannot do without them. Not that we all come to that conclusion. For me that insight dawned gradually with our first child. As soon as she could crawl, we sought to make our home secure against little hands that probed everything within reach. And the single word NO!—with emphasis—was heard throughout the house. "No, don't touch that stove!" "No, not the stairs!" Having heard it so often, "no" will be one of the first words a child learns (and repeats endlessly). No doubt, protective No's become the one-syllable rule indispensable for raising babies to infants, infants to teenagers, and teenagers to young adults. Indeed there may be no end to it. Parents will find it difficult to cease, to stop with the No's, the negative spoken expression of parental care.

Growing children may be more sensitive here than parents. Teenagers tend to find parental rules annoying, brushing them off as unnecessary micro-managing. They protest with eyes rolling in helpless exasperation. This suggests that rules are easier to offer than to receive. Nevertheless, eventually surely the cycle will repeat. And the case for rules as necessary, and probably unavoidable, stands.

A pragmatic argument for the importance of ethical rules parallels the roles of technical standardizations. We expect and insist that our world be manageable and predictable. We expect that electrical plugs fit anywhere in this country and become aware of how inconvenient it is when we cannot plug in our electric gadgets elsewhere. Unless we have adapters, also standardized. In the modern world we can and must take some regularities for granted. Stop signs should have the same features everywhere. General standards prove indispensable in drug and food safety. Moral rules work analogously. Standardized ethical norms function to reduce unpleasant surprises, make behavior more predictable and safer, enable us to take reasonable behavior for granted.

This analogy misleads, of course, when it comes to *enforcing* standardized moral behavior. We put up with the rule to drive on the same side of the road and not to smoke inside. But enforcing moral conduct beyond childhood would require discerning what is morally offensive and manageably avoidable. Yet every harmful, nasty or evil deed can surely be defended with an attractive moral rule. Besides, ours is the land of the free.

Another pragmatic reason for affirming ethical rules, principles, guides for conduct is that without them, one would have to start from scratch every time that problem of what to do arises. We would not learn from experience, our own and that of others. We find it too insecure and perplexing to live in a world without signposts. Driving through traffic intersections without signs can be unnerving. And life generally works out better with certain consistent directions. We admire steadiness (of the right sort) and praise that person's character. Letters of recommendation, helpful in one's own past and indispensable for our students' future, cite patterns of responsible conduct over time. We recommend with examples of steadfastness inferring underlying moral rules, virtues and character. We infer and praise integrity and the ingrained responsibility it implies.

Occasionally we realize the importance of moral rules because they are missing. It is no longer rare to read about someone in high political office, who will not be named, who lied. Not just accidentally or mistakenly but repeatedly and boldly—with never an admission or an apology. He charged our institutional truth-seekers in the press and in law-enforcement with malicious intent in their criticism of him and with spreading fake news. He seemed unaware of Constitutional rules that separate our government into three institutions, assigning each a limited share of power and responsibility. Nor has he grasped the most important rule of democratic governing—that all in governmental service are called to serve this nation, not themselves.

Faced with what many hope is an anomaly, amoral conduct in high places alarms and puzzles us. Psychologists offer diagnoses of irrational and abnormal conduct invoking suspicions of mental illness. Others look to upbringing and conclude parental failure. Some reduce objectionable conduct to style, a move that mitigates moral objections by removing them from ethics to esthetics. And who can establish a measure or norm for style—as the proper length of dresses or the style of beards? Some see and object to the absence of moral norms but can live with the results. In politics "one cannot make omelets without breaking eggs." And if traditional moral rules be akin to egg shells, who is going to clean up the mess?

I have been using biblical texts to evaluate immoral texts and practices. It turns out that the New Testament author, Paul, had a pragmatic side. Paul's Letter to the Romans, *written under the Roman emperor Nero*, insists "Let every person be subject to the governing authorities; for there is no authority except from God, and those authorities that exist have been instituted by God. Therefore whoever resists authority resists what God has appointed, and those who resist will incur judgment. For rulers are not a terror to good conduct, but to bad" (Rom 13:1–3). Being biblical, some conservatives will see this text as timeless, flawless, and as settling the issues of political protest and resistance to immorality and amorality in high places.

A close secular parallel to Paul's peace with perilous politics appeals to a nature metaphor. The troublesome political amorality, just as the weather, is out of our hands. Nature and Government will do as they please. People may complain about both the weather and amorality in high places, but we remain powerless to change either. That holds as true even when candidates pledge reform. Spirits divide over whether such political amorality is realistic or cynical. Perhaps all might concede that acting on moral rules in politics and government proves more demanding and has wider implications than in individual irresponsible conduct. Yet political a-moral apathy appears and reappears despite the great harm that results eventually.

Moral rules count. They are good not just for children but for us all. They mitigate unpredictability, keep chaos at bay, create security, respect, and trust. Their absence in high places shocks and threatens many of us.

Making America Great Again, *MAGA* (not "Good" but "Great") may be attractive in an amoral context. But a vision of the USA as a nation set apart never implied the absence of moral rules.

Before considering some weaknesses and misuses of moral rules, the concept of normative rules deserves closer scrutiny or analysis. As noted, conceptual and linguistic *analyzing* probes the meanings, uses and implications of words. Moreover, analyzing a text should precede evaluating it, lest one judge a text without adequately understanding it.

How might one begin *analyzing* the concept of the truth-telling rule? The most noticeable assumption of this rule may be that truth telling should not be taken for granted. We may not tell the truth naturally, consistently, or reliably. Witnesses in a court of law may be required to take an oath to tell the truth—expecting that the oath itself will not be a lie since there are legal penalties for lying under oath. One metaethical implication here would be that the human word, and humans themselves, can be less than honest and trustworthy. The need for moral rules acknowledges doubt or pessimism about any human inclinations to do the right, just or good thing spontaneously without advisory prodding or threatening. While we may admire the man who assures all that his word is his bond (this does seem to be a male expression), we know better than to regard that as fail-safe.

The history of lying is ancient. The Genesis story of Creation and The Fall involves a lie. But it is the snake, not either human that lies. In tempting Eve, the snake promises a different outcome than God's warning: "You will not die; for God knows that when you eat of it [the fruit of the tree] your eyes will be opened, and you will be like God, knowing good and evil" (Gen 3:4–6). The cost of acting on that lie when knowing better included expulsion from the Garden and death—not a promising start for humankind. Insistence on truth telling, then, implies a certain pessimistic realism about human nature. The Enlightenment light of reason can fail to ignite, can flicker, but it can also illumine amoral schemes.

The rule always to tell the truth also reflects something vitally important about context. We, the human community, need to rely on each other and on our word. We are social beings. We make contracts enter covenants, make promises and long-range plans. We vote for terms of two, four, and six years. We rely on the promises of politicians for a better future, on bankers for safety of saving accounts, on the oath of office, skill and integrity of our law enforcement agencies, judges, and courts. In begetting children we assume that the world into which they would be born will be a good and safe place. Democracy itself presupposes an informed citizenry as indispensable for making informed communal decisions. Confidence in our political and government leaders erodes without trust in their veracity. Trusting and relying on each other as citizens, and generally as human beings, requires knowing and acting on the truth. We need to know the truth so that we can make good or even reasonable moral decisions. Truth-telling, then, acknowledges our social and communal identities (a metaethical claim).

What else might one conclude about the rule and role of truth-telling? If the rule is needed because we depend on and need each other individually and communally and yet we do not always reliably stick to the truth, how should we handle lies big and small? When truth-telling fails and is discovered we need ways to reassess, respond and to mend broken relationships. Insisting on the rule of telling the truth despite inclinations to lie requires reflection on what to do when we violate the rule and the persons and institutions protected by the rule. Perjury, willfully telling an untruth in a court after having taken an oath or affirmation, is a serious criminal offense. Courts punish accordingly. But what then?

While our highest government leaders may pardon offenders (one hopes for good reason), we need more inclusive readiness to pardon each other. Not all injustices can be atoned by reparations. Nor need all sleeping dogs be roused. Resurrecting harm committed decades ago may still call for admission of guilt and regret. But how can we survive without limiting and ending the harm of the past? Without the chance for forgiveness and new beginnings? Christian worship being preceded by individual and communal confession and forgiveness implies the need for analogous mending of our civic and social ruptures. Civic reconciliation presupposes and requires truth-telling in admissions more than in accusations. As one small (yet apparently inconceivable) step in this direction, might Presidential speeches and Congressional prayers end with the insertion, "May God bless *and have mercy on* America"?

Religious traditions refer to *sin* rather than *crimes*, as mentioned, the word is no longer invoked publicly in our secular culture. Sin offends not just against neighbor but against God. Biblical traditions abound with accounts and consequences of moral failures. The privacy of national leaders gets no respect when it comes to Ancient Israel's prophets or the scrutiny and judgment of the Lord. Broken relationships between humans and between them and God require confronting (truth-telling), judgment, repentance (truth confessing), and healing restoration. Where once the fear of God might have motivated civic repentance and reform, it may become clearer in our secular age that divided we fall—a pragmatic more than a moral or religious judgment. Besides, the biblical God, while once predictably stern, has been known to be rather soft on sinners. (Reflections on creedal claims of a last judgment appear in a later chapter.)

Enough of analyzing moral rules. The more discerning reader may object that the task has just begun. But other analytic efforts and scrutiny of key terms will be unavoidable henceforth. And a critique of moral rules belongs into this introduction.

PROBLEMS WITH ETHICAL RULES

Though pragmatically highly useful, mostly unavoidable, providing direction, consistency, and stability for individual and institutional responsibilities, ethical rules have drawbacks. They should come with a warning label: Toxic if misused! Again, the specific rule will be truth-telling.

My most memorable experience with being told the truth, was truth about myself in my first teaching job. A senior department member, Swiss by birth, felt obligated repeatedly to tell me the truth about myself—in German. She was right in part when she charged that my work took too much time away from my family. But she also objected to shortcomings new to me, matters that were not open to question. To be sure, beginners, including assistant professors, need help and good counsel—the supposed purpose of these dreaded imposed truth sessions. But only in a limited tone range, in small and infrequent doses, and never in German!

Again, misuse: The resolve always to tell each other the truth can seem romantic to young newly-weds (such aspirations seem age-related). Years of married life can diminish the attractiveness of such honesty. For unrelenting truth-telling may provide cover for expressing inevitable grievances, resentments, and comeuppances that we did not think of at the time. The resolve, the rule, to love each other no matter what, may well trump saying all we could say. Especially when true.

Truth-telling has been an issue in medical ethics. Patients afflicted with serious or fatal diseases press their doctors for the truth about their diminishing prospects. However, for some patients already weakened physically and emotionally, the shock of an unadorned medical prognosis might be the death of them. Yet the first medical professional rule is "Do no harm." Surely there is some space between not telling the straight-out truth and lying benevolently. Especially when medical predictions can be uncertain. More to the point, truth-telling in the practice of medicine should reflect the professional identity of physicians—a metaethical consideration—that their calling is to *care for* the sick.

A serious weakness of moral rules lies in their tendency to become ends in themselves rather than to serve human needs and flourishing. A familiar example of such inversion appears in books about lying (lying being a more interesting topic and title than truth-telling). The German philosopher Immanuel Kant insisted on the priority of telling the truth even if a murderer who is pursuing your friend (who has taken refuge in your home) is with you.[2] "To be *truthful* (honest) in all declarations is therefore a sacred command of reason prescribing unconditionally, one not to be restricted by any conveniences."[3] Following the ethical rule outranks intentionally misleading the pursuer. For "truthfulness . . . is an unconditional duty . . . which holds in all relations."[4] The rule of truthfulness "does not admit of exceptions."[5] One wonders if Kant in fact had any friends. Perhaps a late friend. And if he did, what kind of friend would Kant be? Protecting a friend from deadly assault by lying classifies as an (in-) convenience?

In an excellent book on lying, Sissela Bok defends the importance of truth-telling but does grant that some justifications warrant a lie, namely "where innocent lives are at stake, and where only a lie can deflect the danger."[6] Surely she is right. For rules should serve humans without becoming ends in themselves.

In religious traditions, textual moral injunctions abound. For example, the Pentateuch, the first five books of the Bible, is labeled "Law." And there is no shortage of laws in those books. However, these books could have been named as Beginnings or The Chosen People. Their designation as Law is not self-evident but reflects the importance of following God's commands. New Testament writers reaffirm the ancient texts. In the Sermon on the Mount Jesus cites traditional commandments and intensifies them as in a new law (Matt 5–7). The letters to young churches as well offer practical instructions (rules) of how to resolve communal tensions and to serve God and neighbors in the advent of the Kingdom of God. Given such importance of laws and of obeying the Law, what is taken as the successful obedience to law can tempt the faithful to claim recognition and standing before God and humans. *Works-righteousness* is the deadly label applied and rehearsed in the Protestant Reformation and in evangelical churches. This pessimistic insight is of course ancient. Paul writes in his letter to the Romans: "For 'no human being will be justified in his [God's] sight' by deeds prescribed by the law, for through the law comes the knowledge of sin" (3:20). If pride be the first or original sin—"you will be like God" (Gen 3:5)—it manifests itself here in the responses to the new law as well. There is nothing essentially

---

2. Kant, "On a Supposed Right to Lie," 611–15.
3. Kant, "On a Supposed Right to Lie," 613.
4. Kant, "On a Supposed Right to Lie," 614.
5. Kant, "On a Supposed Right to Lie," 615.
6. Bok, *Lying*, 45.

wrong with most biblical laws as such. It is their misuse for self-justification that elicit their religious condemnation. Acceptable uses of law would instead call for gratitude for God's guidance and repentance for falling short.

A low-key or more modest version of using God's law for gaining religious standing is the notion that all that God asks of us is a decent life. No scandals, no run-ins with the law, no divorce, no mistreatment of others, no supererogatory ambitions. Some of the Ten Commandments might be invoked here: no misusing God's name, no theft, no adultery, no perjury (Exod 20). The selective connection is with God's law but not with the living God. The command to love God in worship and in a transformed life fades out to be replaced by a respectable moralism.

A different misconception of religious law is that one cannot be moral without being religious. Yet God's generosity when it comes to distributing virtues of wisdom, charity, compassion, and a profound sense of justice disregards *religious affiliation*—to use the jargon of religious questionnaires. That includes "none of the above." The upside of this, in addition to divine generosity, lies in enabling believers to learn from the secular.

Another pervasive problem with relying on moral rules: Rules conflict with each other. That is when they become interesting. Assuming that such conflict is self-evident, one needs a rule for prioritizing rules. For biblical believers, the rules commanding love of God and of all neighbors can serve as the anchor and denominator for all other commandments and rules. "You shall love the LORD your God with all your heart, and with all your soul, and with all your might" (Deut 6:5). And "you shall love your neighbor as yourself" (Lev 19:18).

The latter rule prevents Kant's prioritizing truth-telling over saving an innocent human life. How would one face God with Kant's enacted conclusion? Did Kant attend worship? How would one face the next of kin of the friend betrayed? (I do admit that these last sentences are leading. Even the best of lies—best in a moral sense as excusable, benevolent, ethically preferable—still come at a price of trust and reputation. Retrospective explanations may mitigate these costs. Those deceived may even be willing to rename the lie as patriotic or as whatever the higher good was that trumped truth-telling. But a price remains.)

None of the above misuses or problems of moral rules deny that we need and rely on ethical rules. My point is rather that moral rules are *necessary but not sufficient*. Their insufficiency lies not primarily in the weakness and misuses of rules and laws described. Rather it is their *impersonal* quality. Rules may speak—we make them speak—so that they have a voice, as it were. But they have no eyes. They are not personal. Yet what we owe each other as Christians and as citizens is personal. And that lies beyond the reach and enforcement power of rules and laws. These personal qualities include attention, respect, consideration, friendship, help. In short, biblical believers are called to love all neighbors. In doing so they reflect the character of God, manifest a likeness with God, and act in God's image. Here lies the heart of Christian ethics: *actively reflecting the character of God*. And the only one who can rightly command that (command, but not enforce!) is God.

Why should the lack of being personal make ethical rules questionable in the context of religious faith? What does that claim even mean? Moreover, members of Abrahamic religious communities insist that God *is* personal. Yet since God is not accessible to humans in terms of seeing, touching, hearing (Moses being the exception), what would God being personal mean? And how would that be relevant for ethics? The rest of this chapter focuses on these questions.

My use of the word "personal" excludes the meaning of *private,* as in *a personal matter.* With dictionary help, it means "existing as a person, not as an abstraction or thing."[7] That shifts the task of understanding our use from "personal," to "person." When applied to God, as in *a personal God,* one ascribes the characteristics of a person. In a modern context, formed by the Enlightenment, that means a rational, self-conscious and volitional being relating meaningfully with other persons. However, such definition may not even do as adequate meaning for the persons who love us and whom we love. Would friends recognize each other in such terms? Would any personal relationship be fittingly described with such words? These modern definitions seem too modern, too rational, too deficient, too impersonal, too weak, too alien to those who have experienced, confess and serve the living God. For Christians (and surely for Jews and Muslims) something less modern, more timeless, more religious, more loving, and more personal is required when it comes to God.

The biblical God is personal. Rules are not. I begin with a contrast. The absence of personal qualities when it comes to deities or their equivalents is striking in philosophical writings. As best I know, philosophical references to God do not use personal pronouns. That may be explained by the fact that the only personal pronouns we have: *he, she* or *it,* imply gender or serve as impersonal references. Or it could be that if philosophers were to use *he* or *she,* such usage would imply a personal relationship with the deity. God forbid! And it is not just pronouns that might mislead, the nouns offered here require cautious ingenuity to remain impersonal. The search for suitable terms avoids any specific religion, since that might imply a preference. Terms for philosophical renditions for a deity include *Omnipotent*

---

7. S.v. "personal" (adj.) in Thompson, *Concise Oxford Dictionary.*

or *Omniscient Being, Ultimate* or *First Cause, Ground of Being, Supreme Being, das Sein an sich* (German for*"Being in itself).* When theologians speak this impersonal language one finds *"That than which nothing greater can be conceived"* (Anselm) or *"The Ground of all Being"* and faith or religion as *"ultimate concern"* (Paul Tillich).

God help us! As best one can tell, these stand-ins for God are not on speaking terms with humans, offer no covenants, do not love and seek no love, command no ethical or religious imperatives, do not call for repentance from us, remain indifferent to human needs, suffering, and prayer. These are not personal names and signify no more personal qualities than the weather or the lottery. It makes sense to ask whether we know or can know if such entities are alive or whether they are hypothetical and abstract philosophical exercises. And, of course, they are not idols. Idols offer more.

The God of Israel and of the Christian church is the living counterpart to the above recitation of fictional impersonal characteristics. The biblical God is a Person with a history, with identity, character and will. (One can only refer to this God in the third person as "he" or "she." So one either replaces all personal pronouns with "God," opts for one of the two personal pronouns with an apology and excuse, or resorts to pseudonyms such as "Lord," though they may not be gender-neutral either). The psalmist makes the point that God is personal ever so simply, "O taste and see that the LORD is good; happy are those who take refuge in him" (Ps 34:8). Tasting and being convinced—reminds me of Churchill's remark that the proof of the pudding lies in eating it. Churchill might well have been a better theologian than those who formulated so-called proofs of God's existence.

The theme, again, is that the biblical God is personal. Almost every verse in Ps 34 makes that point. The New Testament parallel to Ps 34 could be Jesus' Beatitudes (Matt 5:3–12). Such verses may not only be read, rehearsed, studied. They may be sung. As in the vocal celebration of a generous and gracious God. Singularly or communally; liturgically or congregationally; with choirs and musical instruments. In time the best such may become hymns. Such singing may be the religious equivalent of love songs. How much more moving than spoken prose, how much more personal! Would one ever sing praises to the Ground of all Being? If our seeing can reflect our soul, our singing can express our hearts. Such singing can be one way of loving God *with all our heart* (Deut 6:5). This is being personal with God. It responds fittingly to God's prior creative, redemptive, personal and loving presence.

To my surprise, I find that there is something amiss here in my trying to describe the personal qualities of God. It seems presumptuous of me, for the task implies that one knows God well enough to offer a faithful rendition—faithful in the sense of *accurate*. While God is personal, God also is holy. The verification of God's personal character is the experience of the encounter. There is no proof of God or of God's character except tasting, meeting, being surprised, overjoyed, transformed by God. Praising God proves more fitting than describing. I stop here. But how to speak about Christians ethics without pointing to our God?

BACK TO ETHICS RULES: RULES ARE NOT PERSONAL

My aim is to question the primary role of ethics rules, good rules, between each other and between God and us. Perhaps I can make my point in regard to a human-human relationship before trying to make sense of our relationships with God. When my son was old enough to drive, he drove too fast, was ticketed, and had to appear in court. I forget whether he asked me to accompany him or not. But I thought about it. Briefly. Was it better to let him face the judge alone, swim or sink? Tough love is said to have its merits. Was there an ethical rule for such a question? Surely there was, since such rules prove ever so adaptable. What made for the resolution turned out to be immediate and convincing: This is my son; I am his father. And fathers stand by their sons. No matter what. How simple! One might phrase that as an ethical rule in retrospect. But for me, our very relationship, our identity—a metaethical conviction rather than normative/ethical rule—settled it. Rules were preempted or co-opted.

I believe that something analogous holds for the God-human relationship. God's identity, God's character experienced and attested by humans over time, can trump ethical rules and ancient commandments. How might one know and justify such a claim? Dietrich Bonhoeffer, a German theologian and member of the Confessing Church (Bekenntniskirche) during the Nazi era, became a member of the group plotting to assassinate Hitler. Of course, he knew and affirmed the commandments to love and not to kill the neighbor. So how could he justify regicide—if that be the right term for what the Nazis called treasonous murder? Bonhoeffer wrote about falling into the spokes of the wheel of state that was crushing the innocent. He understood himself and his fellow conspirators to be resisting genocide at the risk of their lives. He might have explained more. But his role was discovered, he was condemned to death and executed. In retrospect, he is honored as one of the few martyrs.

I take Bonhoeffer's attempt to kill Hitler to be an expression of compassionate intercession that trumped God's commandment. He would not have joined the plot without showing it to God. I do not know but suspect that Bonhoeffer concluded that God would endorse the plot by suspending God's own, "You shall not murder" (Exod 20:13). If so, it holds that in extremis God can and will trump traditional ethical and religious rules. Rules do not have the last word. Discerning love does.

A caution: Appealing to God for acts that contradict good ethical and religious rules can be highly questionable and worrisome. "God made me do it" or "God told me to do it" sounds like an insanity defense. And as best I know Bonhoeffer would *not ever* have said anything like that. He was a Lutheran. That means that he was schooled in guilt. But he also a relied on forgiveness as God's conclusive word and act.

A provisional conclusion: Thank our parents, our teachers, our laws, our ancestors, our God for good ethical rules! They protect us, make life more manageable and predictable, prevent chaos. They confirm themselves over time by their pragmatic value. When missing we take steps to protect ourselves. In short, we cannot do without them for long. But good rules should not always have the last word. And sometimes they should not even be invoked. But there are two exceptions: loving God and loving neighbor. For persons of faith, our moral responsibilities anchor in what is not man-made, in God's character, will, and presence. By contrast, we create rules (even in religion); God creates us. God lives; rules do not live except when we give them life. God loves; rules only command. God forgives; rules demand but do not pardon. Rules can be made-to-order; God cannot be manipulated.

2

The Biblical God and Triangular Ethics

IT ALL BEGINS WITH GOD

CHRISTIAN ETHICS TAKES ITS bearing from biblical religion and expresses Christian faith. The New Testament offers the origin and meaning of Christian faith. Indeed, Christianity remains bound by birth to Ancient Israel and Judaism and to the texts of the Hebrew Bible or the Old Testament. Christians claim that the God who spoke to ancient Israel was revealed uniquely and decisively in the Jew Jesus, whom Christians acknowledge as the Messiah or savior of humankind. In both Hebrew/Jewish and in Christian scriptural texts *it all begins with God*. These are not the stories of humans searching for God—the cultural anthropocentric or human-centered sequence in which everything begins with human initiative. Rather, the biblical God initiates, meets, confronts, calls human beings. That biblical sequence is expressed in the title of a book on the philosophy of Judaism, *God in Search of Man*, by Abraham Joshua Heschel.

It is God, un-invoked, who commands Abram to "Go from your country and your kindred and your father's house to the land that I will show you" (Gen 12:1) and binds himself to this man, his wife, and their descendants in covenantal promise (Gen 12:2–3; 15:18–21). The same Lord hears the groaning of Hebrew slaves in Egypt, surprises Moses with a burning bush, and addresses him by name (Exod 3:1–4). This God initiates covenants, calls and enables prophets, baptizes Jesus with the divine Spirit (Mark 1:1–11), blesses those who hunger and thirst for righteousness (Matt 5:6), so loves troubled humans as to sacrifice an only child thereby to reconcile a fallen and alienated humankind with its God (John 3:16).

THE BIBLICAL GOD IS PERSONAL, JUST, LOVING

Biblical traditions and Abrahamic religions refer to God with personal metaphors and pronouns. Both the initial divine approach to humans and the responses are personal, as speaking, being spoken to and replying implies. While hearing and seeing can remain detached and indifferent, when the biblical LORD "hears" the groaning and cries of slaves (Exod 3:7) and "observes" the misery of this people, it is with the intervening perception of a mother or father. "Indeed, I know their suffering, and I have come down to deliver them from the Egyptians, and to bring them up out of that land" (vv. 7–8.). This Person speaks and hears, blesses, demands and commands, judges, forgives, heals. The human responses as well include the range of universally familiar personal reactions. The psalmists thank, petition, praise, implore, invoke the presence of God. Israel's prophets not only obey God in preaching the divine word but argue, complain, accuse, and seek to change God's mind.

Almost all of the roles, metaphors, and qualities ascribed to God in biblical traditions assume the *personal nature of God*. Whether father, creator, lord, bridegroom, judge, redeemer, warrior . . . these are the roles and functions of persons. And the one personal characteristic that underlies them all—even in the harshest encounters—is love. God commits God-self in covenant-making and by inviting humans to make covenant commitments in turn. Describing the range of loving relationships—from joy and delight to jealousy and anger, from pleasure in the moment to impatience over time, from turning toward to turning away—every human aspect or version of personal and loving relationships, seems to find expression in some biblical text as characteristic of God's love. Two specific biblical examples of love from God's side shall suffice.

The Prophet Hosea proclaimed fierce scenes of judgment against an idolatrous and oppressive people. Nevertheless, in the midst of the harshest prophetic and therefore divine denunciations, one finds this "and yet":

> I led them with cords of human kindness, with bands of love.
> I was to them like those who lift infants to their cheeks.
> I bent down to them and fed them. (Hos 11:4)

> How can I give you up, Ephraim?
> How can I hand you over, O Israel? . . .
> My heart recoils within me;
> my compassion grows warm and tender. (Hos 11:8)

The Gospel according to John, despite its cosmic prologue, offers deeply personal language when it describes Jesus' relationship with believers: Not only the Spirit of God "abides with you and he will be in you" (14:17), but Jesus himself as well as God will be present and love the disciples:

> I will not leave you orphaned; I am coming to you. In a little while the world will no longer see me, but you will see me; because I live, you also will live. On that day you will know that I am in my Father, and you in me, and I in you. They who have my commandments and keep them are those who love me; and those who love me will be loved by my Father, and I will love them and reveal myself to them. (14:18–21)

That God should indeed care puzzled ancient Israel and continues to astound the faithful.

> It was not because you were more numerous than any other people that the LORD set his heart on you and chose you—for you were the fewest of all peoples. It was because the LORD loved you and kept the oath that he swore to your ancestors, that the LORD has brought you out with a mighty hand, and redeemed you from the house of slavery, from the hand of Pharaoh king of Egypt. (Deut 7:8–9)

That begs the question of why God should care in the first place. Nor was the reason any moral superiority (Deut 9:4–7). Biblical believers lack explanations that would make sense by finding reasons for God's love in the qualities of the beloved. One simply begins with God's love. "O give thanks to the LORD, for he is good; for his steadfast love endures forever" (Pss 106:1; 136).

Of similar importance for biblical ethics as the claims that God is personal and loving is the conviction that *God is good*. Not only good in the sense of the psalmist's text just cited, good as in good-to-be-loved-by-God, but good in the moral sense, as in good-and-just. Since the words "ethics," and "ethical" derive from Greek rather than Hebrew one will not find them in biblical texts. Instead, key biblical terms for God's character are "good," "righteous," and "just." The very notion of God as caring or loving already includes a moral dimension. In contrast to the loves of the Greek pantheon of gods, the steadfast love of the biblical God has a moral quality. The community of the faithful can count on it over time: "O Give thanks to the LORD, for he is good; for his steadfast love endures forever (Pss 106:1; 136:1 and throughout). The Psalms explicitly join moral qualities with divine love through poetic parallels (in which the second stanza amplifies the first): "He loves righteousness and justice; The earth is full of the steadfast love of the LORD" (Ps 33:5).

This biblical moral quality of God is not identified with strict even-handedness or impartiality—qualities implied in representations of blindfolded Justice holding both a scale and a sword. The justice of God is only impartial in the sense of being incorruptible. The biblical God sees and sides with the oppressed and other losers: "The great God, mighty and awesome, who is not partial and takes no bribe, who executes justice for the orphan and the widow, and who loves the strangers, providing them food and clothing" (Deut 10:17–18). So also the psalmist: "The LORD works vindication and justice for all who are oppressed" (103:6). Given ubiquitous human oppression, the moral character of God expresses indignation: "God is a righteous judge, and a God who has indignation every day" (Ps 7:11). Moreover, an even-handed justice misleads since God's justice inclines toward mercy. "Gracious is the LORD, and righteous, our God is merciful" (Ps 116:5). The prophet who calls a people to justice also appeals to divine mercy: Therefore the LORD waits to be gracious to you; therefore he will rise up to show mercy to you. For the LORD is a God of justice; blessed are all those who wait for him (Isa 30:18).

LINGUISTIC TRANSFORMATIONS

The personal and moral qualities ascribed biblically to God exert a remarkable effect on key ethical words. Always metaphorical when used of the Holy One, words undergo moral transformation by being linked with God. Rather than justice and mercy seeming mutually exclusive, a just God moves justice toward mercy. Human or legal justice subsequently may be measured by a new standard. God's love both redefines and throws new light on what love and justice should mean. Analytic philosophers insist on attention to words: the very nature of ethics can be shaped by the meaning of key ethical terms. That holds for religious ethics as well: the very nature of ethics and of justice may be transformed by the metaphors ascribed to this personal, just and loving God. Their ascription to God transfuses ordinary words with new meaning and can make them ethically extraordinary in the sense of becoming normative for what human justice *should* mean.

This *linguistic transformation* of moral vocabulary offers a believer's response to the Socratic challenge about the good: does God command the good because it is good or is it good because God commands it? That ancient poser seems a surefire winner for the secular critic. For if God commands an action—as the love commandment—because it is good, one assumes that something higher and better than God exists that guides God and should guide humans. This might be an ideal, a concept that exists independently of God. On the other hand, if it is good because God commands it, a divine-command concept of ethics, then God risks being capricious. Adopting this option would mark believers as less than autonomous rational beings, simply doing blindly what they are told. Seemingly unaware of the implied self-criticism, the logic of the bumper sticker insists, "God said it. I believe it. That settles it."

If, however, believers' relationship with a personal God conceptually transforms key ethical words, as I have claimed—one hesitates to invoke "verbal baptism"—a certain linguistic conversion does occur. It would not be flippant to explain that believers learn new meanings of key ethical words in their relationship with God. The contexts for such transformations may be worship as well as biblical and liturgical traditions. Persons of faith learn what "loving," "good," and "just" really mean in being loved by God who is both just and merciful. Here as in so much of ethics attention to words proves indispensable.

A linguistic clue to Christian conceptions of God lies in analyzing how God is addressed. Both French and German have two personal pronouns, one formal and the other informal. Strangers are addressed formally, family and friends informally. Children may get confused in conversations with strangers. Addressing God, one would think, requires due respect and formality. Yet in German, God is not a stranger but is addressed as "Du," not with the formal "Sie." The French language is said to undergo a similar switch to "tu" from "Vous." The English "thou" in addressing God now seems ancient and unduly formal. Assuming that God is Creator and Lord, one would think that only *Sie* would do. Nevertheless, German prayers use the informal address. One assumes that God is not offended and remains on speaking terms with those who call on God's name informally.

MISCONCEPTIONS OF GOD?

In a secular culture one should not assume that the meanings of the word "God" remain generally shared and clear. Several contemporary uses or meanings of "God" prove to be incompatible with biblical assumption or with texts that describe God's character as loving, good, or just. Indeed, the conviction that God is conceived as a person rather than a force (as radiation or magnetism) cannot be assumed. The basic conviction that God hears and responds to human prayer, that is, that God is personal, may have faded for many. And if the personal meaning of the divine name is lost, so is awareness of the love and mercy of God.

The God of Israel and of the church is not the Unmoved Mover, First Cause, Ultimate Ground of Being—the preferred impersonal language of philosophers (those who still have an interest in religious concepts). These abstract words resist personal coloration and life. The biblical God is certainly a person; philosophical *Being* or *The Good* certainly are not. Despite the *Star Wars* movie's generic benediction, "May the Force be with you!," such an impersonal deity does not bless and does not respond to human suffering, prayer, pain and death. In contrast, the God of biblical traditions speaks out of a burning bush, calls and wrestles with a man, leads a chosen nation out of slavery, groans over a wayward people, becomes human, lies in a cradle, and suffers on a cross. To speak of God abstractly in words detached from time, place, or persons, with words other than those that form the web of human life, loses sight of the Lord of Israel and of the church.

To be sure, biblically based communities of faith also confess that the LORD transcends any conceptual human grasp. For example, the biblical appellation "the Holy One" points to God, as it were, while averting one's eyes. Such pointing describes the otherness of God. It bespeaks fear of divine grandeur too mysterious to fathom and too great for any human to witness and survive. Nevertheless, though aware of the holiness of the biblical God, of divine transcendence or otherness that precipitate human awe and fear, though ascribing to God cosmic creativity and universal concern with all living beings, the Holy One is still a personal presence. Even if God transcends human naming, this God is more than the "power that bears down upon us." The biblical God is a Father, Mother, Redeemer, Savior, Lover who seeks out children created in the divine image—kin of God all. To cite the amazement of the psalmist, "what are human beings that you are mindful of them" (Ps 8:4)? The parallelism or second part of that verse offers a stronger word than the bland *mindful*: "[what are] mortals that you care for them?"

Raising the question of whether there is a personal God cannot be resolved by offering character descriptions. That merely focuses on what or who God is. Proving the existence of God may not have become crucial before the Age of Western Enlightenment. None of the proofs works. Besides, such efforts condescend. The biblical and historical God attest to him- or herself (even personal pronouns resist getting a grip on God). God attests to God-self. God takes the initiative in confronting, addressing, commanding, blessing and redeeming humans. The nature of the divine confrontation with humans is life-transforming. And the experience speaks for itself: "O taste and see that the LORD is good, happy are those who take refuge in him" (Ps 34:8).

WHY BEGINNING WITH GOD IS IMPORTANT

The first two pages of Chapter One began with the concept of God. This chapter presents a more extensive introduction to the identity of the biblical God. Contemporary American secular culture resists the very notion of a living, active, loving and moral divine presence—who calls nations to account and cannot be reduced to a mere ingredient of private piety. A secular nation, by definition, avoids religion, except to add ceremonial dignity to special occasions. Despite the naive but popular claim, America is not a Christian nation. That holds even if religious blessings may be invoked on exclusively secular and political decisions. Separating church and state should exclude state support of religion. That should not be interpreted to mean that God becomes a private deity without a public and political voice. The biblical Lord is the God of nations, not the Roman household god, private and compatible with political idolatry.

The thought of looking to God for ethical bearings in secular and political dimensions now strikes many Americans as odd. It is rarely a topic for sermons and will only deserve an honorable mention when invoking God's blessing on America. Relating religious faith to public policy and politics threatens to alienate church members from each other. Here the options of Christian ethics are constrained. Political differences can evoke religious disagreements. Pastoral and pragmatic concerns incline to avoid disruptive ethical issues. (The meaning of *issues* is *matters on which people disagree*.) Yet Christians cannot leave God out of any dimensions or sphere of human life. The biblical God is the Lord of nations whom Jews and Christians are called to serve, in all dimensions or spheres of life.

The real and present God may make a moral difference in any or all dimensions of life, including social policy and politics. Similarly, as I shall argue more explicitly in the section on ethics and worship, God's scrutiny makes a difference in discerning and judging what is right or wrong in small things or in great. Whatever Christians decide morally, the results will have to be shown to God. And therefore beginning (and ending) with God makes sense for believers in matters of what to think and what to do in both private and public contexts. How to do that in depth as well as in charity may border on the miraculous. Taking a stand on vital but controversial issues seems expected of theologians and church leaders. It is when such issues reach into local church discussions that they can become incendiary and divisive.

HUMAN RESPONSES

In biblical texts, God initiates the relationship with humans. While it all begins with the downward or vertical move (if God be *up*), this encounter calls for human response. A psalmist's poetry offers a response of gratitude and praise:

> O God, you are my God, I seek you, my soul thirsts for you; my flesh faints for you, as in a dry and weary land where there is no water. So I have looked upon you in the sanctuary, beholding your power and glory. Because your steadfast love is better than life, my lips will praise you. So I will bless you as long as I live; I will lift up my hands and call on your name. My soul is satisfied as with a rich feast, and my mouth praises you with joyful lips when I think of you on my bed, and meditate on you in the watches of the night; for you have been my help, and in the shadow of your wings I sing for joy. My soul clings to you; your right hand upholds me. (Ps 63:1–8)

Responses in a less celebratory tone are also easy to find. Abraham disagrees with God over the fate of Sodom and Gomorrah (Gen 18:16–33): "Will you indeed sweep away the righteous with the wicked? Suppose there are fifty righteous within the city; will you then sweep away the place and not forgive it for the fifty righteous who are in it" (vv. 23–24)? The LORD—reminded of his own character by this feisty bargainer—is finally persuaded to reduce the saving remnant from fifty to ten. Human argument can change God's mind—a biblical rebuttal to secular cynicism!

This is a God with whom one can argue. And no one does that more consistently than Moses. He may initially have hidden his face, being "afraid to look at God" (Exod 3:6), but undaunted he raises one objection after another to being sent to Pharaoh: the English text offers "but" four times before he runs out of excuses (Exod 3–4). Less successful in arguing with God than Abraham, Moses finally simply begs off: "O my Lord, please send someone else" (Exod 4:13). Running out of patience, God insists and Moses goes. One thinks not of a voluntary and rational choice but of a parent-child argument. Here the parent has the last word.

THE SCOPE AND NATURE OF CHRISTIAN FAITH

In a secular culture, the world is secular. Secular majorities have certain advantages, beginning with numbers. More importantly, the secular see a different world than believers. They see "our world" with different eyes.

Without a religious upbringing, experience or conversion, the known world reasonably remains devoid of divine presence. Seeing is believing. And not ever seeing or hearing or tasting God, the universe remains self-evidently godless. It then makes reasonable sense to leave God out of it, even if echoes of a religious past still linger. Secular cultures tend to delete or seek to eradicate religion from the present by consigning it to a distant past, to an otherworldly future, or to an inner and private self. In a democracy, tolerance should rule. The secular and the religious can be good neighbors. However, engaging in public policy issues reveals diverging perspectives, assumptions and convictions.

By contrast, biblically focused faith sees with different eyes. It focuses on a present God who creates, loves and claims all of life. When remembering rightly, biblical believers confess a living God who is personal and nearer than hands or feet but also calls nations to account. Biblical morality means being responsive and responsible to this living God—with every heartbeat and in every dimension of life. For biblically-grounded faith, all of reality is religious. No dimension of life remains either external to it or autonomous. And the challenge of Christian ethics is discerning and fittingly responding to the diverse suffering and needs revealed by the human condition.

Self-evident to believers in traditional settings, just what reasons support the modern claim that for the eyes of faith everything is religious? Responding to that question from the side of God, as it were, biblical texts referring to God as Lord of all offer a partial answer (Josh 3:11; Ps 97:5). The very nature of God as loving and moral, seeking justice and human reforming response, resists encapsulating faith in any dimension or sphere of life. Divine character traits are not a limited or sometime thing. Divine caring is ongoing and all-inclusive. From the human side, the command to love God is inclusive as well: "with all your heart, with all your soul, and with all your might" (Deut 6:5). Believers are warned against divided loyalties in not being able to serve two masters (Matt 6:24; Luke 16:3). Christian faith affirms that "In him we live and move and have our being" (Acts 17:28). That transforms everything in the name of God. Believers see reality as religious because their vision has been transformed by the living, personal, and present God.

Seeking to make sense of the world surely is a universal task for humankind. That becomes a theological and ethical obligation for Christians and Jews. That task has implications and features that are not always self-evident or just. Citing a biblical text or offering religious justification for clarifying or resolving complex issues may reveal where the speaker "is coming from." Religious claims tend to go against the secular grain. While cultural secularism is tolerant of religious commitments in principle, in practice it prefers that religion remain personal and private. For the secular, the appeal to religious reasoning in public and political controversy remains alien, unreasonable and unfair. Political and social issues, the common good seems too important to leave to "religionists."

Modern reproductive technology provides an example. Federal support and legal control of embryonic stem cell research remains controversial. Embryonic research endangers its subjects. But embryos and fetuses have no legal standing. In the US being a legal person begins at birth. Lacking legal rights, human embryos and fetuses may become expendable and unprotected. Even the naming of the lives involved differs: are these human "products of conception" or "the human unborn"? Cultural secularism or biblical faith may identify and judge this issue in controversial ways. Continuing with another aspect of this issue, appointment of members to national bioethics commissions—the entities created to advise president and Congress on new bioethics issue—must choose prospective members prudently. To acknowledge the secular critic, such inclusion should aspire to *reasonable persons* who can think in wider than sectarian terms and will not impose outdated religious idiosyncrasies on a wider public (intentional leading language!). Here "reasonable" and "religious" may conflict. "Reasonable" tends to be defined flexibly or à la mode, in the fashion of the day.

RELIGIOUS OR SECULAR RESPONSES

In a secular context, biblical religion is not just countercultural in affirming a real and personal God, it is pre-modern in describing and understanding this God-human relationship in communal rather than in exclusively individualistic terms. While texts may refer to key individuals in Israel's and the church's traditions, the context for these stories are communities of faith. Abraham and Sarah are the progenitors of a people. Moses leads the slaves out of Egypt and becomes a lawgiver for a people for all time. Ancient Israel understands itself as a people of God serving as light to the nations (Is.49:6, 42:6). The Christian church inherits that communal focus and regards itself as the body of Christ (1 Cor 10:16; 12:27).

The Bible is always the story of a people. Biblical scriptures assume that the moral life is never just a matter of individual character and conduct. Rather, such texts remain communal. They are to be located in and held accountable within the faith community. That community in turn is called into being by the graceful activity of God. And it is through the life and witness of the community that individuals are related to God and seek to understand the implications of their faith for moral life in all contexts.

A HISTORICAL CHANGE OF PERSPECTIVE

Biblical and medieval communal self-understanding contrasts with Enlightenment individualism. René Descartes' well known beginning point for all knowledge is familiar philosophically. Willing to doubt everything—sense impressions, tradition, philosophy, religion—in order to test all for its rational reliability, the father of modern philosophy concluded that the one conclusion he could not doubt is that he exists: I think; therefore I am. No doubt a toothache may have yielded even stronger proof. For biblical believers, the starting point of all that counts and can be known is not the doubting, skeptical self but is personal, relational and communal. Rather than the skeptical self, it begins with God, and the communities of Israel and of the Christian church. Specifically, it is the self-revelation of the Lord of Israel and of the church that becomes the self-identifying starting point and focus that calls Christians into a transformed and renewed existence. While Christians may continue to have doubts about themselves, God's love is assumed, even if not always discerned. A Cartesian (à la Descartes) parallel motto for biblical religion would be: We are loved, therefore we are. The Christian contrasts include: community rather than individual; awareness of God rather than self-awareness; awareness of being loved rather than self-focused or self-absorbed; religious rather than secular.

THE ETHICAL LANGUAGE AND LOGIC OF BIBLICAL RELIGION

This as well as the first chapter began with an introduction to the biblical God. Jews and Christians look to biblical texts not only for learning of God in generations past but for comprehending their own relationship with God and therefore in order to understand their own identity and to find their moral bearings. The biblical witness forms and transforms their memory. But the ancient languages of biblical texts may not always serve or describe contemporary biblical faith. In turn, some modern words can serve biblical, faithful and moral meanings. One such word that lends itself to serve faith-relationships is "responsibility."

RESPONSIBILITY

Responsibility describes both personal and communal moral relationships. The word serves morally in both secular and religious contexts. Responsibility also has a family relationship with *being accountable* or *being answerable*.

(In fact, in German *responsibility* is "Verantwortung" where "Antwort" means "answer" or "reply.") Christian morality/ethics is the working out of what it means communally and individually to be confronted, addressed, and to be held accountable by God. Using nouns instead of adjectives, Christian ethics finds its origin, its enabler and model, its ultimate critic and judge, its source of life, forgiveness and hope, its bearings and guide . . . in Christ, God's Messiah. This is not in a deity generically or abstractly (as "Nature's God") but is the Living Presence, attested in biblical stories and in the good news of Jesus as Christ, experienced in worship and empowered by God's Spirit. And it is to Jesus, the Son and Messiah of God, that Christians are responsible, accountable and answerable. *Responsibility* will be a major moral/ethical term used in this text.

Responsibility, the word, is relationship-friendly. Surely humans do not just *have* relationships in the sense of additions to already formed selves. Rather, their very identities are relationally formed. Humans *are* their relationships. And biblical religion acknowledges and responds to life-giving and life-constituting relationships with God that can be lifelong and is believed to be resumed in an afterlife. God does not just create humankind but sustains, loves, commands, judges and redeems these creatures made in the divine image. The metaphors remain familial and social. These links constitute the goodness, joy, strengths and meaning of human lives. In a sense, being responsible not only describes imperatives of the Christian life but extends beyond life to resurrection and Judgment: Will we be found to be *responsible* by God with the life we were given?

TRILATERAL CHRISTIAN ETHICS?

It may be possible to illustrate basic features of God-human and inter-human relationships diagrammatically with trilateral links between God and humans. These links are relationships that interconnect persons with the living God and with each other. Humans do not create themselves but find themselves in life-giving and supportive human relationships. Humans find themselves supportively raised and linked with others, as family, friends, teachers, fellow citizens. The meaning and purpose of these relationships is the double love commandments, to love both God and neighbor. That creates unique trilateral links. Expressed in religious terms, humans are created in affinity or similarity with God, in whose image they are created (Gen 1:27).

Of course, none of that is literal or visible. God may be nearer to humans than hands or feet. But for the sake of describing God-human relationships, here God is up and humans are down in communal contexts.

The diagram (below) assumes the communal nature of human beings by creating relationships (links between A and B) and between humans and God. Biblically, God initiates personal contact with humans after having created and sustained them. The aim of God's presence with humans is to establish loving relationships and godly purposes. God's call offers forgiveness and invites humans to covenant and serve God in blessing humankind through God's covenant people, Israel and the church. The triangular sides signify personal and relational ties that reflect love in every direction. That holds true for God's care for humans (in the diagram, from God to A and B). And that should be true for responses to God from A and B as well. Moreover, human dealings with each other, neighbors in God's eyes, should aim at love as well.

The diagram lines indicate personal relationships and are two-directional. Worship looks up and is symbolized by the upward lines. Morality/ethics should transform the horizontal or community dimension morally. The character of God, God's action over time toward A and B, should inform the horizontal or human conduct, interactions between A and B as well. These relationships of humans with God and fellow humans forms the meaning of life and of ethics/morality. Given a good God, human life as gift and blessings, is good. Moreover, the relations from God to humans become imitable for interhuman conduct.

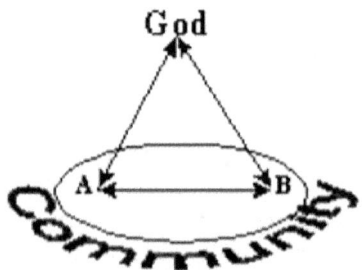

These three-sided human-God interconnections also lend themselves to depicting the rupture or alienation—sins—between humans and between God and humans. The interconnecting lines (relationships) break down. Human relationships with God suffer from indifference and alienation or through injustice among humans. Not only murder but even an insult can have deadly consequences (Matt 5:21–26). The triangular lines remain inseparable as God's creation and intended meaning of human life. Violating one relationship also distorts or ruptures the others. For example, in the book of Hosea idolatry, the worship of false gods, not only severs Israel's relationships with its Lord but destroys human community:

> Hear the word of the LORD, O people of Israel; for the LORD has an indictment against the inhabitants of the land. There is no faithfulness or loyalty, and no knowledge of God in the land. Swearing, lying, and murder, and stealing and adultery break out; bloodshed follows bloodshed. (Hos 4:1–2)

Christian ethics should direct and guide human conduct to sustain, serve and protect the three relational lines created by God as the meaning of human life. Aggression, exploitation, injustice not only ruin human community but also precipitate the rupture of the human/God relationship. In terms of the diagram, horizontal sin ruptures upwards connections. Every one of ancient Israel's prophets expresses this logic. Amos offers a most memorable text. He confronts a prosperous but unjust people in which "religion" is seemingly flourishing. Amos denounces such religion:

> Thus says the LORD: For three transgressions of Israel, and for four, I will not revoke the punishment; because they sell the righteous for silver, and the needy for a pair of sandals—they who trample the head of the poor into the dust of the earth, and push the afflicted out of the way." (Amos 2:6–7)

> "I hate, I despise your festivals, and I take no delight in your solemn assemblies. . . . Take away from me the noise of your songs; I will not listen to the melody of your harps. But let justice roll down like waters, and righteousness like an ever-flowing stream." (Amos 5:21, 23–24)

HUMAN COMMUNITY

The initial meaning of "community" in the diagram refers to *human* community. Human beings are communal or social by nature. Community, then refers primarily to the fact that humans exist from each other, for each other and should live peacefully and caringly with each other. The diagram implies that human community is created by and remains linked with God. As God's creation, it remains good. The author of the initial biblical chapter in Genesis itemizes the divine creation and declares it all to be good—seven times (Gen 1)! In Genesis, creation was and remains good. Its goodness lies in its source from God.

Human community is created and blessed by God. Human abuse threatens that goodness. Even when biblical stories read as mundane and as realistic as contemporary scandals, biblical stories ultimately invoke God, who may transform human evil into a blessing that serves God's intent.

Thus, the story of Joseph reads like fratricidal jealousy, offers intrigue and betrayal, spans decades and a dozen chapters, and only at its end refers to God: "Even though you [the brothers] intended to do harm to me, God intended it for good, in order to preserve a numerous people, as he is doing today" (Gen 50:20). When things go wrong, God intervenes and commands repentance and reform to restore an alienated community with God and with fellow humans. When things go right, more in aspiration than in fact, communities of biblical faith thank and praise God.

Biblical concepts affirm human community as the creation, intention and blessing of God. Biblical self-understanding assumes the givenness and presence of God who creates and loves humankind and in turn calls for human love, love for God and for one another. Yet the inclination that humans prefer their own interests to that of others must be as ancient as humankind. The secular rendition of individual motivation conceives of relationships arising from mutual interest and consent.

The inclination that humans would rather do their own thing can disrupt and alienate all involved. God's participation in human affairs turns into divine efforts to salvage a self-serving humankind. Human turning away from God, and from one another, creates the need for divine rescue efforts. And it is the un-invoked and uninvited Person who insists on repentance and moral responsibility all around. While the effect is judgmental—a word definitely out of season in modern times—God's aim is the human good. Divine judgment expresses redemptive and restoring intent even in the midst of human self-serving. In all but an eschatological context (that of a future and final universal Judgment) it seeks to reestablish the broken triadic relationship.

Three biblical stories that manifest trilateral communal logic of biblical ethics follow: Adam and Eve in the early chapters of Genesis, David-Bathsheba-Uriah-Nathan in 2 Sam 11–12, and the Great Judgment in Matt 24.

GOD, ADAM, AND EVE

In the beginning chapters of Genesis, it all begins with God. The creation of Adam, earthling or man, originates from divine speaking. But this vertical relationship—God and Adam speak with each other—proves insufficient for Adam. God concludes that "[it] is not good that the man should be alone" and resolves to remedy that. Something more than even man's best friend is needed. But then there is Eve! Adam joyfully welcomes her: "Here at last is bone of my bones and flesh of my flesh" (Gen 2:23). Eve completes the triangle. Here the purpose of creation is established in unbroken relationships between humans and God and between humans themselves and the rest of creation.

For a time. A short time, less than a generation. For inexplicably these earthlings seek more than created status, aspiring to "be like God" (Gen 3:5). Defying the only existing commandment, they break their relationship with God and now can no longer face their Creator or each other. Adam and Eve become estranged from each other. They now see each other differently. Their nakedness now needs covering. Adam's alienation from Eve expresses itself in his excuse to God: "The woman whom you gave to be with me, she gave me fruit from the tree, and I ate" (3:12). If it were not for the woman, and if it were not for God who created Eve . . . attested in the rupture of the most personal of relationships, the vertical proves inseparable from the horizontal. Violating the God-relationship, ruptures human solidarity. All three sides of the triangle rupture. The No! to the Creator echoes in blaming the partner.

If that had been the last word, the whole biblical story would have ended there. Instead, God persists, insists, mitigates the damage and makes continued life possible. Here humans prove to be less than heroic. Indeed, the story might well be set into a contemporary context. If it were not for God, who did not foresee the outcome of the script, the story—and humankind—might have ended there. The story witnesses to God's efforts to restore a fallen humankind to what it was meant to be.

GOD, DAVID, BATHSHEBA, URIAH, AND NATHAN

Second Samuel 11–12 tells the story of Israel's greatest king, David, at the height of his power, arising from an afternoon nap when "he saw from the roof a woman bathing; the woman was very beautiful" (11:2). The fact that she was also the wife of one of his mercenary soldiers, Uriah, who was at that very time fighting the king's war, did not deter David from inviting her over, from one thing leading to another, and from Bathsheba becoming pregnant. Resourceful, David has Uriah come home for rest and recreation, expecting that soldiers on leave will do what soldiers on leave do. But Uriah, a non-Israelite, is faithful to the divine law that David has defied. Soldiers stood under a vow of sexual abstinence while consecrated for war, and Uriah will not enter his house nor sleep with his wife. Even after the king gets him drunk! David can only think of the option of Uriah becoming a casualty of war and sends that hint to his general, who knows how to read between the lines. Indeed, Uriah is killed in battle. And after a decent interval, David takes Bathsheba into his house and harem where she bears him a son.

There the story might have ended, but for the LORD and the LORD's man, Nathan. The prophet brings a report of glaring abuse of the poor to the king, who is called to ensure justice in the land: In a culture that insists on hospitality to strangers, a rich man with very many flocks and herds welcomes a visitor by depriving a poor man of his only lamb—that had shared his meager fare and would "drink from his cup, and lie in his bosom, and it was like a daughter to him" (12:3). This kindles David's anger: "As the LORD lives, the man who has done this deserves to die; he shall restore the lamb fourfold, because he did this thing, and because he had no pity" (12:5-6). And Nathan springs the condemning words: "You are the man!" What David did with Bathsheba and Uriah was covered neither by privacy nor royal privilege but "despised the word of the LORD" (12:9). The prophet pronounces judgment that will take the very form of David's violence toward his victim. And David—amazing in a person with political power—David acknowledges: "I have sinned against the LORD" (12:13)! The violation of the horizontal relationship ruptures the vertical. And there, again, it might have ended but for David's repentance and for divine mitigation that continues life and covenantal loyalty toward David and Israel.

THE GREAT JUDGMENT

Jesus' story of the Great Judgment in Matt 25:31-46 describes a universal accounting at the end of this age in a time beyond time. The human relationship with God proceeds with an agrarian metaphor: Sheep will be differentiated from goats, the righteous from the condemned, by their moral or immoral conduct. "[F]or I was hungry and you gave me food, I was thirsty and you gave me something to drink, I was a stranger and you welcomed me, I was naked and you gave me clothing, I was sick and you took care of me, I was in prison and you visited me" (25:35-36). To the surprised question of when any of this might have been done for God, the answer is the familiar but nevertheless startling, "as you did it to one of the least of these who are members of my family, you did it to me" (25:40). The Hebraic/Jewish and Christian God so identifies with the poor, the oppressed, the despised, with "the least of these" that what is done to them is done to God, who is personal about such human caring.

As to those who refused to mitigate the plight of the human poor, perhaps even failing to notice such want, the results are not ambivalent. What is done to God's poorest children is done to God. God's self-identity with those in great need explains the contrasting judgments. Biblical religion insists on compassion and help for humans in dire need! Indifference—here a matter of neglect—remains without prospects of divine forgiveness There it ends! In a tolerant culture, there will not be many sermons on the concluding verse: "these will go away into eternal punishment, but the righteous into eternal life" (25:46).

The threat of this Matthean text is not bracketed by the possibility of repentance and avoidance of eternal condemnation. Jesus may have referred to a very similar earlier Hebrew text in Isa 58:6–9 that focuses on what God expects: God is not asking humans to fast but

> to loose the bonds of injustice, to undo the thongs of the yoke,
> to let the oppressed go free, and to break every yoke?
> Is it not to share your bread with the hungry,
> And to bring the homeless poor into your house;
> When you see the naked to cover them,
> And not to hide yourself from your own kin?
> Then your light shall break forth like the dawn,
> And your healing shall spring up quickly;
> Your vindicator shall go before you,
> The glory of the LORD shall be your rear guard. (Isa 58:6–9)

The prospect of divine patience and of human compassion and reform in Isaiah do not reappear in the text of Matt 25.

Each of these biblical stories expresses the inseparability of the horizontal or of social-communal relationships from the vertical, the God-human dimension. The right relationship with God requires fitting practical care for those most vulnerable. These texts in fact express a pervasive biblical logic. Much as a wedding vow affirms covenantal loyalty with the pledge to honor and to love, ancient Israel's laws constitute the moral affirmation of the covenant at Mount Sinai, the vertical binding between God and Israel. "For I am the LORD who brought you up from the land of Egypt, to be your God; you shall therefore be holy, for I am holy" (Lev 11:45). *Holy*, when referring to God, is considered at some length earlier in this chapter. *Holy*, when speaking of humans, means set apart for serving God. Here, Israel is set apart as the servant people of God. The moral shaping of the horizontal, of communal relationships, constitutes the affirmation of the God-relationship: "But this command I gave them, 'Obey my voice, and I will be your God, and you shall be my people; and walk only in the way that I command you, so that it may be well with you" (Jer 7:23). The same logic reverberates in the Sermon on the Mount (Matt 5–7) whose radical demands reflect the nearness of divine rule in the kingdom of God. The pattern of the radical sayings of Jesus, "You have heard that it was said . . . but I say to you . . ." is the horizontal acknowledgment of the renewed relationship with God: Repent, for the kingdom of heaven [the ruling of God] has come near (Matt 4:17).

In this broad pattern of the inseparability of human relationships (morality/ethics) from the relationship with God (worship, God-relatedness of everything), human-induced rupture—sin—can sever God-human ties. Initially bilateral between humans, as indifference to human need and suffering, it always becomes trilateral. Idolatry, breaking the relationship with God, precipitates horizontal or communal repercussions of disaster. Communal moral indifference, injustice and exploitation also violates the relationship with God. Even approaching God with a gift becomes unacceptable without first requiring human reconciliation (Matt 5:23-24). Forgiveness from God assumes prior human reconciliation: "forgive us our debts, as we also have forgiven our debtors" (Matt 6:12). The horizontal testifies to the vertical. Jesus: "By this all men will know that you are my disciples, if you have love for one another" (John 13:35).

TROUBLING IMPLICATIONS

The preceding paragraphs under "Human Community" insist on the moral importance of practical help for those among us in greatest need. That implies caution for those who remain indifferent to human suffering, poverty and distress. Indeed, the text from Matt 25:31-46 concludes with a blunt warning: those who do not respond to the needs of strangers, of the hungry, the thirsty, the sick, the imprisoned, the naked poor were indifferent to the king (God, who identifies with such). "And these will go away into eternal punishment, but the righteous into eternal life" (Matt 25:46).

CHRISTIAN SALVATION: FAITH OR GOOD WORKS?

Such drastic consequences of neglecting needy neighbors may surprise those who take their bearings from the importance of saving faith. Justification of sinners by faith rather than by good works has been a firm and early affirmation of Christian conviction. Actually, both faith and works are involved. But their right sequence and context matter. The acceptance of God's loving and saving forgiveness of sins *by faith* or trust creates a transformed self. That effect is also described as being born anew. This gift of the Spirit of God saves sinners. Again, the experience of being loved, being forgiven, being transformed creates the birth of a new self. The notion that sinners could achieve such standing with God by their own effort misleads. The label of "works righteousness" condemns such self-deceptive effort.

Doing good for the wrong reason may be an almost universal human temptation. It assumes the ability to do so on one's own strength. Yet, since the fall of Adam and Eve, such self-salvation is more than humans can accomplish. Here Martin Luther condemns human self-centeredness: Humans are curved in upon themselves. Yet self-rescue proves impossible since it resembles hauling oneself out of a swamp by pulling on one's hair. Pervasive sin requires external rescue. That rescue has been created by God in the life, teaching, self-sacrificial death and God's resurrection of Jesus. This is the heart of the Gospel, the story of good news of the gift of forgiveness and redemption by the Son of God. At that redemptive point, Christian love of God and neighbor becomes not only possible but imperative. The motive is no longer self-rescue by good works but gratitude for what had been impossible to achieve on one's own. This is the beginning of the Christian life.

While that might be the conclusion of a life rightly lived, the final answer awaits the end of time and the resurrection of all humans. There is still an inclusive and final Judgment (a later chapter here as well). Christians as well as all humankind remain answerable for their lives. And the measure of ultimate Judgment is to serve the needs of the poorest among us. The capacity to lead such a life is being provided gratis by God's Spirit in the name of Jesus.

IS GOD IN CHARGE?

For those who acknowledge the biblical designation of God as LORD, the term of the Revised Standard Version of the Bible for God, one might ask whether God is really in charge of this world and of humankind. "LORD," the title, seems aspirational rather than descriptive. The name denotes authority, power, rule. To count the ways that divine lordship may apply, creative power certainly holds for creation and preservation of the universe. Raising Jesus from death befits lordly status. Raising all humans and judging them at the end of all ages is clear manifestation of divine lordship.

There is also a biblical precedent of God's redemptive intervention in the story of Joseph and his brothers. This story at the end of the book of Genesis offers a celebratory and transforming divine authority secured by God redirecting the betrayal of Joseph by his brothers to create a redemptive outcome. In a position of power, Joseph forgives the brothers who fall prostrate before him: "Joseph reassures them, 'Do not be afraid! Am I in the place of God? Even though you intended harm to me, God intended it for good, in order to preserve a numerous people, as he is doing today" (Gen 50:19–20). The RSV textual note refers to "God's overruling providence that has already turned evil purposes to a good end." Such confidence in divine authority and rescue is appealing and widely shared. But it is questioned here. Not that asking is wrong. But *relying* on divine intervention alone may be irresponsible.

Clarifying and enacting the respective roles of God and of humans invite simplistic solutions. A perennial Christian spiritual reassures believers: "He's got the whole world in his hand." A believer might waffle between affirming and doubting the ruling (lordship) of God. Yes, all creation depends on its Creator. And God may perform saving miracles, mitigate human evil, forgive, and create a new and better future. Moreover, the theme of divine lordship, while problematic to discern historically, may hold for a time beyond time. Only then the ruling, the reign or kingdom of God, will become discernible. But no, divine lordship is not or is not yet self-evident. At least not in the sense of a divine backup or warrant that will keep the worst from happening. More realistically and more ominously, *God places the world into human hands*. And humans readily assume that thereby this world is indeed safely placed. However, given the record or the odds, *God help us!*

The Joseph Story may reflect how many believers conceive of the character and role of the biblical God in hardship contexts: God is aware of human betrayal and works in the wings, as it were, to transform what was humanly conceived and enacted as betrayal into redemptive results. However, in fact human aggression and betrayal can and does result in unmitigated disaster, into holocausts, into slavery, into fatal suffering and early death. Naïve assumptions about the lordly protective roles of God inevitably become complaints: "where was God *then*!?"

REFLECTIONS ON DIVINE AND HUMAN CHARACTER

God's love of humankind creates special standing for humans in that God created humans, us, in the divine image (Gen 1:27). [Whatever the correct use of *image*, the meaning invoked here is *ethical/moral* similarity or *resemblance*.] Biblically, God places human welfare and human lives, indeed the whole world, into human hands. Yet the biblical creation stories assume that God did not foreknow Adam's or human responses to God's generosity. Given human nature as presented in realistic (read: *troubling*) Genesis texts as well as in historical bloody hindsight, Adam's descendants inherit a good but a hard and demanding earth. Moreover, human beings, while unique in creation and blessed with a certain affinity with God, prove worrisome: Cain kills Abel, his brother. These early Genesis chapters offer a sober and troubling assessment of human nature. God's disappointment, while not explicit, expels and ends human inhabitants from the Garden and makes continued human life difficult, demanding, and mortal.

The biblical Story of the Garden (Gen 1–3) unexpectedly becomes relevant here as warning against the loss of a livable world. The Garden Story contrasts the goodness of God's creation with unexpected and disappointing human responses. The Story is overshadowed by human failure to obey the one commandment God imposes. The first couple eat the forbidden fruit, find themselves at odds with each other and seek to avoid God. If Adam (earthling) and Eve foreshadow humankind and if the Story reflects abuse of the good Garden God had prepared for humankind, human prospects become worrisome. Not just immortality but the Garden were lost forever. Hardships became unavoidable. Humans remain careless with each other and with a world created for them. How could God not be disappointed by human conduct, early and late? Nevertheless, God continues to sustain and bless humankind.

A good creation does not remain safe from human indifference, abuse or neglect. Ecocide, the destruction of all life, may follow genocide. The uniformity of nature, that grand assumption of the natural sciences, becomes questionable. Given human aggression and overreaching, the human future may not always resemble the past. Indeed, the means exist to end all human futures! Surely, God has had second thoughts about placing the world into human hands. Growing environmental threats to human self-preservation and survival may elicit more effective efforts to preserve a livable world. But naïve religious platitudes ("He's got the whole world in his hand") will not save humankind from itself. Christian ethics must remain realistic about human indifference and self-interest. Ethics must play an active role in realistic assessments aimed at planetary survival. Appeals to God mending human misuses of our vulnerable world will not do.

The Creation Stories, assuring human survival under hardship conditions, may now seem benign and unrealistic. Where was God when the snake made its move? The popular notion of God as all-powerful, as in charge of everything, as LORD de facto, as having matters in hand is muted in the biblical Garden accounts. Human responses to a good creation must disappoint God. While God has rescued humans from self-caused disaster, is that an assured precedent? Human character remains unheroic, even though good intentions avow, "your will be done." Human survival remains uncertain. The divine intention offers life within limits. Christian hopes rely on God's steadfast character rather than on their own nature and character for human survival and a livable future. But could it be that current generations are living on borrowed time?

It may be disappointing to raise a problem for which one has no solution or alternative. To be sure, human freedom is an immeasurable gift, It enables humans to become responsible, to be *persons*. Perhaps this freedom is what the biblical author had in mind when he described humans as in God's image (Gen 1:27). If only human character measured up to what we take to be God's intent in creating humans. God's character—creative, generous, loving—offers the model for human conduct. But while humans have obeyed God in being fruitful and multiplying, human mistreatment of humans and of "our" earth remain perennial. Such harm is not confined to individual conduct but assumes communal and legal forms. Such inhumanity must trouble God more than humans. And there are biblical warnings of eventual Judgment and final punishment.

Surely there is a link here with the biblical hope for God's universal resurrection of the dead and inclusive Judgment. God does not owe humans answers. But may we be given insight and resolve sufficient to recognize human abuses of "our" earth while that is still possible?!

CHALLENGES TO CHRISTIAN ETHICS: ASSIMILATION

The remaining paragraphs in this chapter focus on challenges to Christian ethics in contemporary American contexts. American Christians breathe national and cultural air just like everyone else. That becomes morally important, because the way one speaks may influence the way one thinks and chooses. Christian faith in modern secular contexts may be threatened simply by assimilation: a gradual transition, largely embedded in speech, that remains subjectively unnoticed. That possibility may be difficult to detect for the same reason that frogs are said to be unaware in remaining in water gradually getting hotter.

LIVING IN TWO CONTEXTS

Living in two contexts, American and Christian, creates the possibility of one identity transforming the other. For example, "Americanism" celebrates individualism, as in the virtues of self-reliance and personal achievement. Christian character, in contrast, self-identifies as the Body of Christ and as being commanded to love the neighbor (and God), not the self. American adds for military recruits would invite citizens to "be all that they could be," seemingly unaware of the implicit self-contradiction. American culture honors individual success; Christian faith insists on serving others. Democratic individual ambition counsels taking advantage of opportunity;

Christian convictions insist on serving others. Christian faith and nationalism may both flourish together without self-contradictions. But modern prophets remain suspicious.

American rights language may challenge Christian perspectives and values. Individual rights did not arise out of biblical or Christian traditions. Appeals to rights offer a trump-like claim in political and other controversies. Rights are modern and post-biblical. And if biblical traditions form the language of Christian ethics, careful word analysis of rights must test rights language for compatibility with Christian faith. While the motto "for God and country" appeals, hard choices become unavoidable for Christians. Thus forgiveness of enemies is a Christian, not an American, obligation. Even the hostile naming of enemies—as well as the refusal to use such terms—involves moral choices. Biblical moral imperatives focus on love, both godly and human. It requires linguistic skill to "translate" such personal term into the non-personal context of social, technical, political contexts. Being Christian in a non-Christian culture requires linguistic dexterity.

Care in choosing and creating words becomes essential for Christian ethics. When it comes to social and political responsibilities, once an issue (a problem) has been raised, it normally has been carefully "presented." That simply means that the choice of words for presenting an issue was not self-evident and may be contested. Most likely, the words selected to name the problem involved choices. The person(s) who raise a moral problem must name the issue before they can present it. And most likely once named, the name and its implications stick. One is reminded of explorers naming continents. It proves difficult to change names once assigned. And the naming, at least for continents and cars, advantages the name-creator.

Linguistic caution, how to speak and write plainly, understandably and well, can pose challenges for Christian ethics. Using foreign terms may impress readers. But what is "other" may not be better. More important, the language of ethics generally and of Christian ethics specifically, cannot function in exclusively technical terms. Environmental ethics, for example, resists relying on economic language of investments or resources—except to analyze and evaluate such leading terms. Responsible stewardship requires an altered sense of wording, of identity and of time. Thus a projected human future must envision a longer time span than a human life. Present generations have responsibilities that extend beyond current lives. A biblical sense of future includes responsibility for those who follow us and for what we left behind or used up. Assuring a promising human future may call for new and more communally responsible language, citizenship, respect and faith.

PAST, PRESENT AND FUTURE

Future humans will expect that we, this generation, will act responsibly with resources and environments, just as we expect from those who lived before us. From a Christian perspective, there are actually three interested parties here, not just two. The obligation to respect future generations includes both the secular and the Christian. The third participant insisting on a livable future is the biblical God. The living God—past, present and future—is the link between generations. We all have the same Lord, Judge and Advocate. While God is the One to whom all humans are answerable, the point here is that God blesses humans not just now but acts for the good of past, present and future generations. God, we trust, will continue to create future human generations. The biblical God links us not just to the past but to future generations. That link, that Person, insists on environmental responsibility over generations. It is, after all, our God's world.

Christian responsibilities for a shared future include more than personal matters and extend into social, public and political dimension. The command to love the neighbor must reach effectively into economics, law, public policy, and into the institutions upon which human flourishing and life itself depend. It is irresponsible to leave the human future to good luck and reasonable others who care for a livable human future. Being responsible to God includes responsibility to future generations. Yet indifference to the human future is perennially tempting. The German proverb, "Nach mir, die Sintflut" ("after me, the deluge") disavows responsibility those who come after us.

LOOKING BACK

Beginning with the character and roles of the biblical God, this chapter has described trilateral bonds between communities of faith, the secular and God. Loyalty to God becomes inseparable from loyalty to fellow humans. Biblical religion and ethics prove to be inseparable because God cares for all—even for prospective or future—humans. Though these relationships are personal, they are never solely private. Biblical faith and morality are both inclusive. And in biblical perspective most everything is religious. Christian moral inclusiveness deepens and expands human responsibility. The conviction that God loves humans, despite human character, yields the commandment to love neighbors, past, present, and future.

3

Christian Ethics and American Secularism

LEARNING FROM THOSE WITH WHOM ONE DISAGREES

CHAPTER 2, DEALING WITH biblical religion and a triangular model of Christian ethics, noted that relationships between God and believers on the one hand and within the human community on the other are inseparably linked. Therefore: No biblical religion or faith without ethics and moral responsibilities. But that is not to say that there is no ethics without religion. In secular as in religious cultures philosophical, professional, personal ethics prove to be indispensable. Open societies require trust, truth telling, promise keeping, free associations and compacts. While such cultures can do without religion, doing without ethics should be seen as an aberration. Even repressive governments, as that of the German National Socialists (Nazis), appeal to ethics within constrained limits. Normally, one has to work toward reasonable solutions even in unreasonable settings. Rather than regarding secular ethics as inimical, Christian ethics needs to understand and respect such versions of ethics, should respond to them openly and cooperate with them when possible. Prudence suggests that in a society that insists on separating politics from religion, good causes can be recognized and supported without religious imprimatur or endorsement.

The reason for such openness and cooperation is theological. All humans are children of God. And God not only creates but cares for and loves them. Given this godly inclusiveness—one thinks of that biblical text that

God blesses both Christians and the secular with rain and sunshine (Matt 5:45) and surely with the love of wisdom as well—Christian ethics can and should learn from those with whom it disagrees. What better critics than the secular? The last pages of this chapter introduce the secular Social Contract Theory as a foundational story for modern philosophical ethics as well as Communitarianism, a secular critique of the social Contract.

HERMENEUTICAL CAUTION

While all biblical believers look to the Bible for meaning and direction, no one should do it precipitously. The process requires preparation and hermeneutical (interpretational) caution. Hermeneutics is the discipline that studies biblical interpretation. It is the study of how to make the Bible speak. Such hermeneutics resists those popular appeals to the Bible that one might call proof-texting: reaching directly for the commandment or verse that supports one's argument and convictions. Such use of texts dismisses context, sources, and original setting. Uncritical or unreflective Bible-quoting also abandons any search for how a specific text relates to other strands of tradition. Rather than encouraging inquiry, "the Bible says . . ." or "God says . . ." can work like a trump and conversation-stopper.

Proof-texting expresses uncritical confidence in citing scripture because it conceives the Bible to be inspired directly, infallibly and relevantly. "God said it; I believe it." That includes confidence that God guided the reader to the right biblical text, prevents misreading of the text and dispenses the reader from discerning the meaning in its original or general context. All biblical believers claim that biblical texts attest to divine actions and purposes. But fundamentalists in effect eliminate the middle man: biblical authors took dictation and recorded God's words verbatim. That assumes that professional biblical scholars are not really needed since the Spirit of God assures the reader's correct understanding of ancient words and context. The divine presence brackets or eliminates human shortcomings of biblical writers and of current readers so that the text remains pure and devoid of human influence and distortions. Here the Bible as God's Word guarantees its own truth and becomes the uncritical foundation for instructing the church morally.

Such an attempt at guaranteeing certainty concerning the Bible as Scripture betrays both a theology of glory that claims the ability to make God transparent to direct human understanding, and the Enlightenment assumption that at the basis of our knowledge must lie an indubitable truth.[1]

---

1. Jersild, *Spirit Ethics*, 47. Especially helpful are both chapter 3, "Determining 'What the Bible Says,'" and chapter 4, "The Ethical Content and Authority of the Bible."

Such naiveté includes additional inspirational guarantees: as that contemporary readers' understand the text as God meant it and that their selection of texts is divinely warranted as well. In contrast, believers who deny that God eliminates the human element in revelation, assume that the times, the culture, the concerns of the reader can affect the interpretation of a text. Understanding and honoring God can be more human than divine. A holy or transcendent God is never within guaranteed human grasp. Respecting the holiness (the otherness) of God creates, should create, caution about "God says . . ." or "The Bible says . . ."

Even the most cautious of textual scholars cannot avoid choosing and interpreting and thereby making texts speak. There is a hermeneutic corrective discipline: all those *criticisms* (the poorly translated German word Kritik that should be rendered as "critical investigation" or "analysis") that form a major part of any introductory course in biblical studies. And there is a theological scholarly community as well. The point of these cautionary remarks is to note that all biblical references have been considered at length by biblical scholars. The reader should not assume that text renditions here form the last and the best word. Rather they may well be an exercise in what Luther calls *sinning bravely*, i.e., risking a new or bold interpretation.

One example of what contemporary Bible readers may assume about biblical texts is that American individualism is not shared by ancient biblical authors. Social scientists caution us that humans are social, time-, culture-, and language-infused beings. Modern believers, too, reflect their age. No one comes to biblical texts or Christian ethics with a blank slate. Thus, contemporary Christians think of salvation in individualistic terms: "how can I be saved?" Yet in the communal contexts of biblical texts, individual salvation is part of the welfare of a people or a remnant people. Similarly, any notion of divine judgment has just about evaporated in a tolerant secular cultural where to understand all is to tolerate all. Contrasts between biblical traditions and current cultural assumptions appear throughout this study. If the mainstream of Western culture is secular, becoming believers and trying to understand Christian ethics can be countercultural. Paul's countercultural advice to believers in Rome elicited the warning, "Do not be conformed to this world [Greek: age], but be transformed by the renewing of your minds, so that you may discern what is the will of God—what is good and acceptable and perfect" (Rom 12:2).

AN ETHICS OF CASE LAW OR A THEOLOGICAL ETHICS?

The task in the next few pages is to identify and to describe two different approaches to interpret biblical and other traditional texts. One is the hermeneutics (interpretive method) of revealed morality similar to case law. The other is a theological ethics approach. While *morality* and *ethics* often function as synonyms, they differ here. Morality focuses on specific cases or precedents. The other, theological hermeneutics, concentrates on one or more general themes. To use a math metaphor, morality-hermeneutics are numerators; theological hermeneutics function as denominators. To use a legal metaphor, morality hermeneutics functions as case law. Theological hermeneutics parallel constitutional law. It may help to conceive of the issues here as matters of distance: Case law looks closely at a specific decision to derive ways of resolving a certain current problem. Theology seeks perspective from distance. Both distances, near and far, promise an improved understanding of what one faces.

CASE LAW MODEL (HALAKHAH): THE HERMENEUTICS OF REVEALED MORALITY

Looking to the Bible for ethical understanding and moral guidance can be and is done by searching for moral or directly action-guiding texts. That might include 613 biblical commandments (someone has counted them!), the Top Ten, the double love commands, specific prophetic calls for justice, the moral specific prudence of biblical Wisdom literature. Ancient biblical moral texts have divine revelatory authority and are carried into the present to be applied analogically to contemporary moral issues, including ethics. Traditional Jewish ethics serve as example of revealed morality. While the title and focus of this book is Christian ethics, Hebrew scripture is a part of Christian tradition as well. I introduce a sketch of Jewish ethics here to honor its importance and as contrast to any theological ethics approach. Actually, both methods include key features of the other. *Halakhah*, a legal and precedent or case law approach, includes theological features.

The traditional Jewish approach to biblical texts seeks a revealed morality. The halakhic method guides traditional law and practice. Halakhah (or halachah), the Hebrew word for "the Way," is traditional Jewish law and the way of life defined by it that obligates every member of the Jewish community. The legal aspect of halakhah should regulate every aspect of life, offering a correct way of responding to each and every situation. This comprehensiveness of the halakhic law reflects the aspiration to sanctify every aspect of human conduct. But halakhah also offers a relational, covenantal or theological dimension focusing on God and Israel:

> the covenantal pole emphasizes that halakhah is not only a formal system concerned with rules of procedure but also an expressive system grounded in the love relationship symbolized by God's invitation to Israel to become his covenantal community. The understanding of halakhah as a covenantal relational experience guards against the mistaken notion that a dynamic living relationship with God can be structured exclusively by fixed and permanent rules. The need for order must not be at the expense of spontaneity, personal passion, novelty, and surprise. . . . The perennial problem that one faces in living by halakhah is how to prevent the covenantal relational pole from being obscured by the massive, seemingly self-sufficient legal framework.[2]

Strongly communal and traditionally authoritative, halakhah connects Israel's historical memory to specific moral imperatives. "Jews have historically adopted this method because they believed that this was the only way to preserve the divine authority of the tradition, but such continuity is also crucial to preserve the identity of a people as widely scattered as Jews are."[3] While analogical reasoning requires judgment and therefore involves risk, one can appreciate halakhic continuity with the past and its historical authority.

This approach to moral biblical texts and their subsequent rabbinic interpretations resembles case law or common law in its appeal to precedent. Collective memory retains past decisions (commandments) and draws on them analogically in contemporary judgments. Thus, ancient rules of respect for the dying become contemporary resources for resolving questions of euthanasia. Rules about when one may silence woodcutters for the sake of the dying guide moral decisions about the use and removal of respirators.[4]

---

2. Hartman, "Halakhah," 310. The covenantal or relational feature of halakhah resists legalism or strict adherence to the letter of the law. The believer who practices halakhah takes the role of a servant of God. "Accordingly, no rule or aspect of Jewish law can be an end in itself. Every dimension and facet of Jewish law should be an expression of the love of God (Ex. 20:6; Deut. 6:5; Is. 41:8), leading the observant Jew to saintliness (Num. 5:40) and *imitatio Dei* (Lev. 19:2). The prophets, therefore, severely criticize those who regarded obedience to God's law as a mere matter of external propriety and legalism (Amos 8:5; Is. 29:13, 58:3), judging such behavior to be based on a fundamental misconception of the law as well as of religion and morality." Falk, "Jurisprudence," 512.

3. Dorff, "Methodology," 164.

4. Newman, "Woodchoppers and Respirators," 144-45.

Biblical texts, surrounded by rabbinic interpretations, can in fact readily accommodate any contemporary bioethics issues.

Retaining even minority opinions, such living memory expands continually with layer upon layer of interpretation. One suspects that the lawyer/court/scholar can take widely diverging paths through the immense field of this legal tradition. Different precedents, alternate texts might be chosen along the way. The non-practitioner of the halakhic method may get the impression that such uses of tradition resemble an unpredictable wandering through the wide field of prior decisions, renditions of biblical texts, and precedents. One scholar picks a precedent here and a usable rabbinic interpretation there. Another scholar might take a different path and retrieve quite different precedents. But of course, that may also be the impression among non-lawyers of legal experts searching for precedents. In both contexts the search for precedents assumes that the past is sufficiently rich and imitable to shed light on all new quandaries. Whatever is found requires stretching to resolve novel contemporary moral dilemmas. The moral/legal outcome might be the same or it might not. The same method—halakhah—can yield different results.[5] But that holds for any method.

My own appeal to hymns, liturgies, and even biblical texts in the chapter on ethics and worship proves vulnerable to the same suspicion of ad hoc, unsystematic, and unpredictable selectivity. My pragmatic justification of such moral uses of worship traditions holds for the halakhic method as well: Communities of faith search their traditions, hymns, and liturgies with different needs in different times but always with a sense of the fitting. Faith communities will judge whether particular texts, hymns, liturgies work or prove useful to sustain the life of faith and its need for moral direction in a given time and place. And the community of scholars probes and argues whether moral bearings from these sources point in the right direction.

The halakhic search for precedent may not be as haphazard as it seems. Acknowledging the rich memory and scholarly creativity of this process, searching for precedents to resolve novel contemporary ethics problems surely presupposes a notion of what to look for. Scholars seem guided by inclusive concepts of justice and of divine and human character. Without widely shared theological assumptions undergirding the halakhic search, no one could recognize a precedent if he stepped on it. If that is true, then the halakhic method may not be as hostile to biblical *revealed theology*—a contrasting hermeneutics (interpretive method)—as it seems.

---

5. "Even when authorities employ the same methodology, they may read the sources of a tradition in quite dissimilar ways." Ellenson, "How to Draw Guidance," 132.

While the traditional approach of pursuing a revealed morality favors the case and precedent method, a few Jewish scholars distance themselves from pre-modern shortcomings of tradition with a different approach, with a hermeneutics that looks to a revealed theology. For the halakhic method, insisting on close moral links with tradition, is prone to have a conservative effect. One may welcome that as a rich and sustaining moral heritage or reject it as a limiting burden of the past, best left behind.

THEOLOGICAL ETHICS

To use the legal metaphor mentioned, while halakhah resembles the legal case or precedent method, looking to the Bible as revealed theology seems analogous to the study of Constitutional law. That discipline is not bound to case law (or ancient moral texts) but invokes larger themes—as the relationships between branches of government (the relationships between God and communities of faith). It seems more internally coherent and predictable since every case can be viewed through a more or less coherent cluster of Constitutional values (theological beliefs). The Reform Jewish theologian, Eugene Borowitz, chooses the key biblical concept of the covenant in writing Renewing the Covenant: A Theology for the Postmodern Jew.[6] Borowitz insists on relational revelation that acknowledges the personal relationships between God and believers. "I reject the normative principle that authentic Jewish continuity requires the halakhic process."[7] Insisting on more personal autonomy than afforded by halakhah, Borowitz claims that "[a] postmodern theology of serious Jewish duty must then take the form of reconciling an effective autonomy with existence in Covenant."[8] The covenant—analogous to the Constitution—then serves as the common denominator for enumerating key biblical and rabbinic texts with which to respond to contemporary moral issues.

THE BIBLE AS REVEALED THEOLOGY
(CONTRASTED WITH REVEALED MORALITY)

While belonging within the Christian tradition, my own approach resembles that of Borowitz in looking to a revealed theology in biblical texts. That assumes that the ethical relevance of biblical texts lies not primarily in

6. Borowitz, *Renewing the Covenant*.
7. Borowitz, *Renewing the Covenant*, 281.
8. Borowitz, *Renewing the Covenant*, 257.

particular moral or religious commands, prophetic pleas, the Sermon on the Mount, or in pastoral advice in letters to young churches. Rather biblical ethics makes better sense when it takes its cues from the character of God as attested by God's relationship with communities of faith. My reason for choosing such an approach is the conviction that normative biblical injunctions—"you shall!" "you shall not!" "do this!" "do not do that!"—originate from something more fundamental. The defining identity of God covenanting with faith communities undergirds biblical commands. That seems to be assumed even in the halakhic method as a recognition-criterion for what may serve as precedent.

To be sure, some commandments (invoked as revealed morality) are sufficiently broad or inclusive that they define the divine-human relationship: The double love commandments characterize the horizontal and vertical faith relationships, insisting that they should resonate with each other. "You shall have no other gods before me!" defines an exclusive God-human covenant. Here the two hermeneutics overlap. But the theological conviction of what God and humans are to each other, their identity and relationship, seems more basic and prior than any specific moral advice or command.

A CHILD RELATIONSHIP ANALOGY

Lest that seems abstract or far-fetched, the same logic may hold for ethics in normal but ever so trying human relationships. Much of what goes on between parent and child is repetitive and invokes precedent: "I've told you a thousand times . . ." But being a parent can be a new and trying experience. While new parents may be grateful for the assistance of how-to books, while law and social mores specify basic parental obligations (a revealed morality of sorts), many problems in raising children are simply not in the book. And even if they were, do they offer genuine precedents or sound advice for our current dilemmas? Being a father requires a prolonged learning curve. And in the really trying situations, it may prove more helpful to remember who one is in that relationship than moral maxims, such as "be patient!" "talk it out" "forget yesterday!" In this complex and trying situation, what do I as father owe my son, my daughter? It helps to remember who or what we are to each other. Of course, that still requires discernment, hope, patience and risk. But whatever needed to be done had to be true to and acknowledge our relationship. That should be plural: had to be true to our relationships. For father-child relations are embedded in the webs of being husband-wife, grandparents, friends as well as members of a religious as well as a civic community. It is hard to be angry with one's child and be either at ease with one's wife or to take communion with a glad heart. Moral maxims abound. But we live by and in our relationships.

NON-PRECEDENTS

One of the difficult responsibilities of relating Christian faith to American culture is the fact that biblical texts reflect their age and pre-modern assumptions that have become impossible to affirm in the present. Whether one looks to specific ethical texts or pervasive theological themes, certain ancient texts can no longer be ascribed to the biblical God. Ancient affirmations of holy war, of the limited roles assigned to women, of the endorsement of human slavery, of the condemnation of homosexual relationships would be among the topics that set the modern reader's teeth on edge. Such texts remain in the canon (authoritative scripture) out of respect for tradition. But, and this summarizes the point, they prove to be *incompatible with the character of God*. A revealed theology compensates with more flexibility (a leading term) since it appeals to the character of God rather than to specific ethical texts. Moreover, it recognizes that time and place make a difference. As the hymn has it, "new occasions teach new duties, time makes ancient good uncouth."[9]

An additional interpretive risk of any text interpretation (hermeneutics) is that it may project religious meaning where there is none.[10] The pragmatic counsels of biblical wisdom literature, moral structuring of economic relationships, family law, echoes of ancient cultures may simply lack any theological meaning. And the reply that for believers everything is in fact religious or should be may bestow textual meanings where there is none. Texts may simply be and remain strange. Finally, when it comes to faith and ethics, one should not assume human progress that would bring the old into conformity with the new. The modern counsel to jettison outdated and morally perverse texts may echo the beguiling voice of ancient or modern times. Not only the past but the present can be wrong.

---

9. The first line of the hymn is "Once to every man and nation."

10. I do not remember the source and cannot make it rhyme in English. But the German doggerel has a point: "Im Auslegen sei frisch und munter. Leg's Du's nicht aus, so leg' was unter." "In laying it out [interpreting a text] be brisk and lively. If you don't lay it out, slip something under [give it a different meaning]." Word-humor may be untranslatable.

A CONSTRUCTIVE PROPOSAL

Seeking more coherence than appeals to moral texts, a theological interpretation appears in what follows here. Specifically, the biblical character of God can be theologically and ethically instructive. God's character—formed by pattern of acts over time, a very long time!—offers a model for human imitation. Imitating God witnesses to believers' identity: "so that you may be children of your Father in heaven" (Matt 5:45). That divine identity—here named as Father—is always more than that of Lawgiver. John Hick offers that argument in regard to Jesus' response to the Mosaic law.

> [Jesus'] objection to the Law was not merely that it needed revision in various particulars. It came under a more radical objection to legalistic morality as such. A system of laws must, in the nature of the case, prescribe and proscribe specific overt deeds. But Jesus' critique of the Law arises from his perception that the kingdom is extended not merely by securing the conformity of men's overt deeds to a stated code, but by changing people themselves.[11]

Changing people themselves would be effected by changing their character, their consistent acts, over time. The goal of such changes would be becoming more like God. That may well be a lifetime calling for Christians as well as for Jews. And the model for Christians for imitating the character of God is the word, life and death of Jesus.

CHRISTIAN HERMENEUTICS

Christian hermeneutics (interpretations and meanings of biblical texts) looks first and last to what it believes about Jesus. All other biblical writings—and most of the ethically interesting texts appear in the traditions of ancient Israel—will be read in the light of faith in Jesus. Yet the interpretive flow surely runs in the other direction as well. To understand the significance of the Jew Jesus is to place him within Israel's traditions and witness to the character of God. Moreover, the Old Testament offers a richness reflecting a long period of living with God through thick and thin. By contrast, the New Testament remains regrettably short and covers only a brief period of years. These texts seem overshadowed by the expectation of an immediate End, that most believers no longer share and that can foster indifference to the long-range future of the earth and of humankind. If one were living in

---

11. Hick, *Faith and Knowledge*, 241.

end-times, giving thought to the day after tomorrow would seem futile. But applied (specific issues) ethics faces some of its most important issues in intergenerational choices for the future.

THE WAYS OF THE LORD

One concept for pursuing coherent biblical themes fruitful for ethics is the inclusive phrase "the ways of the LORD." This is not a clearly moral text or concept, since these are God's rather than human ways—the latter being the topic of morality. God's ways constitute all that believers actually experience or know of God, since revelation limits itself to divine action by definition. The eyes of faith do not penetrate into God's thoughts. And God's motives remain human conjectures. God's ways constitute the divine character. Character, to repeat, is formed and discerned through repeated consistent and coherent patterns of action. Over time communities of faith construe discernible patterns within divine actions and therefore believe that they discern God's character. That can enable the faithful to distinguish the voice of the times from the voice of God, both in the texts themselves as well as in subsequent uses of the texts.

In biblical traditions *the ways of God become imitable*: "So now, Israel, what does the LORD your God require of you? Only to fear the LORD your God, to walk in all his ways, to love him, to serve the LORD your God with all your heart and with all your soul" (Deut 10:12). Though the continuation of this texts insists on obeying all of God's commandments—a text supporting a revealed morality hermeneutics—the Deuteronomist returns to the ways of the Lord, to a God "who is not partial and takes no bribe, who executes justice for the orphan and the widow, and who loves the strangers, providing them food and clothing" (10:17–18). These ways set the pattern for human imitation: "You shall also love the stranger, for you were strangers in the land of Egypt" (10:19).[12]

The task of practical Christian ethics is then to see and hear, to reason, to decide and to act in ways that *resonate with the ways of God*. The ways of God create a hermeneutical guide, a canon within the canon—criteria for judging texts by means of the text. In terms of the triad diagram offered in chapter 2, the two sides from the apex to the base, the patterns of action

---

12. This pattern of joining the ways of God with the commandments reappears in Deut 26:17. "Today you have obtained the LORD's agreement: to be your God; and for you to walk in his ways, to keep his statutes, his commandments, and his ordinances, and to obey him." Also in Deut 28:9; Josh 22:5; 1 Kgs 3:14; 8:58; 11:38 (with a bit of stretching); Isa 2:3; Jer 7:23; Mic 4:2.

from God toward humans, offer bearings for imitation for the base, the horizontal, for Christian ethics. Moreover, this appeal to the ways of God here takes a theological rather than a case law approach.

THREE STORIES OF THE WAYS OF GOD

Three biblical stories offer clues to God's ways: Israel's beginning as a people in the story of the Exodus, the beginning of the human race in the first chapters of Genesis (reflecting memory of the Exodus), and the new beginning to which believers attest in the gospels and letters of the New Testament. Each expresses divine intent, purpose, and character: the ways of God. Each offers theological bearings for a biblical ethics.

THE EXODUS

The Exodus story begins with a LORD (YHWH) who identifies with the sufferings of a slave people: "I have observed the misery of my people who are in Egypt; I have heard their cry on account of their taskmasters. Indeed I know their sufferings, and I have come down to deliver them" (Exod 3:7–8). These are God's people, not Pharaoh's. This personal God acts in political, economic, and liberating ways. The Exodus story narrates suffering, promise, deliverance. It is not a "spiritual" story in the sense of being otherworldly, removed, or inward. Nor is it a story reflecting ideals of human or divine nature, given Moses' reluctance (4:13) and the people's repeated complaint, "what have you done to us, bringing us out of Egypt?" (14:11; 16:3; 17:3), or God's impatience with the whole sorry lot (Exod 32:10).

The Exodus story turns pessimistic when it focuses on humans. Moses is not an American hero. These former slaves are not a freedom-loving people. The text remains realistic throughout. It centers hope not in Moses or the people but in the LORD who "comes down." Psalm 136 celebrates this liberating event with a repeated congregational response at the end of each verse: "for his steadfast love endures forever" (vv. 10–26). This is a beginning that brings Israel to life as a holy (set apart for God's purposes) people. The divine purpose is to bring life sustaining justice to all: "and in you all the families of the earth shall be blessed" (Gen 12:3). Believers read this story as one of compassionate and saving love, providential in the sense that God seeks life and offers hope in the context of enslavement and despair. While death and violence play an important role in the Exodus, believers discern a pattern that is pro-life. Pro-life not only for Israel but for humankind.

Subsequent traditions invoke this key event in Israel's life normatively. "You shall not wrong or oppress a resident alien, for you were aliens in the land of Egypt" (Exod 22:21; 23:9; Lev 19:34). More positively, "You shall also love the stranger, for you were strangers in the land of Egypt" (Deut 10:19). The triangular logic, repeatedly explained in this book, is implied: What God has done for Israel now becomes imitable. This beginning of Israel's life also expresses the meaning of all human life: This holy people, singled out for God's purposes, exists not for itself but for God's universally redemptive intent. That is the required response to God's literally saving love. Israel's calling is to love God and neighbor by seeking and serving life. Subsequently the Christian church, designating itself as the New Israel, appropriates not only the name but the mission. Whatever the issue, Christian responses must be true to this fundamental vision of faith as life-affirming love of God and of neighbor.

GENESIS

The stories of the beginnings of the human race in the first chapters of Genesis are confessional. They express faith. In Adam ("earthling") and Eve the believing community describes itself and all human nature. The stories profess a good God whose words create life and declare it good. As creatures, Israel acknowledges itself to be dependent, not self-made. The text describes a deity who seeks a loving relationship with beings in God's own image (1:26), a resemblance or kinship that lies not in looks, power, or wisdom but in character (at least in aspiration). The likeness will become apparent when humans act like their divine parent. They flourish while their relationship with God remains intact; they wither when they violate it—a No! that echoes in their infidelity to each other.

PESSIMISM REGARDING HUMAN NATURE

These stories also express a deep pessimism about human nature: created good, humankind is not content with its dependent relationship on God but aspires to be like God (Gen 3:5). Pride, claiming to be more than one is, is the universal sin. It spoils what humans were meant to be, reverberates as fratricide between the first children, and sweeps toward the inclusive alienation of all creation from God. Things go from bad to worse. And by Genesis chapter 6,

> [t]he LORD saw that the wickedness of humankind was great in the earth, and that every inclination of the thoughts of their hearts was only evil continually. And the LORD was sorry that he had made humankind on the earth, and it grieved him to his heart (6:5–6).

How might these first Genesis chapters inform ethics? Beginning with positive features, human standing or worth, dignity, intrinsic value, the claim that a human life counts—all used as synonyms here—finds its origin in God. Here fundamental human standing grounds itself in God. It does not originate in humans or base itself in human capacity (as rationality and free will, now Liberalism's key good). Human beings count not for what not for what they have done or can do. Here human dignity is not self-referring but other-relational. Again, in contrast to a Western, Cartesian (à la Descartes) self-focused rational starting point, the biblical claim affirms that human standing (or worth) arises from an external source: from God's love. That love—explained no further with possible reasons for God's love—is the beginning of the biblical Story. God's love for Israel creates the beginning of God's efforts to redeem a fallen humankind. Human lives count because God creates and cares for them. Parents are to be respected because they serve as God's agents of creation. The honor due parents—one of the commandments—is indirectly due to God.

MODERN SECULAR ASSUMPTIONS

Biblical perspectives begin and continue with a personal God who creates, loves, redeems but also obligates humans. No further explanations required. Enlightenment self-evidence begins and continues with rational human beings who owe their lives to no one and take responsibility for their own lives. No further explanation required. Along with biblical human dependence on God for life itself comes the stark and unnerving—Liberally unacceptable—recognition that one's life is not one's own.

In biblical stories of beginning human life the meaning of being human remains pre-modern and strange. God creates humans as enlivened bodies, as dust now formed and animated by God's breath (2:7). Humans *are* their bodies as well as *having* bodies. To be sure, they are also persons, to use the modern term. Nevertheless: bodies are us! For better and for worse. That is bound to have relevance for an understanding of illness, of handicaps, of mortality and of the nature, function, and limits of medicine and medical technology. If in fact to dust we return (3:19)—and hope for a personal afterlife does not appear in Israel's traditions until very late—then such absolute mortality sets respect and care for life into sharp relief against non-existence. The facts of aging, of dependence, of needing care are not unnatural in these biblical images. To be human means to be dependent on God and others. Dependence therefore must not become a reason for being ushered out of life.

A more sobering implication of the early Genesis chapters is their realistic assessment of human nature. Again, pride is the besetting sin. It manifests itself in the overreaching that violates the relationship with God and alienates persons from each other. The allure is that "you will be like God" (3:5) expresses human overreaching. I have never seen a good use of "playing God." But those words do come to mind when reading about fetal tissue experimentation and more recently human embryonic stem cells research. The envisioned benefits, when they promise so much, must make even their advocates uncomfortable.

NEW TESTAMENT TEXTS

Turning to Christian beginnings, Christian ethics is the study of what it means to be human and of what humans are to think, be, and do in light of the creative, loving, and redemptive relationship of God with all creation. Specifically, that calls for ways of thinking and living that attest and express the redemptive divine acts in Jesus, the Messiah. One can describe both Christian faith and Christian ethics simply in terms of relationships or connections. Christian faith and ethics are bound to God through Jesus, for in him God heals the broken relationship with an alienated humankind. Christian faith and ethics are also bound to biblical texts since scripture attests to these divine acts and to the living God. And Christian faith and ethics are bound to the church since through baptism believers become members of the body of Christ, receive a new identity, and strive to think and to live true to their new identity.

What, then, are distinctive features of this new beginning? Jesus' key affirmation is this: "The time is fulfilled, and the kingdom of God is at hand; repent, and believe in the gospel" (Mark 1:15). Kingdom of God might be more usefully translated as the ruling presence of God. For the One who has always been understood as Lord approaches humankind, is "at hand," manifests divine presence in new and powerful ways. This divine nearness not only brings but enjoins "righteousness and peace and joy in the Holy Spirit" (Rom 14:1). The fitting human response is to repent and to affirm this new divine presence. The verb 'repent' implies action. It means to turn away from the old way of life and to turn toward and entrust oneself to God.

This encounter with the present God is so powerful and radical that it calls for a language of death and rebirth.

The examples of this new life, as in the Sermon on the Mount (Matt 5–7), are possible only because they presuppose the transforming presence and power of God. Moreover, the moral commands of Matt 5–7 are examples of what it means to walk in the ways of God's ruling presence. They are not definitive, as if one could add up and itemize them, much as 613 laws in the Old Testament. If these examples have a common denominator, it reaffirms the sum of the law in Israel's traditions: "You shall love the Lord your God with all your heart, and with all your soul, and with all your strength, and with all your mind; and your neighbor as yourself" (Luke 10:27 citing Deut 6:5 and Lev 19:18).

This new nearness of God calls for a renewed ethics. The ways of God again become normative. The Gospel of John offers a new commandment (13:34), "Just as I have loved you, you also should love one another." Since the Christian confession understands Jesus' love to include his sacrifice of himself for others, Christian ethics reaches beyond the Golden Rule, beyond "love your neighbor as yourself," beyond equity, to "as I have loved you."

A NEW/OLD MORAL LOGIC

Christian faith claims that God's ways manifest themselves in a new and universally redemptive action in the life, teachings, death, and resurrection of Jesus. Jesus not only proclaims the nearness of God's ruling—"the kingdom of God is at hand!"—but lives out of its power and reasons morally in its light. Indeed, Christian faith sees the ways of God ultimately and decisively revealed in Jesus. This Jesus is who God is and how God acts for humankind. This is the model for believers.

Yet both the identity of Jesus and its implications for him and for disciples proved difficult to discern and accept since they went against the grain of messianic expectations and against the logic of human self-assertion. The clearest textual example of this unexpected and unnatural quality of God's ways appears in the turning point of the Gospel of Mark at 8:27–38. The question over Jesus' identity elicits Peter's response, "You are the Messiah." Given that the gospels were written by Christians, that should be the right response. And yet immediately Jesus "sternly ordered them not to tell anyone about him" (8:30). In the following verse Jesus counters Peter's (and everybody's) concept of the messiah: "Then he began to teach them that the Son of Man must undergo great suffering, and be rejected by the elders, the chief priests, and the scribes, and be killed" (8:31). Peter objects to any such notion, eliciting a harsh reaction from Jesus as well as the repeated insistence: "If any want to become my followers, let them deny themselves and take up their cross and follow me. For those who want to save their life will lose it, and those who lose their life for my sake, and for the sake of the gospel, will save it" (8:35–36).

This counter-intuitive divine logic of God's ways renouncing self-centeredness may not have persuaded disciples until after Jesus' resurrection and vindicating manifestations of the Spirit of God. This logic certainly opposes contemporary cultural self-realization. "Be all that you can be!" seems antithetical to "take up your cross and follow me." Actually that U. S. Army invitation turns out to be either more misleading or more profound than it seems. Given that both soldiers and disciples put their lives on the line, their potential may be limited by their dedication.

One may call such reasoning a new/old logic because biblical beginnings and both Judaism and Christianity insist on living life for others. Ancient Israel understood itself as a servant people called to be a blessing to the world (Gen 12:2). A holy people (Isa 62:12) set apart for the aims of God, for walking in the ways of God, for honoring the name of God. Aspiring to self-realization requires a different context. If Jesus' "you have heard... but I say to you" (as in Matt 5) contrast new with old, that reflects divine nearness demanding deeper dedication. It is not so much an ethics new in content as a renewed and deepened vision of the moral life. Loving God first and then neighbor has always been the right way to walk in God's ways.

These New Testament texts constitute ground much plowed over. Little if anything in the preceding paragraphs is new or controversial. The goal here is to probe how such texts might contribute to a contemporary Christian ethics. The triadic diagram (chapter 2), once again, helps. In that visual conceptual aid, Jesus' proclamation, life, death, and resurrection appear as a renewed divine initiative that transforms those who receive and affirm it. The power of this divine presence, God's new move, now not focused on the ancient People of God but offered to all humankind, enables those empowered to live a new life, redirected from focus on themselves toward God and fellow human beings. The presence and love of God flows downward, as it were, to these believers in life-affirming ways. And it flows through them as well, horizontally, to others. The pattern is ancient and biblical. But the range and power of this new divine initiative is new. Enemies are now included within the range of divine and therefore of human love (Matt 5:44–45). Lepers, outcasts, gentiles, IRS agents, prostitutes, the poor, the insane, the handicapped, the incurable, the "harassed and helpless" (Matt 9:36), the naked, the imprisoned experience themselves to be loved by God. Both in New Testament texts and for subsequent Christian communities, the vertical divine moves—God's ways—become normative and imitable for Christian ethics, for the normative shaping of the horizontal, of morality.

Discerning what might be God's ways or what is loving in particular complex ethics issues, however, seems rarely to be self-evident. But the inclusiveness, unexpected range, and indiscriminate quality of divine love does promise ethical bearings for contemporary believers. Whatever they might conclude normatively, it must be congruent with divine active love on behalf of "the least of these who are members of my family" (Matt 25:40). Here salvation is this-worldly. It means feeding the starving, accompanying the sick, welcoming and including outcasts. This love not only includes the unexpected, it is sturdy, robust, practical, solid.

THE CALLING OF HUMANKIND

The three biblical stories in the previous pages provide content for "the ways of the Lord." Again, the three are Israel's beginning as a people in the story of the Exodus, the beginning of the human race in the first chapters of Genesis, and the new beginning to which believers attest in the gospels and letters of the New Testament. Each expresses divine intent, purpose, and character, offering patterns for "God's ways." Though none of these texts was definitively probed here, they do yield general directions. Since characteristic divine ways relate to human ways, these texts also reveal biblical concepts of human nature or of what it means to be human. That holds in both a descriptive and a prescriptive sense—both for who believers and all humans in fact are and for who they are called to be. When it comes to their calling, both Jews and Christians, are to walk in the ways of God. Indeed, that is the calling of humankind.

One challenge of contemporary ethics lies in learning to see and to speak, to reflect and to respond to ethical issues with God in mind. "God in mind" refers in large part to the biblical memory just sketched under "the ways of the Lord." Rephrased, the task of Christian ethics is to reconceive and to envision everything with eyes and mind transformed by God's redemptive love. A coherent rendition of that love—whether as revealed morality or revealed theology—must also function as the glasses that bring reality into focus. That holds from start to end, from the beginning of morality when a moral issue first presents itself, through the deliberative and communal process, to decisions and conclusions that can be shown to the church and to the living God.

This foray into biblical texts has offered a theological vision or what is named *metaethics*—a view of reality, of the meaning and purpose of life, of the source of the value and status of human beings, an inclusive view of faith as a triadic relationship between God, individuals, and communities that connects believing with doing. The Christian name for metaethics is simply *theological ethics*. Paraphrased that means a biblical/Christian vision applied to ethical/moral reflections, issues and decisions.

RELIGION: THE STUDY-OF, THE ADVOCACY-OF

In a secular context, the study and teaching of religion differs fundamentally from the advocacy of religion. Teaching and studying religion at a public college or university are academic in nature. Neither faculty nor students are asked if they have religious commitments. Teaching and studying at a divinity school or seminary is also an academic matter, except that the context differs. Seminaries seek to educate persons preparing for religious professions and therefore involve future advocacy in diverse forms. Seminarians may be assumed to have religious commitments. But even in such a context, a sermon differs from a lecture. The study-of remains a quest for learning and understanding. The practice-of expresses personal and communal commitments. The advocacy-of is the calling of Christians to witness to God's redemption in the life, death and resurrection of Jesus.

BIBLICAL FAITH IS INCLUSIVE

For biblical believers everything is or should be religious. The simple reason for believers conceiving everything as religious is that God created it all, sustains it, and declares it to be good: as in Genesis, chapter 1. God's creative and sustaining care is not only a thing of the past. Moreover, biblical believers acknowledge themselves to be responsible or accountable to God as LORD of everything. In effect that creates a trilateral relationship between individual believers, the community and God. And, if one expands the vision to include the environment, that becomes a four-way web of relationships. (The triangular diagram of chapter 2 can visualize the wider circle of biotic life as encircling *community* but is not shown.) The nature of these relationships should evoke gratitude. Human gratitude for being alive relates to parents, to friends, to communities, to our world—God's world, actually—expresses the goodness of it all. Human relatedness or connectedness, though easily assumed as given and ordinary, is in fact precious and sustaining. Anyone who has lived in cities bombed, levelled, silenced by war recognizes normally crowded streets as alive, reassuring, sustaining and good.

The complexities of modern life may at times frustrate anyone. But they tend to improve life together. Such relationships involve ethical responsibilities That includes political and governmental responsibilities. Christians may and should serve in government as a *religious vocation*, enlarging the meaning of that phrase. The security and reliability of government services provide firm ground for our shared lives in ways that we only recognize when government threatens to fail or actually fails. For example, when public servants risk their own career in telling truth to power, in public witness that shames the selfish or thoughtless actions of superiors in words that will not be forgotten, they serve us all and honor God.

HONORING GOD'S NAME

Biblical believers are called to honor God's name. That includes Christian ethics. Being tasked with honoring God's good name may imply the responsibility of not speaking too readily in God's name on behalf of what are deemed to be Christian causes. American political traditions and exemplary precedents prove diverse and rich enough for Christian citizens to witness to God's justice initially *without* invoking God's name. God's justice reflects divine self-identification with the poorest, the neediest, or simply the least among us. Egalitarian secular democratic values also speak against glaring economic inequalities and injustices and oppose the hardships imposed on those who see no way ahead. Moreover, it is important to be self-aware that, whether rich or poor, politically Right or Left, white or black Americans are one people, one nation. In a secular age, no longer acknowledged as "one nation under God," but we are all Americans. And that may call for hospitality for those on the way there: asylum seekers, refugees, and the human unborn. Speaking American, as citizens respecting and self-identifying with those among us with little or no hope, should precede, if possible, speaking explicitly as Christians when it comes to public policy. Respecting God's name includes discretion in when to invoke it.

AMERICAN MODERN SECULARISM AND ITS RISE

Modernity, a term defining contemporary Western culture, distinguishes itself as technologically, scientifically and progressively advanced, in contrast to what preceded it. It reflects the belief that human reason rather than religion should govern public life, politics, law, national organizations and the like. A major reason for objecting to religion in a public or political roles were the European wars of religion during the sixteenth, seventeenth and early eighteenth centuries. Fought after the Protestant Reformation began in 1517, those wars disrupted the religious and political order in the Catholic countries of Europe. The Enlightenment or the Age of Reason, a philosophical movement that dominated in Europe during the eighteenth century, was alienated by such violence in the name of God. It insisted that human reason rather than traditional religious faith should be the primary source of authority and legitimacy. Humankind, as it were, had matured and had outgrown its spiritual tutelage and its religious hostilities. Enlightened by its rediscovery of human reason Western humanity should rely on reason. It was time to grow up and become rationally independent of religious dominance.

In terms of values, the Age of Reason advocated liberty, progress, tolerance, fraternity, constitutional government, separation of church and state. Such values also influenced American revolutionaries and the creation of the Declaration of Independence and the United States Constitution. The practice of religion was and remains protected as a human right. But religion was privatized, individualized, and in a political sense neutralized. Christianity, including Christian ethics, was left to personal individual choice, banned from politics except for ceremonial occasions.

4

The Social Contract

THIS PHILOSOPHICAL-POLITICAL AMERICAN THEORY includes a reference to a deity, yet it remains secular. It played a role in the American Revolution and continues in popular justifications of American democracy. Why would it be included at some length in a book on Christian ethics? The reason is that the social contract played a role—and may continue to have a role—in the secularization of this nation. The theory preempts a Christian metaethics (view of reality) of the nature and role of citizenship. The justification of this national secularism may be its longevity. Moreover, its logic appeals to enlightened self-interest. And that is not a easily compatible with religious perspectives.

The social contract is a story of how Western society was modernized or transformed and secularized during the Enlightenment. It is used here as a focal point for the secularization of American culture and for its influence on Christian ethics. The social contract theory became popular in the eighteenth-century Enlightenment, was an answer to the search for a better form of government than that resulting from the traditional divine right and rule of kings, hereditary monarchy, and the social stratification of inherited status and privilege. Such venerable institutions and practices had been integrated into religion, were blessed by it, and benefited the church. Increasing dissatisfactions with established political institutions also cast critical light on the political role of traditional religion. Indeed, it initiated a growing secularism that extends into and now permeates American culture.

The social contract offers a story that explains and seeks to justify the inclusive shift from a religious to a secular culture and from support of monarchy to a justification of democracy. As such, the contract story resembles the biblical creation story: this is how it all came about and how it should be. Except, of course, the stories are antithetical. One is modern and secular, the other ancient and religious. Both offer imaginative stories of the beginnings, of how and why communal life began. Both aim to portray human nature and offer a reasoned explanation of how and why current humanity came to be what it is now. Neither story is historically or literally true. Their truth is metaphorical and existential: This is how government makes sense.

The contract legend begins in a fictional state of nature in which human beings had fundamental natural rights but no government or law and order. In this imagined original time humans were not yet members of groups, communities, or states. They were by nature equal and free but without the safety or support of laws and civic order. Persons were born with certain rights to secure the necessities of life and to protect themselves. In short, each person was free, equal, and independent—but not secure. Individuals still lack the civil and social institutions that might secure rights. Thus life, while free, might also be nasty, brutish, and short (Hobbes). Humans, being rational in the sense of being self-interested, decide that their rights would be better served and more secure by creating laws and order, establishing a state, and prudently relinquishing some rights in order better to enjoy the remaining ones. Thus, one gives up one's right to all property with the understanding that others do the same. One forsakes any right to harm or injure as all others do so as well.

SECULAR AND RELIGIOUS STORIES OF HUMAN BEGINNINGS

In terms of ethics, both the biblical origin stories and the Nature God's story (in the Declaration of Independence) eventually integrate with and transform worldviews. They offer to make sense of civic and political life. They become intrinsic features of inclusive worldviews. In metaethical ways, they do not directly guide human conduct but endow human conduct with meaning. The link with ethics is derivative. Thus, an understanding of human nature forms the background against which vital values should shape moral conduct. Given who humans are, conduct should be guided by or reflect that nature. And if such conduct is deemed natural or normal, that endorses and recommends that conduct. The biblical and social contract stories remain different ethically. The Bible appeals to God and the imperative for believers to love God back and to share that love with the neighbor. The social contract remains secular and relies on individual self-interest and rational egalitarian consent. It calls for citizen respect and fairness, for justice but not for love.

The social contract's underlying logic of why humans create and obey the law is the pessimistic/realistic insight that human nature can be aggressive and overreaching. Civilized life needs security and protection from chaos. There will always be threats and abuses by those who take advantage and violate fundamental egalitarian justice. One thinks of free riders who take advantage of the rules but do not abide by them. The American lawless West—without sheriffs—comes to mind. To secure property generally, law and order must back and enforce the rules of the social contract.

In the words of secular advocates, the American founders' insights secure the foundations of democratic government as self-evident: The world based on rational self-interest and individual freedoms makes more sense than one in which religious believers resort to torture, undertake crusades and perpetuate religious wars. Democratic government as well makes better sense than any God-ordained self-serving monarchy denying subject-rights. Social contract foundations offer the prospect of a better future than the traditional hierarchical Christian world.

The social contract is not just a theory or a social and political idea but takes on life and legality in the Declaration of Independence and the US Constitution. Rather than monarchial power concentrated in one person, the memory of bad experiences convinces American founding fathers to divide government it into three branches. The intent is to build in safeguards, checks and balances. This contract derives its authority from "The people of the United States" (the opening words of the US Constitution), not from God. Natural rights, again, not God or religion, guarantee the right to life, liberty and the pursuit of happiness, and protect citizens. These rights proved to be revolutionary, successful and lasting. The social contract remains the real (though initially fictional and assumed) political agreement between people and their government. The contract tacitly defines the spirit of mutual obligations is now spelled out and enforced in positive law.

Lest one be absorbed by the details of the Social Contract in the Declaration of Independence and in our Constitution, what proves most important and remarkable is that this social/political contract proved to be revolutionary and successful. It replaced the existing monarchial authority of the British empire over American colonists with democratic governance based on the will of the American people. What was claimed as self-evident by the American colonists was obviously not self-evident to King George III. The colonials themselves were largely British and, if it were to come to military conflict, could be regarded and executed as traitors. Much was at stake. Striving for independence needed effective grounds to justify rebellion. The solution, self-evident to the founders and with assumed visionary universal appeal to all rational persons, is democratic government of the people, by the people and for the people. Just government must rest on the consent of the governed. The logic of the social contract insists on government by and for the people.

CHANGING THE WORLD BY DECREE

Historical hindsight assures American contemporaries of a good outcome of the American Revolution. Such retrospect may obscure the daring and courage expressed in that revolution. Contemporaries may well hold the claims of American revolutionaries to be self-evident, having been raised with such certitudes. To claim self-evidence *at the time*, however, is quite different. "We hold such truths to be self-evident," as the Declaration of Independence proclaims, declares natural human rights into existence then and there. It does that for all human beings and for all time. Surely that is daring, visionary, and amazing in the age of monarchies! One wonders whether the revolutionaries themselves were amazed by their own courage or by their eventual success.

SAYING SO CAN MAKE IT SO. SOMETIMES.

To pause in regard to how the revolution began, changing the world politically *by decree* deserves ethical analytic attention. The world was indeed changed by decree or declaration. But that took vision and involved serious risk. Revolution was for better or worse. Nor was such creating-by-decree wholly unique. The explorer: "I declare this land to be the property of the British crown." The judge: "I pronounce you husband and wife." A legal court: "We find you to be innocent." In my case, a judge declaring a US soldier who has taken the oath of allegiance to be "a citizen of the United States." Saying so can make it so. In the right context and by the right speaker(s). Language analysts call that *performative language*. In a revolutionary context, affirming individual rights into existence could cost the speakers their freedom and their lives! Gratitude to those who risked revolution and succeeded remains fitting. A grateful nation honors the memory, courage and sacrifices of its national founders!

THE POWER OF RIGHTS

Amazement over the creative power of words extends to the vitality and power of a specific word and concept that played a major role in the American revolution: *the declaration of rights*. A legal or political right is a claim recognized, justified and enforced by law. A moral right remains a claim but lacks legal standing. Legal rights come into being by decree in the context of legislators and juries and in certain other contexts. The right to national independence (and a war to back it up) justified the creation of the United States of America. The declaration of natural rights also created standing, legal, political and moral for colonists and eventually for slaves. Declaring rights, in the fitting context, can liberate and protect. What seems so simple remains remarkable nevertheless. The right to privacy, expanded to women seeking abortions, was created by a majority of the Supreme Court that denied the human unborn any right, including the right to life. Human rights were declared as endowed at birth—and not before! A few justices said so and made it so. And millions of beginning but unborn human lives were doomed. (*Rights* is the title of one of the subsequent chapters. As is *abortion*.)

THE SOCIAL CONTRACT: CRITICAL QUESTIONS

The social contract assumes and relies on prudent self-interest and natural rights. One needs to be clever and prudent when it comes to self-interest. Being rational sounds better. But "rational" remains morally questionable. That holds true for "self-interest" as well. Self-interest might indeed be deemed natural in the sense that it arises naturally and need not be taught. What is said to be natural is assumed to be descriptive and universal, but it may fall short of being acceptable and moral. That holds for self-interest as well—ubiquitous but rarely a moral concept.

A biblical perspective may conclude that such self-focus and self-interest reflects the Fall, the human fall from grace and alienation from God and from neighbors. In effect the assertion and priority of self-interest makes the love of self its highest good. In contrast, the biblical imperative is to love God and neighbor. That points away from self. Turning to the context of the creation of a new nation, the grounds for long-term success of a new nation and democratic self-evident individual rights may not actually be as sturdy, as promising or as self-evident as claimed. If the State of Texas were to declare secession from the United States with the same or similar justification as those cited in the American Revolution, its self-evidence might be intuitively contested by non-Texans.

A closer look at the assumptions of the social contract of the role of self-interest leads to serious questions. How can any community survive if love of self is assumed as prior to communal needs? In case of war, national enlistment posters will appeal not to self-interest—no longer rational or natural—but to what is needed and right: love of country and willingness to risk self in order to protect this nation. Not just a call to arms but the duties of soldiers and their effectiveness assume and rely on loyalty to serve country and on solidarity with comrades. The Declaration's inborn right to the pursuit of happiness bows out in times of communal or national distress such as war. At that point self-interest loses any self-evidence or rational status. As every soldier knows, in times of crisis no one needs even to be told what the priorities should be. Could it be that self-evident truths depend on circumstance? As to the biblical response to self-interest, Jesus insists, "strive first for the kingdom of God and his righteousness" (Matt 6:33).

A CONTEMPORARY VERSION OF THE SOCIAL CONTRACT

In 2018, Robert Reich used the title of the social contract to counteract growing divisions and political dissonance in American society. He did so with five moral propositions that express the positive values Americans share and that could create a new social contract to unite citizens. The five statements do not appeal to the traditional story of the social contract but invoke its spirit. Here they are:

1. Everyone should have an equal chance to get ahead.
2. No one should be discriminated against because of race, religion, gender or sexual preference.
3. No one who works full time should have to live in poverty.
4. People should take responsibility for themselves and their families, but deserve help if they need it through no fault of their own.
5. No one should have special privilege and power based on wealth or class.

These democratic social justice principles constitute a *declaration* and vision of what American workers need and deserve.

Analyzing these statements ethically, one might distinguish them in two ways, first in terms of human equality that reflect the appeal of the traditional contract story. Secondly as ways that go beyond or insist on more than the traditional social contract. First: Propositions 1, 2 and 5 insist on equal and fair standing and treatment. No more, no less. These three propositions insist on equal treatment. In the context of a democracy such equality is a version of fairness or egalitarian justice. The propositions almost affirm themselves. Propositions 3 and 4 seem more complex and more demanding to analyze.

Proposition 3 says, "No one who works full time should have to live in poverty." This is the claim for "a living wage." And while it holds for all who work and is equal in that sense, it goes beyond the equalities of the three statements in the first group. The US has minimum-wage laws. But it is doubtful that anyone would consider such laws sufficient to escape poverty. Therefore, Robert Reich proposes something new: *a legal living wage*. It implies that full-time work is valuable enough to lift working individuals and families out of poverty. Employers would be legally restrained from paying as little as possible and would predictably complain of being victimized by Socialism. But what remarkable innovation! From a humanist or Christian perspective this improvement would be fitting and just. This proposed change acknowledges human dignity and contributions of those who labor. Moreover, this innovation would imply something commendable about this nation. The concept of *citizen solidarity* should encourage Americans to care enough about each other that no working person or family should have to live in poverty. A Christian response may find these recommendations not only reasonable but compassionate and just. It resonates with biblical imperatives to care for those most in need.

Proposition 4 says, "People should take responsibility for themselves and their families, but deserve help if they need it through no fault of their own." That people should take responsibility for themselves and their families is nothing new. In fact, one would think that this has been true in the US since the end of slavery. That workers should receive help in cases of undeserved hardship is new. Yet how difficult to decide what is their own fault and what is not. Alcoholics deserve no help but accident victims do? A large family would receive more help since childcare is expensive. But large families are not environmentally responsible.

It seems that the specifics of the Contract Theory have yet to be worked out. Legal judges would have to become judges of human character. But the recognition that human beings encounter unforeseen hardships or emergencies and deserve help (from employers, unions, government programs) is not just humane but remains needed and right. Such changes would create a practical expression of loving the neighbor when the neighbor and his or her family face unanticipated and undeserved hardship! Note that both proposition 3 and 4 insist on better or more than is available now. As acts of citizenship solidarity or of loving the neighbor in hard times, these two recommendations might indeed offer constructive help and reconciliation in divided and difficult times.

ENLIGHTENMENT WITHOUT GOD?

American founding fathers may in fact have initiated a second revolution in their political separation from the British Empire. Politics and government, law, public education, justice, the practice of the professions, in short, American public life became a-religious. Secular changes may have been less noticed than the political transformations in the founding of a new nation, because this secular revolution was successful as well and became the new cultural norm. Here secularism means the avoidance of public and political religious speech, education, practices and worship.

The following paragraphs make the case that there was indeed that second revolution: The Enlightenment precipitated a cultural revolution from the medieval to the modern world in which traditional Christianity, hierarchically structured and culturally definitive, was replaced with an egalitarian and humanistic secularism. Secularism has since become the default positions of American public life, and perhaps of most Western nations, as the given or default assumption for culture and its institutions. Though stylistic references to God remain acceptable, the social contract and its priorities are secular.

Historians support the claim of a Western cultural transition from religious and hierarchical to secular and democratic. The historian Jon Meacham, in an interview describing the century or so before the American Revolution, noted that "The world was going from being vertical to being horizontal. It was vertical for a long time—with the divine right of kings, your entire destiny was shaped by the station to which you were born, and you had no other alternative. Everything came from above."

That changed when Thomas Jefferson shifted from a traditional hierarchy to a democratic ethos in which human rights, or the rights of all men (!) being created equal, came from the Creator. Mecham acknowledges Jefferson's role as "the great articulator of the manifestation of the Enlightenment that shaped the modern world." In the same interview, Meacham describes a difference between Benjamin Franklin and Jefferson that relates directly to religion and secularism at issue here: in an early draft of the Declaration, Jefferson had written the adjective "sacred." Franklin changed that to "self-evident"—"that these truths are self-evident." The point was that the appeal to reason would be more effective over time than invoking religion. Jefferson supported the revision.

Leading scholars of the Enlightenment do not seem to claim that the major figures of the Enlightenment were irreligious. Secularization was more subtle. Enlightenment figures redefined the meaning of religion in their own image. They invoke a Creator in terms unrecognizable from a biblical perspective. Biblical traditions point to God; Enlightenment reformers point to humankind. The Enlightenment historian Peter Gay implies a critical judgment when he sub-titled the first volume of *The Enlightenment: "The Rise of Modern Paganism."* He introduces this volume with Enlightenment figures' quest for a host of new freedoms, and summarizes, that freedom of moral modern persons lies in making their own way in the world. The author focuses on the European Enlightenment but claims that its American counterpart arose in close conjunction with European philosophical as well as political developments. Indeed, he insists that for American Enlightenment figures "the substance of their ideas came from a handful of European thinkers." Gay concludes that the heart of their charge against Christianity was that it made God the proper study of mankind [humankind] whereas the Enlightenment, as the ancient Greeks, insisted that the focus should be man.

BUT WHO IS THIS CREATOR?

May one ascribe secularism to our national founding fathers though they invoke a deity of sorts—"Nature's God"—in the first paragraph of the Declaration of Independence? Who is this Creator, this deity who endows and protects humankind with rights? In more devout times this may well have been thought to the biblical God familiar to Jews and Christians. But human rights are not mentioned there nor anywhere else in biblical texts. Perhaps a "Nature's God" is vague enough to be acceptable to the more traditionalist founding fathers. Moreover, Enlightenment deists would be assured that a deity would have a place in the new nation. A Nature's God was sufficiently flexible (undefined) to fit into the Enlightenment. As with human rights, this Creator was also declared into existence. But performative language normally does not extend to creatures creating a Creator. Here the traditional sequence is reversed. This may be as close as secularists ever come to deity. Could this be a case of invoking a sponsoring deity out of political prudence?

In fact, beyond the hope of saving these revolutionaries from British monarchy, there was another, long-term political reason for invoking such Creator. Our founding fathers were critical of established religion and meant to prevent religious interference in the governing of the envisioned nation. An amorphous deity without a history of choosing and judging rulers lent itself to separation of church and state. That, in turn, would offer a prudent preventive measure against religious meddling in the governing of the envisioned nation.

The religious identity and context for this Creator newcomer is *Deism*. Deism regards Jesus as a teacher who offered moral insights but lacked any transcendent status. And it is not Jesus who is invoked in the Declaration of Independence. The cited deity is the or a Creator, who lacks a personal name, does not speak or confront humans, does not express, seek or command love. If a person, this deity remains impersonal. Conceived as the mechanic of the universe: "He had built a superb machine, given it laws to run by and then [had] withdrawn. From such a view it followed that the only reliable road to knowledge of God's plans was through science, not religion, through observation and experiment, not dogma and revelation.

One does not cry out to such Creator or invoke its presence, forgiveness or guidance. Thought to be compatible with natural reason, this Creator seems closer to philosophy of religion than to Christian or Jewish faith. Removed and inaccessible, this deity was a construct, an invention, a deity ready-made (ex machina), helpful but discrete. Useful in declaring independence from British rule, this Creator's authority trumps British royalty with divine authority and with human rights! But this deity was also prospectively modest, since it would not interfere in founding and guiding the nation.

This Enlightenment Creator has little if any resemblance to the God of Jews and Christians. The invocation of a deist Creator seems to have been a concession to political necessity as well as an extension of secular social contract logic. This Creator appears as a counterpoint to British authority, remains unrecognizable as the biblical God, and fades out after having served the nation in three ways: justifying American independence, validating human rights, and replacing traditional religion with secularism as the default position. The secularizing goal was achieved with a newly minted and temporary Creator. Political religion becomes literally self-effacing!

CONTRACT AND COVENANT

Analyzing and contrasting the terms *social contract* and *biblical covenant* may help to clarify the differences between religious and secular perspectives. A contract involves more conditions or stipulations than a covenant. That implies that the parties creating the contract need to spell out the arrangement to be relatively secure. One thinks of bilateral business contracts, such as the sale of a house. By contrast, a covenant is an agreement that presupposes considerable trust. A marriage vow forms a covenant for life that takes a lot for granted. Conditions or stipulations here seem inappropriate and are simply lumped together generically into "for better or worse, for richer or poorer, in sickness and in health, until death do us part." After all, the couple loves each other. That will not be assumed for contracting parties—who proceed at arm's length.

CONTRACTS ARE AGREEMENTS ENFORCEABLE BY LAW

Covenants must rely on mutual respect, character or love. That may leave the participants more vulnerable. Covenant-makers pledge themselves, not just their property or services. Biblical covenant texts witness to God pledging God-self to individuals and communities. No matter what! Except, of course, for infidelity, which violates and may end the covenant. Given the character of the biblical God, whose word, promise and love endure forever, the chance of infidelity here remains one-sided.

The deist Creator endows human rights at birth, a gift that seems unilateral, asking nothing in response. In other words, this newly minted Creator offers neither a contract nor a covenant when endowing humans with rights at birth. The contract remains an agreement solely between humans to refrain from the violence and resulting insecurity of a state of nature. In contrast, the biblical covenanting God pledges loving presence but makes demands! That God obligates covenanting individuals and communities—to love God and to love neighbors. That holds for everyone—for life! That is, for a lifetime as well as "that they may have life, and have it abundantly" (John 10:10).

American founders of our nation, though familiar with the word *covenant*, chose the word *contract* to found a new nation. Was that because they considered citizenship to be a less demanding bond than the ancient term covenant? Or did they prefer *contract* because *covenant* was taken and was too difficult to secularize? "Taken," in the sense of being associated for eons with the name of the biblical God?

BIBLICAL COVENANTS

The Genesis story presents God as key actor. The early American secular vision dispenses with the historical God (God acting in history), leaving humans on their own except for an unknown Creator—newly minted, rights-granting but then fading out. The contract is made between human equals. That contrasts with biblical covenants between the LORD and a servant people. The biblical Creator insists not on rights but on love. Only the biblical covenant-originator has personal characteristics. That God also creates. But that ancient God is personal and loves, reasons, angers, decides, speaks, insists, acts and makes covenants. Only the biblical God is said to walk in ways that humans should choose and follow (Deut 8:6).

One more contrast between the social contract and a biblical covenant involves a difference in what each expects and assumes about human beings. The social contract assumes that enlightened human self-interest proves astute and persuasive enough to create communal justice. Here humans in a state of nature were wise enough to limit their own greed and aggression sufficiently to assent to fair limits, just dealings, and equal rights. Contractual prudent self-interested insight chooses law, endorses limits, maintains mutual respect and equal justice. A biblical perspective would regard such natural virtues as unrealistic. Such social-contract character knows nothing of the Fall. *It remains* prelapsarian (before the Fall). Biblically, that would seem not just counter-factual but fictional. In biblical contexts, humankind cannot ultimately help itself without God's aid. Moreover, even if humans could act reliably, justly and fairly, what is required of humans to get it right biblically reaches beyond justice and equal rights. The fact that God relates to humans in love requires love of humans for humans in turn. Love proves more demanding than respect and equal justice.

The social contract is a foundational story created by Enlightenment thinkers to explain and to justify the secular rationale for democratic government. The contract intends to justify democracy to replace traditional monarchy and a vertically structured social system. In effect, the story disowns the British monarchy and shifts government authority to the general will or the will of the American people. The story of the social contract remains secularly horizontal. It omits existing religious traditions. It buttresses human natural rights with an anonymous Creator, who bows out after endowing all humans with human rights, justifying a revolution, and evoking a new democratic nation. The secular Creator-story in effect prepares the way for the creation of US democracy and for the US Constitution. Thereafter, that Creator bows out.

AMERICAN BEGINNINGS AND SECULARISM

American founding fathers, aware of European traditional problems of linking politics and religion, sought to avoid repeating such connections or inter-relationships. Secular policies promised avoiding such long-standing errors. Separation of church and state coupled with freedom of religion promised a better future for both. In a context of political freedom, of revolution from England, religious freedom from politics made sound sense. In the formation of American national beginnings, the legal separation of state and church goes back to the First Amendment to the US Constitution: "Congress shall make no law respecting an establishment of religion, or prohibiting the free exercise thereof." Similar exclusion of religion now applies to public institutions such as education, law, economics, and the military services (except for chaplains). Secularism's most pervasive influence in modern American culture now lies in being self-evident and assumed. Living, speaking or voting religiously now seem to be the exceptions.

POLITICAL ADVANTAGES OF SEPARATING CHURCH AND STATE

From the perspective of politics or government, it seems prudent to separate state and church. Counting the ways, separating these institutions avoids religious interference from gaining political standing, power, or influence. Religious institutions, free-standing, so to speak, would not be able to claim financial support—which is always contested already. Religionists—that label reflecting a certain mistrust—would not have standing or political connections with authority to affect legislation. They would lack any right to *meddle*, as politicians might put it. Churches would simply not be "players" in state or political contexts and competitions. And, of course, religious organizations would have to pay for their own expenses. Church members are faced with more responsibilities than in times past.

MEANINGS OF SECULARISM

The American social contract was and remains secular. It now pervades American culture. The *Oxford English Dictionary* defines secularism as "The doctrine that morality should be based solely on regard to the well-being of mankind in the present life, to the exclusion of all considerations drawn from belief in God or in a future state" (2nd ed., 1989). Another definition appears in the *Encyclopedia of Global Religion* (2011): "Secularism may indicate a nonreligious world-view, an ideology, a political doctrine, a form of political governance, a type of moral philosophy . . ." The latter definition, in the context of a brief essay, insists that secularism cannot be reduced to anti-religiousness. It is also guided by a vision of society and of the Enlightenment with the goal to institutionalize secularity and the ideas of secularism in law, education, politics and economics. In effect, all dimensions of public national life should remain humanistic. And humanism defines itself as philosophy of life that, without supernaturalism, affirming human ability and responsibility to lead moral lives that aspire to the greater human good. In secular times, religious self-understanding and practices become more complex.

A less formal version of secularism would be that, if one had to mention religion at all, a secularist might regard secularism as an honest way of living, including all the complexities, limits, hardships and disappointments with realistic honesty and without recourse to supernatural reassurance. As a courtesy to believers, the last word in the preceding sentence is not "illusion."

Sociologists are also taking a closer look at secularism and go into some depth in their research. They distinguish hard from soft secularism. Hard refers to an irreconcilable opposition to religion. It includes militant atheism, thorough eradication of religion and replacement with an ideology, as in Marxism. Soft secularism is what describes American secularism. "[T]he U.S. Constitution set politics on a new course by wisely prohibiting a religious test for public office. This is an example of a political initiative to establish soft secularism at the societal level of institutions that leaves matters of conscience to individual choice." The author offers no explanation of why excluding religion may be endorsed with "wisely." Another example of soft secularism extends secular Americanism to law, politics, art, and learning. Such soft secularism respects religious convictions. A free society includes respect for human diversity and choices, that is for a range of human convictions and practices, The freedom to make diverse life choices should be respected unless harmful implications threaten the self or others. Such liberty, too, is justifiable with the logic of the social contract.

OVERLAPPING AND CONTRASTING VISIONS

In looking back to American national beginnings, the purpose was not historical but focused on two versions of American self-understanding, two metaethics, secular and Christian. Americans now live in secular times. Even if one affirms both America and God, it cannot be simple addition. "In God We Trust," the motto on US currency, serves as a sample of simple addition. "Simple addition" here means that religion is simply tacked on to decisions based on other grounds.

The conviction that Christian patriotism is a genuine option and not an oxymoron or a simple addition to secularism is assumed here. Serving God and serving a community or nation may conflict, but not in principle. Relating social contract themes to Christian faith may endorse the social contract's vision of human beings as individually worthy of legal and moral standing and protection, inherently equal, rational beings—able to recognize their own self-centeredness and of constraining it sufficiently to make democracy possible. Of course, the contract vision was aspirational initially, since those who proposed and supported it often remained slave owners. Initially this democratic vision of the nature and meaning of government and of natural rights was applied only to white men. Extending it to all men cost America a bloody civil war. Extending the vision of equal human standing to women took an additional century and remains a thing in progress. Given this ambivalent national history, confidence in the social contract becomes muted. Historical inequalities, as pervasive poverty or the inability to afford medical treatments may resist inclusion in the equality assumed in the social contract. The equality expressed in the social contract may not be able to serve those of us who experience expensive disabilities or illnesses—or any ill that exceeds the dimensions we ascribe to the social contract.

THE MODERN AMERICAN VISION IN DISTRESS

American individual human intrinsic equality and standing remain aspirational. The large gap between rich and poor disheartens the many without work, without medical insurance, without sufficient earnings to raise a family, without means to repay educational debts. Factional party deadlock, the grip of the rich and powerful on legislators, the resulting difficulties of the losers—all weaken the loyalties, pledges, oaths, bonds, trust and indeed the assumed contract that unites and protects citizens. The mutual respect and expectations implied by the social contract—equal citizens must respect as well as deserve respect from each other—recedes when political partisan politics overwhelm dedication to country and Constitution. Adversarial divisions may numb legislators to the plight of the least among us.

The desperate among American citizens may well hope that a strong man might save this nation from itself. The individual rights warranted by the social contract and Constitutional protections may fail to unite the nation in hard times when human needs threaten to outweigh human freedoms. We the people may fail the vision that has survived through thick and thin for two centuries. When either the House of Representatives or the Senate become so dependent upon or controlled by an autocratic executive and rich donors that their sworn allegiance to country and Constitution fails, we all lose. Our founding fathers may not have foreseen that democracy not only needs the Constitution but requires a certain character quality in political leadership as well as in the electorate.

The social contract's assumption that humans incline to be self-centered resonates with the ambivalent biblical image of human nature. While God's creation is good in all of its aspects, including human beings, from the very beginnings, humans disappointed God and each other. Created in God's image and blessed with a Garden that met all their needs, the image of or likeness to God proves hard to discern in the conduct of the first couple. The temptation to be like God, conceived not in terms of divine generosity and love but in human overreaching and pride seems perennial. So are the dire consequences.

CONTRASTING VIEWS OF HUMAN NATURE

In contrast to enlightened confidence in human reason and progress beyond crude self-interest, Christian faith perspectives judge the human condition of ego-centricity to be flawed beyond self-improvement and self-help. An actual liturgical confession of sins may exemplify Christian pessimism about self-help. Christian liturgies, including confessions of sins both past and present in their worship services, reflect believers' self-understanding. Speaking as one, they confess, "Almighty God, to whom all hearts are open, all desires known, and from whom no secrets are hid: Cleanse the thoughts of our hearts by the inspiration of your Holy Spirit, that we may perfectly love you and worthily magnify your holy name, through Jesus Christ our Lord."

The definitional difference between social contract secularism and Christian faith—one claiming that humans are on their own for better or worse, the other insisting that humans are created by and called to love God and each other—biblical texts have less confidence in human nature than the prospects of enlightened reason. A secular pulling-ourselves-up-by-our-bootstraps seems so much more inviting and dignified than a Christian and biblical admission of needing help. The words of the judicial oath, "So help me God" becomes a plea that includes all aspects of Christian life!

In a biblical sense, human dignity, its worth and standing, derive not from rational, resolute and self-relying mature effort. Rather, human standing originates from God's creative, sustaining, and redemptive love. That source originates beyond humans. Moreover, biblically humans count not because they can think—along the line of liberals or of philosopher Descartes' "I think, therefore I am." Nor do they count because of some other worthy capacity or quality. Rather humans count because they are loved. Passive sentence! Loved by God. The biblical God names humans as special in a relational sense. God creates humans in God's image (Gen 1:26-27). And that bestowed relationship assures their standing.

THE IMAGE OF GOD AND THE MEANING OF LIFE

The meaning of "in the divine image" biblically ascribed to human beings remains contested. There is probably not a theologian who has not written about the meaning of that image. Since the word *image* is ambiguous, and making images of God is biblically prohibited, one may be at liberty to find coherent meaning as best one can. Here, image is taken to be a relational term, as in the expression "like father, like son." But it cannot be a visual likeness for obvious reasons. Humans are kin and akin to God in some other sense. Inheritors of the Enlightenment find human reason to be the self-evident meaning of the image of God. Yet being smart seems never to be as important in biblical texts as in American popular culture. And even in a secular culture, gravestones lauding the dead "he knew much" lose out to "he loved much." The likeness, then, may relate to character.

The prevailing and pervasive character of God in biblical traditions is that God loves humankind. The origin of such love seems to lie less in humans than in God. What God asks of humankind—commands, rather—is to love God in return and to share God's love with neighbors. That, in fact, is the biblical meaning of life. Its simplicity may disappoint. Christians discern such love in the message, life and death of Jesus. When humans practice loving God and neighbor in word and deed, humans come into their own as children of God.

The key difference between Christians and the secular does not lie in some human quality, ability or inclination. It is simply the experience of God's presence. Experiencing God's love surprises. The New Testament speaks of being born again (John 3:1-10). I have used that expression myself. That may mean that one's identity changes. Tasting God's love, when welcoming it, transforms the self. One sees differently, thinks and plans differently. One joins a new community, the church. One becomes a new person, even though the old one still hangs around. Except of course, it takes time to get adjusted, to focus differently, to work out how things relate to each other, to make sense, and to adjust to increased responsible living.

The *first* of the two great commandments is to love God. That is possible only because God initiated love first. The present tense—loves us first—would be more accurate since the relationship is lifelong and may begin before birth. Indeed, the relationship between humans and God is believed to extend beyond death. God's resurrection and judgment of humankind constitutes the initial postscript.

Modern secular life in an American context regards the individual as owning his/her own life and of being responsible for oneself and to those linked with oneself. That holds true for the social contract. One's life is one's own. One can make a life-contract/covenant with it without asking for permission. Of course, once one commits to contracts/covenants one commits oneself. The social contract obligates for life. So does the traditional wedding vow. And responsibilities to one's children, while diminishing as they mature, may be lifelong as well.

5

Love and Faith

THE THREE WORDS OF the title, "love and faith" might be found at the close of a love letter that expresses both affection and confidence. Or the words might be part of a prayer, expressing gratitude, devotion and commitment. Christians worship the God who is personal, who creates and sustains the cosmos, listens to us, helps us, loves us, blesses us and expects us to share that love with our neighbors. Perhaps most remarkable, this God in turn asks us to return God's love. The goodness of our lives and the joy of living reflect the creative love of God. We may be awed by God's magnificent creation and sustained care. But how remarkable that God knows our names, seeks to share our lives, redeems and sustains us!

In continuing to describe aspects of Christian faith expressed in the diagram of chapter 2, this chapter focuses on love and faith, key Christian virtues. Human love and faith form affirmative human responses to God's revelatory initiative. When both love and faith function as they should, they create relationships that interconnect Christians with God and with each other. The main task here is to analyze love and faith for their meanings for Christian ethics.

It begins with God's initiative. This means not just that God creates and forms humankind but that God loves humans individually and communally and seeks their company, hoping—in fact commanding—to be loved, trusted and served in response. It is important not to reduce love or faith to feelings. Love can and should continue when feelings fade or cease. On God's part, love as divine commitment to humankind lasts a lifetime at a time.

LOVE AND FEELINGS

In humans, feelings, including religious feelings, may only make cameo appearances. We incline to ascribe loving feelings to God as well, in whose image or likeness we are created. Since God is holy, the divine character transforms its features.

Yet God's love is understood as God's care for humans, care expressed in creating, loving, blessing, redeeming humans. Such love has manifested itself at great cost. Christian witness insists that God's care and friendship with lost humans became most evident in Jesus' crucifixion. Jesus' self-sacrifice intended to reconcile an alienated humanity with God. This crucifixion expressed God's and Jesus' conviction that such sacrifice would reconcile an alienated humanity with its God. This was God's manifestation of love expressing itself at great cost: seeking, forgiving and redeeming sinners, God offered his only Son. If one dares to ascribe thoughts to God, could God have expected that "surely now they will be reconciled with me!" If one ascribes feelings to God, we can suspect how painful it is to a parent to lose a child. No doubt, there is enough misery in the world to trouble God. To keep on redeeming a sinful world expresses God's love and care. But God's love and character must be made of sterner stuff than feelings.

AMERICAN SECULARISM

Since America is largely secular, personal experience of God may come as a multi-faceted surprise. That God seeks out humans to bless, to redeem and to call may surprise in a God-forgetful context! There were times when it was thought that God's existence could be proved—proved by reasoning and argument. Such attempts prove to be futile. More to the point, how condescending that humans would do what only God does—prove that there is a real God. God reveals God-Self. The experience of the living God—revelation—speaks for itself. Yet not in a way that leaves no other interpretations or rendition,

God may surprise us. Who knows God's ways? Good news in a secular land! There is a God after all! The personal presence of God surprises and convinces. Descriptive words fall short of proof. Converts witness to being filled with the Holy Spirit. They describe the experience as "being born again." Experiencing God's love transforms humans. It changes who they are. At times they insist on a new name to indicate a new self. One searches for analogies. Experiencing God's love can resemble close friendship or—one hesitates—being married. One begins to see life from a new or transformed perspective. And, of course, one is surprised, changed and grateful. Experiencing God's presence has communal implications. Loving God, being friends with God, can transform individuals into members of new communities, that is, the Christian church.

NEW SELF-UNDERSTANDING

Becoming and being Christian changes or transforms the self. The experience of God's presence affects one's way of perceiving reality. Now all that is may be experienced or recognized as related to God. Becoming Christian should alter our former understanding of just about everything. This world is God's world. And human beings have new inherent worth as children of God. Strangers, outsiders, lawbreakers, the poorest of the poor have new standing in being linked with God's special care. The sick, the old, the outcast, the hungry, the socially unattractive should be respected and cared for by Christians. Humans being linked with God's special care count not because of what they have achieved or deserve but of who they are in relation to God. God links their identity, as one's own, with God. Being friends of God should break down social barriers and bias of long duration. Nor do such effects of being known and loved by God remain a one-time thing. Once discerned they persist for a lifetime. Indeed, longer than that. Christian traditions note that God remembers, resurrects, and holds humans accountable for their lives. Such remembering, too, expresses God's care and love. God's friendship is forever, even in judgment and accountability.

Christian ethics concerns the human-human dimensions of the covenantal triangular relationship (in the diagram of chapter 2). Both love and faith transform the inter-human dimension by linking it with God. Christians and Jews regard this connection with God to be a great blessing. Without the divine initiative of loving humans, human life may become godless, might well be meaningless or become brutish, nasty, and short. That holds not just because humans do not do well on their own. More importantly, humans tend to be inordinately focused on themselves and their own individual prospects. Yet God creates them for each other and for God. Christian faith should respond gratefully to God's love and is called to share that love with the neighbor. Absent the presence and love of God and given human indifference or aggression, what would or could keep humans from despair?

GOD'S LOVE AND THOSE DISLIKED

Love is a characteristic of the biblical God. God loves sinners, without being repulsed, one assumes. Or despite being repulsed? Sinners count as far as God is concerned. Given any sort realism about the depth, variety and continuity of human sin, such divine patience, endurance and grace must be among the greatest of God's miracles. The phrase "to know him is to love him" is great praise. Applied to God's *knowledge and love* of human sinners, the phrase loses its triteness. Both God's knowledge of sinners and the dimensions of God's love for those sinners extend beyond measure. One implication of that judgment is that God need not like someone to love that person. And if Christian ethics takes its bearing from the character of God, humans, too, are called to love those whom they do not like.

What, then, might be a reasonable Christian definition of love? Endless patience comes to mind first. So as well, liking a person is not a prerequisite of loving that individual. The biblical command to love enemies comes to mind (Luke 6:27). In a family context, liking individuals is not required. We love parents, our children and friends because they are ours, not because we like them. The same holds for the poor, the imprisoned, the outcast. The great commandments are to love God and neighbor. And neither of them has to be likeable to be loved.

Does that shed light on the meaning of "love"? Love seeks the good of the person loved. Love seeks to bless, to make whole, to restore, to redeem. Again, no affection or liking required. The thesaurus adds kindness, caring, compassion, generosity and altruism. For biblical believers, God's character defines the meaning of love. And that does not bode well for the persons we dislike. And, in turn, it does not bode well for those of us who simply avoid the unlikable.

GOD'S LOVE AND HUMAN RESPONSES

When secularism dismisses God, that prevents any attempt to understand the concept or the reality of God. Attempts of believers to prove the existence of God has gone out of fashion, thank God. As mentioned, there is something condescending about seeking to establish the reality of God. Assuming that God creates and sustains humans, that the creature should seek to verify the reality of its Creator patronizes God. Secularism, to repeat, dismisses God. From the perspective of faith, God does not coerce human recognition, worship, faith or love. Yet since God is real, personal and loving, as Jews and Christians claim, what condescension to deny or to ignore God's care for the unliked. Agnosticism (the claim that God is unknown or unknowable) seems more modest and defensible. Christians should admit both the condescension and impossibility of proving God's existence. God reveals God-Self to those who seek. The low-key version of that recommends, "taste and see!" (Ps 34:8). The presence of God creates its own verification.

The fitting witness of believers to God would be worship, praise, dedication, service and love of God. That love in turn would extend to God's love of humans. God, the biblical God of Israel's and Christian traditions, verifies him- or herself. (God-Self? "God" is personal but resists gendered pronouns). The traditional term for naming God's self-manifestation is *revelation*. The subjective reception of such revelation is *conversion*. "Meeting God" can be one of the most transforming experiences of life. Regrettably, the expression now implies death. The dead, by definition, do not have relationships with anyone. But Christians look to God restoring the dead and the hope of eternal life.

ENCOUNTERS WITH GOD

What follows here are implications of the experience of God's love. The joy of the moment of experiencing God's presence and love may well overwhelm any reflections about its implications. Therefore . . . what? Therefore, everything changes. Akin to getting married or giving birth, nothing quite remains what it was. For the young, occupational options must be reconsidered. For example, a serving profession may become an option. Income is no longer all that counts. Marriage may take on new directions. Planning for children may expand beyond personal wishes to include the fact of an overpopulated world. The term "transvaluation of all values" fits here. Human responses to God' love, just as responses to others who love us, is a back-and-forth thing. The conviction that God knows human thoughts is not a conversation stopper but an incentive to converse.

The biblical God is personally accessible to those who seek. Important for Christian ethics, the church community is a forum in which Christians seek to understand the renewed moral dimensions of their lives. Believers do not just show their reflections to God but to one another. The first and greatest commandment forms the context for communal reflection: "You shall love the Lord your God with all your heart, and with all you soul, and with all your mind" (Matt 22:37). And that is best done together in Christian community and with God.

GOD AND THE LIMITS OF HUMAN LANGUAGE

In a Christian reading of biblical texts, God expects two related human responses to God's creating and blessing of humankind: faith and love. Both words name relationships. Both are used in God-human and interhuman relationships. But when human words describe the actions and character of God, those terms become metaphorical rather than functioning literally. "Metaphorical" means that language for God retains the meanings ordinarily ascribed—and yet it differs. The meaning is transformed when linked with God. Human language is all we have. Believers assume that God is a linguist and understands all tongues. How to speak with God can be problematic.

For example, referring to God as "Father," as in the Lord's prayer, "Our Father," is similar to what "father" means but also differs. God as Father is one step removed from what that word ordinarily means. God is Father of all fathers. Indeed, God is the Father of all humans. The word belongs into the context of family. And, again, of all human families. To be fatherless can imply serious deprivation. Having God as Father implies human safety and protection. "Father" also makes this earth into our trusted home. A key word in describing the character of this Father is love: "God is love, and those who abide in love abide in God, and God abides in them" (1 John 4:16). Biblical believers trust that God's love not only lasts through human lifetimes but manifests itself beyond life in a universal resurrection, Judgment and an eternal life with God.

Speaking of God tends to become grandiose and ever so serious. But what of small things? Does God enjoy or make jokes?

MATTHEW'S GOSPEL AND ETHICS

The Gospel according Matthew reflects about the Great Judgment and the decision of who shall be saved or lost (Matt 25:31–46). Those approved by God for aiding humans in need did *not* cite religious reasons, faith or love. Without offering motive or reason, the story focuses on actions. That action is an example of the second great commandment: love of neighbor. In terms of the Great Judgment, those who helped the least of humankind will be saved for eternal life. The story omits motives. The charitable helpers were surprised that God knew or was involved. The fact that Jesus told the story makes it Christian. It certainly is a story of practical love and rings true to the biblical witness and to the character of God. The key text is Matt 25:40: "And the king will answer them, 'Truly I tell you, just as you did it to one of the least of the these who are members of my family, you did it to me" (25:40).

The fact that God identifies with these compassionate persons is news to them. They acted without awareness of God. They just did it. And that was good enough for God and for Jesus, who tells the story. Who knew? As for the story, given that Protestant Reformers insisted on salvation by grace, not by works, were those Reformers aware of this Matthean text? Again, were the authors of ancient Christian creeds aware of this text? (Those creeds insist on the right beliefs when it comes to salvation rather than on acts of human love and kindness, as in this key moral text in the Gospel according to Matthew.)

Faith simply played no explicit role in the Matthean text. But love in the form of compassion, also unmentioned, may be its point. What Jesus was advocating in this story were acts of stout help for those without human standing and support. Jesus regards and declares such acts of kindness and helpfulness as done to God. God makes such deprived humans into members of God's family. Those forlorn individuals are declared as kin, family, relatives of God. God transforms their standing or status by adopting them as family.

Something seems missing, however, in this Matthean text. The modern reader looks for motivation for such charitable help for persons at the social margins. But the text offers no motives of those who were helpful. The text focuses on the acts of those who helped and on God's self-identification with those who needed help. God's approval of such charity was initially expressed by the fact that in this Great Judgment these helpers were included with the blessed at the right hand of God (Matt 25:33–46). The meaning of the story seems clear. God identifies with acts of loving neighbors in need. Looking for motives may simply be a modern sophistication. As to the relationship between love and faith, here love reigns.

HUMAN LOVE OF GOD: DIRECT AND INDIRECT

The biblical story begins with God's love. And, when it goes well, love begets love. God certainly expects such a sequel in demanding that humans love God back. Jesus summarizes that first and greatest commandment. Trusting that it is not misleading to describe love as flowing, love flows from God to those who hunger and thirst for God's presence. That love effects (creates) human love. And when responses follow, as they should, human love begins to flow in two directions, to God and to fellow humans. Those blessed by

God's love, love God back—gratefully—in worship, praise and in a transformed life. That is loving God directly.

But there is also an indirect human love of God. Indirect because it is directed to those whom God loves: humans in trouble, in need, in poverty, in low repute. God so identifies with persons at the social margins that God identifies them as God's family. "Truly I tell you, just as you did it to one of the least of these who are members of my family, you did it to me" (Matt 25:40). It is God who identifies such practical love of humans existing at the margins of human community as done for God. Christian ethics as a flow chart!

Such charting of divine and human love simplifies and assumes that human charity is as effective as intended. It assumes consulting, showing and sharing decisions with God and with others. Faithful decisions do not prove fail-safe. Not even God may foresee all outcomes involving human moral decision-making. Nevertheless, it still makes sense to reason together. Showing or sharing moral decisions with God or with the church will not assure right outcomes. Such consultation is necessary but not sufficient.

THE BIBLICAL GOD LOVES AND DEMANDS LOVE

The sequence of love begetting love is natural but not guaranteed. Love offered or given calls for love returned. That is how friendship begins, romance happens, children come to exist. Moreover, God's initiating love insists and persists. When the sequence of love bearing fruit fails, God persists, as in the Story of the Garden of Eden. And the Christian church, communally and individually, is grateful for such unreasonable divine patience.

The biblical identity of God differs from the impersonal and nameless deity of philosophy (when philosophers still have some interest in God) or from Nature's God invoked in the Declaration of Independence. The biblical God is personal. That God loves, angers, judges, saves, blesses, grows impatient, becomes jealous, redeems, saves. The biblical God has a name. And one can call on that name, confess, thank and praise, petition and trust, argue and complain with that Person. The biblical God sent God's Son to reconcile and to redeem humankind. That Father raised his Son from the dead to everlasting life. Christians hope for the same for humankind.

KINSHIP-LOVE DEMANDS RESPONSIBILITY AND HELP WHEN NEEDED

Loyalty, friendship, long-standing promises and sustained care, all practical expressions of love, may be invoked. Humans need help, especially at the beginning and ending of life. Without love as active care few would survive birth or old age. Speaking of the absence of love, the importance and vital goodness of love can become evident through its absence. Loneliness or death of loved ones may reveal the importance and power of love when it ends or is lost. Human vulnerability reveals itself to survivors through the loss of those who shared their lives. Looking to a larger than personal or family settings, the legal penalty of solitary confinement imposing long term isolation on offenders constitutes a version of social death. The measure of legal penalties may need adjusting to account for the severity of human isolation. The measure of justice includes the severity of punishment and its length.

One practical expression of love is *sharing*. "How does God's love abide in anyone who has the world's goods and sees a brother or sister in need and yet refuses to help?" (1 John 3:17). That seems reasonable in a context of Christian identity in which the church is the body of Christ, and all are members of the same body. But the same letter of John also insists on something that goes beyond sharing. "We know love by this, that he laid down his life for us—and we ought to lay down our lives for one another" (1 John 3:16). Self-sacrifice expresses a love of others greater than self-love or the willingness to share. Jesus' love exceeds what seems fair or reasonable. The letter writer of First John declares such self-giving love to be obligatory. That goes beyond equity, fairness or justice. It exceeds all the other generous characteristics of love. The model is of course the sacrifice of Jesus (1 John 3:16). And the time context is "the last hour" (1 John 2:18). Here love becomes a matter of life or death. Being a Christian may become costly.

THE INCLUSIVENESS OF LOVE

The word "love" is so inclusive that most, perhaps all, ethics and moral requirements can be implied by it. The biblical Ten Commandments (Exod 20:2–17) attest to that. Ordinarily, stealing, killing, envying, adultery, idolatry, dishonoring parents and the like violate love. Not only in such major violations but in smaller and unnamed ways of moral indifference one recognizes the absence of love. Such absence of love reveals its importance. Augustine was convinced of the inclusiveness of loving God: "Love God and do as you will." But that omits one other necessary ingredient. Doing what is right also requires good judgment or discretion. "He meant well" honors intent and resolve but implies that something went wrong. Augustine should have insisted on "love and good judgment."

GOD, LOVE, AND FORGIVENESS

Stepping back from love and the task of judging or guiding moral conduct, there is something liberating and enabling in the experience of God's love in the forgiveness of sins. The sacrifice of the crucifixion granting God's grace in forgiving human sin, frees the recipient from preoccupation with his or her own salvation. The calculus of weighing one's good deeds against the heavy weight of sins—as in the reckoning of Purgatory logic—simply disappears. If there is anything like theological-moral liberation, forgiveness is it!

God's forgiveness enables human forgiveness. Divine liberation from sins becomes imitable. Being forgiven, when experienced and acknowledged, calls for and enables forgiving others. And it may be true that *not* forgiving others obstructs being forgiven oneself. The Gospel according to Mark is clear about the sequence of forgiveness: "Whenever you stand praying, forgive, if you have anything against anyone; so that your Father in heaven may also forgive you your trespasses" (Mark 11:25). Lacking forgiveness should block and disqualify an individual from receiving God's forgiveness.

Forgiveness for oneself, for others and even for nations makes it possible to start over. But actually letting go of deep resentments is difficult, because humans cling to their grievances. Resentments can have a long shelf-life. They tend to remain and breed new grievances. And they can be heavy. Heavy in individual life as well as in national grievances. The instability of Balkan states come to mind, where grievances go back centuries and nothing is ever forgotten and therefore cannot be forgiven. Grievances require strength of character to acknowledge openly. Perhaps love as forgiveness is not misplaced in politics after all.

God's forgiving and life-enabling love is vital and normative in Christian morality and ethics. Being forgiven enables and requires forgiving others. That is the logic of the Lord's Prayer, "forgive us our sins, for we ourselves forgive everyone indebted to us" (Luke 11:4). The linkage between divine and human forgiveness arises from solidarity between humans and between God and humans. The family or kinship model again applies: Husbands and wives need forgiveness to continue in love and in marriage. Families cannot survive without the grace of forgiveness. Holding on to grudges prevents God from forgiving, since receiving and giving love are linked. Retained grievances and resentments invoke self-inflicted incompatibility and impotence to receive forgiveness. That holds for both individual and communal contexts. The Prophet Jeremiah proclaiming Israel's transformation by God in establishing a new covenant: "I will forgive their iniquity and remember their sin no more" (Jer 31:34).

For Christians, repentance of resentment is built into worship. Effective confession clears the deck and makes new beginnings possible. One awaits political ingenuity in creating occasions for facing and resolving national and international grievances and sins. There are times in American politics when grievances and resentments swell, when journalists write about losing the ties that bind. The storming of the Capitol Building in Washington, DC in January of 2021 expressed national resentments and accumulated deep grievances. As of this writing, more than a year later, grievances continue to fester without courageous national leaders who might name, confront, and seek to resolves such bitter political resentments.

LOVE AND DISAGREEMENTS

The meaning of love or the meaning of faith need not include being of the same mind. Indeed, it is on the basis of loyalty, trust and courtesy that persons find themselves free to disagree. Surely the pun that wherever there are two Jews, there are three opinions is a tribute to the dedication with which that community of faith approaches its responsibilities to God. While Judaism has not avoided schisms, the inclusiveness with which that community remembers, invokes, and imitates rabbinic disagreements—halakhah (Jewish law)—attests to the possibility that such diversity can be a strength rather than a scandal, an expression rather than a failure of faith or of love. Moreover, given the harsh expressions of the Christian quest for theological certainty, the Jewish theme recommends itself that the divine test of a man's worth is not his theology but his life.

GOD'S LOVE AND HUMAN RESPONSES

In secular times belief in God falls on hard times. And with such disbelief, the claim that God is a Person and loves human beings must seem even stranger. Yet that has been the testimony of biblical believers forever. And it is the experience and claim here. What follows are implications of the experience of God's love. That includes ethical/moral inferences. Yet one must avoid giving the impression of limiting the range or nature of God's love. Love can be and will be creative. And when God acts, there will be surprises.

The joy of the moment of experiencing God's love may well overwhelm any reflections about its implications. But eventually one's breath and thoughts catch up. God's love experienced, therefore . . . what follows? Therefore, those blessed may reconsider the direction of their lives. The emphasis shifts to serving others, as in the serving professions or simply in any occupation. Earning a living cannot be all that counts. Again, there is God. Thinking of marriage as a Christian makes a difference. A prospective partner deserves fair warning about marrying a Christian, about limiting bringing children into a crowded world, about the political implications of Christian faith. The term "transvaluation of all values" has already been introduced but applies here as well. Experiencing God's love may change just about everything. Indeed, it may well alter the self-identity of those who are blessed by God's love.

COMMUNAL EXPRESSIONS OF LOVE

There is a tendency to restrict love to individual and personal expression. Defining love as personal relationship, as in these pages, also has privatizing implications. "Personal" usually means one-on-one. While one surely learns of and experiences love in personal contexts, love should also be conceived and envisioned in wider dimensions, namely in all dimensions of life. Love in general, undefined, may well sound right to believers. But living in a secular (Western) world presupposes that political and national issues are always already spoken for. Political policies and practices have their advocates. A reason for excluding love from public and political settings may be that these contexts remain matters of competition, of power struggles and hard deals, where the devil takes the hindmost. Arguing for love as guide in politics, some argue, would be sentimental, unrealistic, misconceived and fruitless and therefore harmful. Idealists, predominantly on the Far Left, call for more or better than what the law allows, such as help for the jobless, the homeless, the disabled—such idealists should avoid politics, realists insist. Yet politics is the realm in which the most important issues for human needs and justice appear and need to be acknowledged.

REALISTS' OBJECTIONS

Continuing that "realistic" perspective, economics and politics reflect self-interest. They do not and should not function as charities. Ethicists who consider themselves realists—meaning that they acknowledge the limits of morality in political and social contexts—resist extending the concept of love or of faith to wider than personal dimensions. The key norm and guide in political and social issues, realists insist, should be justice, not love. Here justice would be defined in terms of equality and fairness, of everyone getting his or her due. Such justice would be close to what the law requires. And, as a realistic virtue, we can all live with that. But of course, that sells "love of country" short. It holds Christian ethics short as well. And it may be that such realism sells God short.

CIVIC CHRISTIAN RESPONSIBILITIES

Faith and love apply to political, economic and public issues because God is Lord of everything. Secularism, in the guise of political realism, finds that inclusive claim to be alarming: Religion distorts politics and should remain non-political. Love and faith should remain personal, and private realists note, with few exceptions. Love of country in times of war proves to be exceptional and fitting. Nevertheless, Jews and Christians may conceive of God as Lord in all dimensions of life. The biblical God will not be quarantined or diminished into a household god. Public, political, judicial, economic (and so on) venues are not off-limits to God. The reader will find this theme of Christian ethics' relevance to the political, economic, and other public institutions repeated throughout this text. That relevance claim may remain controversial in any secular culture.

THE ROLE OF "NECESSITY"

A linguistic way to avoid conceiving God in relation to public institutions and public life lies in invoking *necessity*. That includes political-, military-, business- and social necessities. Again, these are spheres of responsibility beyond the personal. These necessities need not be publicly posted, because they have become self-evident truths. "Necessity" leaves no options and offers no choices. For example, "There is no alternative than to prepare for effective national nuclear deterrence. Denial of such necessity places America at unacceptable risk." "Maintaining a realistic minimum national wage is a business necessity." Appeal to "necessity" may avoid any need for forgiveness. In a secular culture, religion is privatized, personalized, individualized. Exceptions tend to remain merely stylistic. When the President concludes a national address with "May God bless America," everyone understands that such prayer can be appreciated by all citizens without alarm, since it remains a matter of style. If the prayer were, "May God have mercy on America," it would be confessional, genuine, alarming, and probably unrepeatable.

AMERICAN SECULARITY AND CHRISTIAN RESPONSIBILITIES

What follows are three modest versions of conceiving of major public dimensions of life as fitting contexts for Christian civic responsibility. The first is a childhood memory of Allied air raids during the last years of the Second World War bombing my hometown, Hamburg. Bomber missions could occur any time, day or night. While not allowed to step outside to see the formations, the air was filled with the low humming motor sound. Until the planes reached their target. Warning sirens had notified civilians to seek shelters. In our case, the basement was fortified with timbers. That's where we sat and waited for the all-clear. The raids came too often and too quickly to find more adequate shelter. Then the bombings began. The third house down the street took a direct hit that left only a crater where twelve persons had taken shelter in the reinforced basement shelter. Just war theory prohibits targeting civilians. Would it be a fitting witness for Christians to support a national policy to prevent targeting civilians? Christian ethics might find the courage to support limits in times of war. Targeting civilians used to be prohibited but now seems to be forgotten. Perhaps hostilities in wartime tend to obscure established traditional limits and require serious renewals.

A second example of the importance of Christian responsibility for the public dimensions of life relates to the choice of jobs, occupations, careers. That begins with questions of preparation. Parental practicality has usually already been offered and may be helpful but not decisive. Of course, one should be able to make a living. But more is at stake. A "Christian orientation" need not be limited to the usual *religious* professions. The *calling* to serve both God and humankind should be conceived more widely in terms of a life's work. What are institutions on which we all depend? What are the practical and essential organizations that support us all? Public service offers a legitimate and promising future for Christians. But so—and more so—are the structures and institutions that form indispensable services for this nation. Such public dimensions of life remain open to responsible choices that can include serving and loving both God and neighbor. Christian students might expand their vision and extend their options to occupations few would ever conceive as accountable or of service to God and to humans.

If examples would be helpful here, serving God in major institutions and businesses might be banks, financial institutions that prove essential for commerce and for funding civic projects. Public service organizations, teachers, police personnel, organizations providing safety, shelter, food. Broadening the concept of a *Christian calling* would be compatible with such a wider concept of serving God and humankind in what are now institutions and organizations that consider themselves to be soundly secular and safe from "religious meddling" "or naïve unrealistic ambitions."

A last and somewhat unusual version of Christian perspectives of what are normally taken to be public matters considers the end of an individual life and its obituaries. Acknowledging the ending of human lives tends to involve assumptions of what makes a human life meaningful and good. Obituaries, serious almost by definition, become public reflections of what makes human lives worthy of praise and imitation. The death of someone well known and dear occasions reflections on the worth of that life. In retrospect we look and hope for both good and caring lives. Importantly, we deem such search to be fitting, reasonable and right. On such occasions, we may look for moral and Christian meaning in all human venues, even those declared by secular *realists* as devoid of love or of God. The social, political and public dimensions of our lives merit inclusion in what are recognized as worthy dedication and service of humankind. A Christian acknowledgment of such lives deserves a public voice.

More explicitly, obituaries ascribe successes of the deceased to talent and hard work, with never a hint about compromises and wrongs along the way. Don't speak ill of the dead! Though not all the successes are mentionable either (as "he died rich"). Moral judgment of the dead may be left to God. Those who speak on behalf of the dead search for acts of generosity, dedication to others, words and deeds of helping or healing, good and caring lives. Kindness and love count. Any human life should manifest those virtues. And when they are found they will be included in obituaries and reminiscences. The point here is that public dimensions and serving professions do count morally retrospectively in obituaries. Such insights should play a role *prospectively*. The essential and constructive institutions and dimensions of public life do not remain alien to God. And they should not remain alien to those who understand themselves to serve both God and humans.

Biblical and Christian ethics insist on love and faith in all dimensions of life. "You shall love the Lord your God with all your heart, and with all your soul, and with all your mind." This is the first and greatest commandment. And a second is like it: "You shall love your neighbor as yourself" (Mark 12:30–31). God creates humans for love, love of God and of humans (neighbors). These commands to love hold for all dimensions and areas of life. Biblical texts include public dimensions of life as being responsible and accountable to God. Separating religion and politics is a modern and secular invention. And Christian ethics may ask whether it can justify or perpetuate such restrictions.

Christian love and faith should reach farther than person-to-person. Love of country is evoked in troublesome times. Medical professionals, in the years of the COVID-19 epidemic, dedicate themselves to serve their patients at considerable risk to themselves. Such dedication is also known as love. Teachers, government servants and what we call "the professions" provide services not always justly respected or rewarded. They may love their work and those they serve, and all others are the better for it. The *helping professions* offers a fitting label for a number of occupations. But even street sweepers serve the common good and can honor God in their work. Designating them as *sanitation workers* acknowledges the importance of their contributions. Words count. And so does respect for all who serve the common good.

The fact that biblical traditions command love of God and of neighbor may also shed light on what love of God and of neighbor mean. If one were to define love as feeling, one could not command love. Feelings have their own ways of coming and going. But love commanded retains its force and status. Love as the recognition of inherent worth and value is at least conceptually independent of feelings. Secularists derive and celebrate human standing for being able to think and to decide. Here human dignity arises from the ability to reason. That makes human worth self-generated, more or less. The biblical and Christian parallel looks elsewhere than human rational nature to find human standing. That is God's love. God's love is expressed in and through creative blessings, nurture, healing, guiding, serving when humans become what they are intended to be (discernible retrospectively?). What defines that success is God's love of human beings and human loving response to both God and neighbor. Thus, the standing or intrinsic worth of human beings in such secular and Christian contexts differs: in biblical traditions, human worth derives from a nonhuman source. That extrahuman source—the love of God—endows humans with infinite worth. That assumption pervades, forms and transforms Christian ethics.[1]

CHRISTIAN FAITH AND SALVATION

This paragraph turns to the second main topic of this chapter, Christian faith. The history of Christian faith is ancient and controversial. The most important historical aspect of faith is its soteriological (saving) function. After God's resurrection of Jesus, early believers' hope for eternal life became dominant. To be saved means to be rescued from the consequences of God-alienating sin and to get right with God by being forgiven. One is saved from sins (one's own) for the asking. Forgiveness of sins is God's redemptive act

---

1. Maguire, *Moral Creed*, 191–92. Chapter 11, "Exploring Love," offers an excellent helpful Christian introduction.

of saving love, offered to all who in faith affirm the life, teaching, death and resurrection of Jesus as acts on their behalf. Christian faith seeks not only to rescue believers from sin in this life but intends to be eternally life-saving.

The prospect of an eternal life seems alien in secular cultures. So are prospects of a resurrection and a divine judgment of all the resurrected. Contemporary Christians find themselves culturally out of step. That holds for the three cosmic events of being raised from death, being judged, and living eternally. Yet there is another difference between the secular and the faithful. Convictions about the future reach into the present. Faith looks forward to end-times events. An anticipated future influences the present. Pending personal judgment concentrates the mind. Awareness of having to answer for one's conduct has present moral implications. Here faith widens the range of responsibilities and magnifies the scope of the anticipated human future.

God raising Jesus from death becomes the precedent for early Christians' hope and trust in God's love for their own resurrection and eternal life. Not all who will be raised would inherit eternal life with God, however, because resurrection would be followed by a universal Judgment. That could thin the ranks of resurrected hopefuls. Given that God has a reputation for being forgiving may improve the prospects. And it might dim visions of eternal hell. Besides, the resurrected saints living eternally with God would not cease imploring a just and merciful God on behalf of eternally suffering sinners. Projections of an eternal human future, however, may say more about their authors than about an eternal future.

FAITHFULNESS ASCRIBED TO GOD

Faith as an affirming personal relationship might best be called faithfulness. Faithfulness more than "faith" emphasizes the relational quality of faith and adds a time dimension. Faithfulness also suggests loyalty in trying times that defy expectations. Biblical texts apply faithfulness to both God and humans. The Hebrew Bible ascribes faithfulness to God repeatedly: "The LORD, the LORD, a God merciful and gracious, slow to anger, and abounding in steadfast love and faithfulness" (Exod 34:6). Especially in the Psalms, divine faithfulness seems to function as a synonym for God's love. "All the paths of the LORD are steadfast love and faithfulness, for those who keep his covenant and his testimonies" (Ps 25:10). "I will sing of your steadfast love, O LORD, forever; with my mouth I will proclaim your faithfulness to all generations. I declare that your steadfast love is established forever, your faithfulness is as firm as the heavens" (Ps 89:1–2).

THE SUFFERING OF JOB AND FAITHFULNESS

Faithfulness calls for constancy when hopes fail. And fail they do when it comes to undeserved human suffering, to congenital disease, to untimely and cruel human dying. All satisfactory explanations can fail. Yet Job, tried and found true, remains faithful—he will not let go of God—even as he accuses God of grave and inexplicable injustice. Job's faith or faithfulness is a relationship in which faith, the human Yes to God, clings to the Holy One for better or worse, in life and in death. "See, he will kill me; I have no hope; but I will defend my ways to his face" (Job 13:15).

Job's patience is proverbial. He understands his trials as evidence that he was cut off from God. For no good reason God's faithfulness threatens to fail. When the divine voice finally speaks in response to Job's litigation, it is not the content of those words that prove decisive for Job but the very fact that God is still on speaking terms with him. Job remains faithful throughout the inflicted trauma. His faithfulness survives, even if he—though not his friends—was utterly at a loss of good explanations. While Job regrets his complaints, he cannot make sense of his suffering. But making such sense is not the point of the story. Job's clinging to his relationship with God is. It is the divine presence itself that turns him around. Job addresses God: "I had heard of you by the hearing of the ear, but now my eye sees you; therefore I despise myself, and repent in dust and ashes" (42:5–6).

FROM JOB TO JESUS

The New Testament is written by a community who faithfully acknowledges God's life-giving initiative in the message, life, death, and resurrection of Jesus. Jesus makes believing as trusting central to his message: "Repent and believe the good news" (Mark 1:15). By faith hearers acknowledge the new divine presence—the near kingdom (ruling) of God at the center of Jesus' message. Such faith or faithfulness requires a personal turning (Repent!) from a former way of life to God. What must be the best-known New Testament text, John 3:16, focuses on faith in God and his chosen one: "For God so loved the world that he gave his only Son, so that everyone who believes in him may not perish but may have eternal life."

The experience of meeting the living Christ, unseen yet life-transforming, is described by two theologians. H. Richard Niebuhr writes of a meeting:

> [The Christ of faith] meets us, we meet him, not as perceived but as one to whom the eyes of others are directed, not as an idea in our minds but as a person who accompanies in unseen

presence those who believe in him, who are loyal to him and who trust him."[2]

Timothy Sedgwick, an Episcopal ethicist, describes faith in explicitly personal and relational terms:

> Christian faith is not first of all a matter of right belief but of right relationship. In this sense, Christians share the conviction that faith is covenantal, given in a relationship with God. This covenant, moreover, is understood as a matter of grace. Grace is a matter of being loved by God, of being forgiven, of being embraced and invited into a new life.[3]

It is not just that the words of Christ come to life. It is the resurrected but unseen person of Christ who continues to live and reveals himself to those who seek him.

FAITHFULNESS AND MORALITY/ETHICS

To clarify the two linked terms, *morality/ethics* are both repeatedly mentioned together, as if they had the same meaning. They do relate to each other and may overlap. But they differ. Morality is applied ethics. Morality focuses on specific issues, practical problems, deciding how to act and acting morally. Morality focuses on specific issues, disagreements or problems. Ethics, by contrast, is the discipline of analyzing and guiding moral thinking generally and inclusively. Theory (ethics) as distinguished from practice (morality) may be helpful in understanding and using these key terms. (End of clarifying "morality/ethics.")

Faithfulness to Jesus is linked with the horizontal, with the human community. Here lies the inevitable link with moral and ethical responsibility: The Yes to God must lead to Yes to those in God's image. The triangular logic that binds the relationship with God to human interconnections reappears in this key religious term, *faithfulness*. Salvation, believers' vertical God-relationships, and ethics, the horizontal, prove to be inseparably linked with each other. Thus, the author of the Gospel according to Matthew presents Jesus not simply as Messiah and Savior (Matt 1:18, 21) but as a second Moses, a second lawgiver whose Sermon on the Mount (Matt 5–7) deepens and radicalizes ancient divine commands. Here Jesus assures his hearers that he has not come to abolish the law but to fulfill it (5:17). "Therefore, whoever breaks one of the least of these commandments, and teaches others to do the

---

2. Niebuhr, *Radical Monotheism*, 116.
3. Sedgwick, *Christian Moral Life*, 21.

same, will be called least in the kingdom of heaven; but whoever does them and teaches them will be called great in the kingdom of heaven" (5:19).

Faithfulness is the term that links humankind with God as well as creating human communal solidarity. In effect, God's faithfulness to humans calls for faithfulness among humankind. And the nature or meaning of such faithfulness proves to be gauged to human need. The "least of these," who are members of God's family (Matt 25:40) come first as far as God is concerned. This is Christian and biblical ethics at their simplest and clearest!

Jesus insists on moral recognition-signs for those who would enter the kingdom of God: "you will know them by their fruits" (Matt 7:20). The same Paul who insists on faith rather than works of the law when it comes to salvation, appeals to faith when it comes to Christian ethics: "the only thing that counts is faith working through love" (Gal 5:6). Similarly, the author of the First Letter of John insists on obeying the commandments for "whoever says, 'I abide in him,' [the vertical to God] ought to walk just as he walked" [the horizontal and moral] (1 John 2:6). The Letter of James asks rhetorically, "What good is it, my brothers and sisters, if you say you have faith but do not have works? Can faith save you" (Jas 2:14)? The self-evident answer is No. [This last quote is problematic, since in evangelical contexts faith in Christ is held to save. The intended meaning might be that faith without works is not genuine faith.]

GOD'S CHARACTER AND MORALITY

Once the divine presence has initiated its transforming rebirth of God-seekers—surprisingly and undeservedly, as both Jews and Christians attest—once the covenant old or new is offered and accepted, then God calls for the human Yes in both worship and moral life. The two great commandments become inseparable: "You shall love the LORD your God with all your heart, and with all your soul, and with all your might" (Deut 6:5), and "you shall love your neighbor as yourself: I am the LORD" (Lev 19:18). And in the New Testament: "If you love me, you will keep my commandments" (John 14:15).

Why should that be so? Why should loving God result in loving humans? Faith or faithfulness to this LORD must take moral expression because of God's character. Character simply means consistent actions over time. A New Testament text identifies God with love (1 John 4:8, 16). One cannot say Yes to this God without a Yes to those whom God loves and redeems. The analogy is to family relationships. Biblical texts speak of God as Father. If the Christian God had a motto, it would be parental: "Love me, love my children!"

THE CONCEPT OF FAITH/ FAITHFULNESS IS AMBIVALENT

These words mean both affirming confessional faith propositions as well as a personal committed relationships between believer and God. Each meaning will be introduced in more detail. *First*, faith/faithfulness refers to affirmations about God to be believed. Ancient creeds insisted on statements that must be truly and sincerely affirmed and believed to be effective for salvation. As the Athanasian Creed characteristically states in the closing sentence, "One cannot be saved without believing this firmly and faithfully." None of the ancient creeds include moral/ethical obligations. There are references to resurrection and accountability in the Great Judgment. But the crucial elements seem to be sincerely believing and affirming, not doing, imitating or following Jesus. Such sincere affirmations of God may be conceived as affirmations of faith/faithfulness and as having saving effect. Belief here is in theological affirmations. Experience of the living God or of "tasting" God (Ps 34:8) remain missing.

Second, creeds are not prayers. They describe personal convictions. Faith as (mere) propositional assent may know nothing of biblical religion as personal experience and as living relationship. Indeed, the insistence on right belief as correct propositional recitation can obscure the meaning of faith as personal and moral loyalty to God. Creeds seem to be shared recitations of the self for itself known and acknowledged by God. Or, if recited communally, they assure themselves communally of their Christian faith. To whom are recitations of these ancient creeds directed? To themselves and to those who share this ritual. The image of pilots reciting safety checks before flight comes to mind when one participates in such recitations. Creeds may indeed function like religious safety checks: believe this credo and you will be safe both now and eternally! Would it improve worship if the oldest Christian creeds were given a rest, perhaps replaced by contemporary creeds that include moral/ethical implications of faith or faithfulness?

This critique of creeds did not analyze the implied concept of God, who is assumed to be listening and responsive to creeds in the present and in the crises of end times. If the reader detects criticism of this concept of creeds, it reflects the assent to propositions without moral commitments.

HUMAN AND GOD INTERCONNECTIONS

Referring to the trilateral diagram in chapter 2, human faith or faithfulness are the affirmative human response to God's revelatory initiative. It is expressed in worship of God (the diagram's upward lines) and morally/ethically in transformed expressions of responsibilities to others (the neighbor and the community or horizontal lines). That God has faith in humans, given God's experience over eons, makes God's trust in humans... God-sized! Such grand faith has importance for Christian imitation. But Christian ethics is for humans. God is assumed good, right, just and faithful to humans. Indeed, God exceeds human moral measures. Where God's character (consistent actions) becomes important for Christian ethics is in providing a model of what love and faith mean and require as well as to provide the inspiration and strength to follow through in practice. Philosophical ethics differs from Christian ethics in that philosophers do not look for deities defining, practicing and enabling love or faith. Philosophers' gods do not seem to be personal. Nor do they have personal names. One assumes that such deities are not invoked in prayers or petitions.

Since both God and humans exist in relationship with each other, one cannot very well understand either in isolation. Related they are, linked by the initiative and grace of God. And human affirming of the relationships should be understood as a life-time or continuing dedication. Again, Christian ethics concerns the human-human dimensions of this covenantal relationship. Faithfulness transforms the inter-human dimension by linking it with God. Christians and Jews experience God's presence as a unique blessing. That holds not just because humans do not do well on their own. More importantly, humans tend to be inordinately focused on themselves and their own prospects. Yet God creates and enables them to love each other as well as God. Christian faithfulness is a human response to God and reaching out to (needy) neighbor. And the guiding norm all around is love.

FAITH/WORKS CONTROVERSY

The meanings of Christian faith have inspired book-length studies. Historically the word "faith" played a major and violent role in wars of religion. The prolonged controversy over salvation by works or by faith divided Christians. A short summary may at least outline the soteriological aspects of that religious controversy. While Christianity had humble beginnings, in pre-modern times it only took a small step to invoke the sword, to silence false faith, to protect souls from damning belief, and to burn heretics. When

Rome made Christianity into the state religion, the sword of the Empire replaced weapons of the spirit, and lambs turned into lions.

The Protestant Reformation in sixteenth-century Europe led to the controversy of faith versus works in regard to being saved (soteriology). Being saved means being forgiven for sins and being restored to the right relationship with God. It is also possible to understand being saved as God's reward for a good life (works, good deeds). That had been the traditional assumption in regard to salvation. Martin Luther and others protested that forgiveness of sins was offered by God in Jesus' sacrifice on the cross. God's grace may not be sold by the medieval church with indulgences (remissions of sins). Protestants claimed that sinful humans cannot save themselves. Salvation is God's unmerited gift to those who accept it. The implications for the authority of the church were drastic. The prolonged struggle over the concept of salvation by good deeds or divine grace precipitated horrendously cruel post-Reformation wars of religion. Hostilities did not end until the Enlightenment insisted on depriving religion of its political clout.

The eventual resolution was to affirm both faith and works as well as insisting on right sequence. Faith, human trust in God's unmerited forgiveness of sinners, comes first. Works, Christian moral responsibility to serve God and neighbor, follows. Faith precedes and enables works. Such faith is active in love. And that is a good description of Christian ethics.

Given the bloody past, Enlightenment philosophes sought something more tolerant than religious dogma for founding human value, standing, and hope. They believed to have found it in human rational capacity and in human rights. Secularization would rescue warring nations from religious hostilities. No matter what the religious belief, natural and civil rights would protect all persons, all who shared the rationality that set humans apart from animals. Modern secularism began there in the eighteenth century. And contemporary secularism still reflects confidence in human reason—despite world wars, genocide and dehumanizing tendencies of modernity. It is not inconceivable that the philosophes of the Enlightenment saved Christendom from itself. Indeed, Christians may discern here the providential hand of God, though one looks in vain for church prayers of gratitude for these secular reformers or for their separation of church and state.

LESS ORTHODOXY, RELIGIOUS CERTAINTY, MORE FAITH ACTIVE IN LOVE

The earlier discussion of the meanings of love in this chapter affirmed the compatibility of Christian love with disagreements. That also holds for faith/faithfulness as trust in God and for tolerance discerning different ways of expressing faith. Certitude about things godly may be left for the next life, when the faithful expect to see God face to face (1 Cor 13:12). Faith/faithfulness as loyal personal relationship can survive and even deepen from disagreements about religious truths, cognitive claims, the nature of faith, of God, of texts. Invoking the metaphors of family, of friendship, of fellow learners, modern theological convictions can be strong and flexible enough to withstand the tensions of reasoned disagreements.

Can one argue for less explicit orthodoxy on scriptural grounds? Biblical texts insist on loving and obeying God. There is no text commanding humans to understand God, which should cut learners some slack. Even the command to love God with one's mind (Matt 12:30; Luke 10:27) is a matter of coherence, covenantal consistency and gratitude. It simply means to love God with all of oneself. The point is the inclusiveness of loving God and latitude about understanding God. Paul expresses realistic modesty when it comes to knowing God. "For now we see in a mirror, dimly, but then we will see face to face. Now I know only in part, then I will know fully, even as I have been fully known" (1 Cor 13:12). In that text, *mirror* translates a polished metal surface, not offering a clear image. Loving God requires no doctrinal certitudes beyond trust, hope, love and faithfulness. As to faithfulness, that need not be an intellectual achievement. Affirmatively, faith can be simple or sophisticated. "[W]ise as serpents" is recommended (Matt 10:16) but is not required.

FAITHFULNESS AND MORALITY/ETHICS

Christian faithfulness originates in vertical or God-linked relationships but manifest itself within the horizontal, within the human community. The Yes to God should be echoed with a Yes to those in God's image. Potentially, the love commandment includes everyone. More urgently and selectively God expresses special concern with "the least of these." That includes the poor, the sick, the defenseless, the oppressed, the outcasts, the friendless, those on their own and at their wits end. In short, Christian ethics finds its bearings in God's compassion and care. Faithfulness reflects the triangular logic that binds the relationship with God to selective human solidarity with those of us who need help.

Salvation, the vertical relationship, and morality, the horizontal, prove to be inseparably linked. Thus, the author of the Gospel according to Matthew presents Jesus not simply as Messiah and Savior (Matt 1:18, 21) but as a second Moses, a second lawgiver whose Sermon on the Mount (Matt

5–7) deepens and radicalizes ancient divine commands. Here Jesus assures his hearers that he has not come to abolish the law but to fulfill it (Matt 5:17). "Therefore, whoever breaks one of the least of these commandments, and teaches others to do the same, will be called least in the kingdom of heaven; but whoever does them and teaches them will be called great in the kingdom of heaven" (Matt 5:19). *Faithfulness* is the term that links humankind with God as well as creating human communal solidarity. More simply, God being faithful to humans calls for faithfulness among humankind. And the nature or meaning of such faithfulness proves to be gauged to human need. The "least of these," are members of God's family (Matt 25:40) come first as far as God is concerned. Christian and biblical ethics at their simplest and clearest!

FAITH/FAITHFULNESS WITHOUT WORKS?

Jesus insists on moral recognition-signs for those who would enter the kingdom of God: "you will know them by their fruits" (Matt 7:20). The same Paul who insists on faith rather than works of the law when it comes to salvation appeals to faith in regard to Christian ethics: "the only thing that counts is faith working through love" (Gal 5:6). Similarly, the author of the First Letter of John insists on obeying the commandments for "whoever says, 'I abide in him,' [the vertical line to God] ought to walk just as he walked" [the horizontal and moral] (1 John 2:6). The Letter of James asks rhetorically, "What good is it, my brothers and sisters, if you say you have faith but do not have works? Can faith save you?" (Jas 2:14). The self-evident answer is No. But salvation by faith is now orthodox. And good works tend to be seen as *expression of faith*, saving faith.

In commenting on this text, H. Richard Niebuhr writes, "Dead faith is belief in propositions, such as that God is one; living faith includes love."[4] As to "dead faith," since "faith" has a dual meaning, perhaps Prof. Niebuhr's expression refers to the absence of a living relationship with God. Dead faith may have lost the relationship with God and subsequently refers merely to the faint echoes of creedal remains, of what perhaps was once living faith. As to the Letter of James, the editorial note in the Revised Standard Version (RSV) of the Bible, refers to faith without works as counterfeit. It cannot save (see note to Jas 2:14–26).

If this issue may be redescribed and reduced to its simplest terms, faith/faithfulness is both a head-thing and a heart-thing. The loss of the first—as understanding less and less about God—may be genuine insight into one's own limits. By contrast, losing the heart-thing is serious. For the

---

4. Niebuhr, *Faith on Earth*, 7.

heart stands for relationship and love. Human understanding of God will always be limited. But love does not depend on understanding. Love delights in presence, it affirms, embraces, strives to be patient, forgives wrongs, reconciles. Love is faithful. And if love and faithfulness die—a human, not a divine possibility—God can restore the dead.

GOD'S CHARACTER AND MORALITY

Once the divine presence has initiated its transforming rebirth of God-seekers—surprisingly and undeservedly, as both Jews and Christians attest—once the covenant old or new is offered and accepted—then God calls for the human Yes in both worship and a moral life. The two great commandments become inseparable: "You shall love the LORD your God with all your heart, and with all your soul, and with all your might" (Deut 6:5), and "you shall love your neighbor as yourself: I am the LORD" (Lev 19:18). And in the New Testament: "If you love me, you will keep my commandments" (John 14:15).

Why should that be so? Faith or faithfulness to this LORD must take moral expression because of who God is. God's character, that is God's consistent actions over time, sets patterns for human imitation. That pattern of divine action describes God's character as love (1 John 4:8, 16). One cannot say Yes to this God without a Yes to those whom God loves and redeems. Again, God's imagined parental motto insists: "Love me, love my children!"

HUMAN FAITHFULNESS BIBLICALLY TESTED

Seeking assurance of having genuine faith or faithfulness is age-old. Biblical authors of the story of Job even include God as one seeking assurance about human loyalty to God. Chapter 2 here considered Job's faithfulness despite God's apparent lack of such loyalty in testing Job. In that story God seems unable to predict lasting human faithfulness to God. Job's faithfulness is tested (and found to be lasting.)

Another example of human faith affirmed or of the human Yes to God, is the story of Abraham's calling. The context is a fallen humanity, alienated from God and from one another. God's intent to restore an estranged humanity begins with God's confrontation and call of Abram. In a world in which family and clan provided the only security, Abram entrusts himself to the divine call and mission. He "went, as the LORD had told him" (Gen 12:4).

Moses seemed to have been harder to persuade. He wonders about a burning bush not consumed by flames, draws near and is startled to find himself confronted by God (Exod 3:1–22) who asks him to liberate an enslaved people from Egypt and to lead them to a land flowing with milk and honey. Omitting the reasons with which Moses tries to evade that task as well as divine efforts to persuade, the point is not simply to note that God initiates the relationship with humans but insists. Key traditional biblical figures do not volunteer but need to be persuaded. As a note in that regard, the pattern of God's initiative is the reverse of the cultural assumption that it all begins with humans in search of God. The actual biblical sequence—that God started it—is the believer's reply to the secular question of why be religious.

Moses repeatedly refuses to accept the dangerous mission. Yet God will not accept a No! God's redemptive intent is to create a people who would serve God in living justly and in offering a model that would persuade and redeem a fallen humanity. The plan is to exemplify and invite, not coerce. God's faith in humans remains invitational rather than coercive. That constrains God into a prolonged argument. God does *command* Moses! Human faith in and obedience to God are not natural or spontaneous. God offers a universal invitation and creates humans to be free, free even to ignore or reject God. In regard to Moses, things turned out well eventually.

GOD'S FAITH IN/FAITHFULNESS TO HUMANS

The conviction that God has faith in human beings—despite all the lapses—is remarkable. As far as God is concerned, God loves humans inclusively—and invites humans to receive, to affirm and to share love (Matt 25:40; John 3:16). Contrasted with the historical patterns of human warfare, hostility, and indifference toward one another and to God, God's continued love and patience with humankind continues to amaze the faithful.

The faith of humans in God in the Western secular world seems residual, a shadow of what it was before the Enlightenment. Ambivalence and doubt are as old as faith. The insight that Christians are conflicted—both sinners and sinners saved by grace—has also been familiar for ages. What may be new in regard to humankind and God is that the word "sin" drops out of common usage. Equivalent secular terms prove to be elusive or deceptively modest. If "sin" will not do, how to name the self-contradictions and lapses that tempt and plague Christians? How to find a modern equivalent of "sin"? The problem of course is not linguistic. A secular culture will insist on secular terms.

THE REACH AND RELEVANCE OF CHRISTIAN FAITH/FAITHFULNESS

The great risk to Christian faith in secular and tolerant cultures may lie in adopting the secular assumption restricting the reach or relevance of Christian faith to personal and private dimensions. Secular cultures, confident of human reason, assume as a matter of course that Christian faith is personal, private and outdated. Faith remains an individual or private choice with the freedom to worship, to assemble, to witness to faith and to pray for divine blessings on nations and citizens. Such faith may remain without critical public functions but will be called upon for certain ceremonial occasions. Honoring the death of important citizens, adding religious coloring to presidential speeches, invoking a blessing on America, or reinforcing the superiority of Western nations over godless Communists offer religious advantages in secular times. These constitute skeletal remains of what used to be a living faith.

FAITH IN A FUTURE BEYOND TIME

Since the beginnings of Christian faith, being in the right relationship with God—being saved—became a matter of life or death. That held true not just for what one might call ordinary or historical time, but for a future radically transformed by God. Such a predicted future would end ordinary time and ordinary life. God intervenes with great cataclysms, ends normal history, and resurrects (recreates) the dead. Divine Judgment of all humans follows. Those who are judged approvingly will live eternally in the presence of God. Those condemned will suffer eternally, away from both God and from those who were saved.

This apocalyptic (catastrophic) end-time and dual outcome, too briefly described here, is the New Testament vision of an eternal future. No sentimentalizing of faith here! The horrifying possibility of eternal damnation, of everlasting pain and suffering offers incentives for taking religious warnings seriously. Even Jesus is recorded as having predicted threats of eternal punishment: "Then he [the Son of Man coming in his glory] will say to those at his left hand, 'You that are accursed, depart from me into eternal fire prepared for the devil and his angels'" (Matt 25:41).

The lack of certainty of knowing where one ends up personally can create anxiety. Apocalyptic visions resist the gravestone inscriptions "Rest in Peace." The anticipation of a divine Judgment focuses attention on itself. That Judgment follows the resurrection of all humans, assuring that no one escapes being held accountable.

Such predicted universal events did not trouble the convert evangelist Paul: "For now we see in a mirror, dimly, but then we will see face to face. Now I know only in part, then I will know fully, even as I have been fully known" (1 Cor 13:12). Of course, Saul/Paul had experienced some stunning evidence of God's actions and character when he was struck blind for failing to see the truth (Acts 9:1–22). He recovered and became an effective evangelist. God was already on speaking terms with Paul, who was serving God as missionary. That may lessen the risks of personal eternal judgment. But what fierce concept of God is assumed in those New Testament versions promising either eternal loving presence with God or everlasting torment! If God be the "Our Father . . ." of the Lord's Prayer, describing God as eternally vindictive creates a divine character self-contradiction.

PROBLEMS WHEN SEPARATING FAITHFULNESS FROM MORALITY

Such confessions of faith in a God who loves and embraces, forgives and restores humans may have become obscured in much of Christian history. Major historical events, such as the Crusades, the expulsion of Jews from Europe and wars between Protestants and Catholics require a range of historical, political, economic, and other explanations not attempted here. Isolating faith as true belief in orthodox propositions—as in defending creeds—may have contributed to these historical failures of Christian conduct and faith. Many defenders of the faith no longer discerned the image of God in Turks and Jews. Modern contemporaries in turn have difficulty discerning that image in medieval and Reformation "defenders of the faith." Devotion to saving doctrines, to "the true faith" can turn defense of divine truths into hateful and even deadly aggression against heretics and "false faith." Such zealots of the faith and of God avowed ultimate justification for deadly religious zeal: God wills it! Such "faith" no longer acknowledges that God is good and seeks the human good. Such hostility also violates God's image in human beings. From such defenders of the faith, may God protect us!

SUMMARIZING CHRISTIAN FAITH/FAITHFULNESS

The concept of Christian faith\faithfulness has a double meaning. The word means both propositional—often creedal—assent to what one trusts to be true about God and the human prospect. Faith/faithfulness also means a vital personal committed relationship between persons. That double meaning holds for both religious and secular contexts. Ancient Christian creeds sought to assure Christian belief and confidence by focusing on creedal faith. Such creedal summation of what must be believed *omitted* moral commitments. That insistence on right belief as correct propositional formulae can obscure the meaning of faith as personal and moral (trilateral) loyalty. Creedal soteriology (theology focused on saving belief) can obscure ethics when believing replaces doing. Faith as personal and communal faithfulness, while seeking understanding and able to make a case for itself, is responsible to honor God in faith and by walking in God's ways. Biblical figures, as Abraham and Moses and of course Jesus, exemplified inseparable connections between faith and ethics. The Christian meanings of love and faith exemplify and express the trilateral diagram of Chapter 2 that link Christian faith with faithful action.

LOVE, FAITH, AND CONTEXT

The two key terms of this chapter have been mostly considered in sequence. Yet surely faith alone or in tandem with love can be differently used and even misapplied. Religious faith without love has led to cruel and destructive consequences. It justified crusades and human enslavement under the banner deus vult, God wills it! Secular faith has motivated countless deaths in the name of the Aryan race or of the classless society. Faith in political leaders as saviors seems never to go out of style. No doubt, what Christians consider misuses of faith can invoke love—of country, of race, of the past, of the future. Even the best of words cannot save, though all "great causes" will invoke and offer superlatives and hyperboles. Both "love" and "faith" are used in religious and in secular contexts. What determines their meanings proves to be their context. To be sure, dictionaries define the meaning of words. Yet actual meanings can and do vary depending on context and use.

LOOKING BACK AND FORWARD

The first two chapters of this book are devoted to identifying the contexts of Christian ethics in biblical texts and traditions. The third chapter seeks to relate Christian ethics to its secular American setting. The chapter on worship identifies the home of Christian ethics in church worship, in contrast with philosophical ethics. The frequent references to biblical texts and traditions in this and other chapters serve to remind readers of the assumed Christian background of Christian ethics throughout.

6

Christian Worship and Ethics

CHRISTIAN COMMUNAL WORSHIP IS the gathering of Christians to seek and invoke the presence of God, to recognize and confess their sins, to ask and receive forgiveness, to celebrate God's love with the Eucharist, to learn the meanings of God's will for their lives, and to thank and enjoy God and each other in word and song. Christian worship is a communal version of loving God back. More accurately, for loving God back in worship since loving God is life-inclusive. Worship is a celebration. And celebrations call for more than individual expression: It is done best in a crowd!

ENFORCED PRIVACY

Crowds, however, were prohibited in 2020–21 to counteract transmission of the coronavirus. That included communal worship. Worship services were made available online. Such public health restraints were not as drastic as the isolation of patients suffering from the coronavirus, surviving in isolation and often dying alone. Yet virus restrictions made all aware of how much everyone depends on the presence of others. It taught a new appreciation of the importance of friends and of our communal surroundings. To be deprived of the right of free assembly tended to make one aware of how much one actually relies on access to others. Surprisingly, even sustained legal incarceration took on more ominous meaning. Being isolated from others is hard on human beings. Though American popular culture prizes individualism, human nature and needs are social. Humans need each other.

Biblical religion, from beginning (Adam and Eve) to end (the Great Judgment), is communal. Theologically, the biblical God creates humankind for each other and for God. The two greatest commandments also reflect the inclusive purposes of life: love God and love each other! Over the long term, the coronavirus epidemic assumed moral and theological implications.

FAITH COMMUNITIES

While believers worship both singly and communally, doing it together matters. Communal worship expresses covenant solidarity for Christians and for Jews. Individually and communally biblical believers invoke the presence of God to learn or to remember and reaffirm who they are. Jews exist as the people of God. Christians consider themselves to be the body of Christ. Such communal solidarity goes against the grain of Western cultural individualism. Confessionally and liturgically acknowledging the need for others contradicts the cultural ideal of self-reliance, self-sufficiency, or simply being content with doing one's own thing.

Christians are communally re-identified. Strangers become sisters and brothers as members of the church that is also the body of Christ. Christians would find it odd that anyone would prefer to worship God in nature alone—as strange as celebrating anything without the people one loves. That anyone would prefer televangelists in the privacy of one's home or drive-in services seems about as reasonable as preferring video-conferencing or zooming to an actual family reunion. Hymns are to be sung together. Prayers prove incurably communal and incline to the first-person plural: "Our Father. . . . Give us today, forgive us our sins as we forgive. . . . Save us . . . , deliver us . . ." In such worship and prayer believers assume that they are in this together. Hymns and prayers are mentioned together here, for hymns are prayers set to music.

CONVERSION AND BAPTISM

While one may grow up in a Christian family and consider faith and worship to be familiar and normal, one does not become a Christian church member without a conscious choice made in a communal context. Unlike common law marriage, where a couple never having exchanged wedding vows may slide into actual marriage gradually, churches insist on a specific and explicit choice for membership and a commitment to Christian communal responsibilities. Christian churches differ as to when children may join the faith community as responsible members. But being born into a Christian family still calls for a deliberate affirmation or confirmation of the faith.

The importance of insisting on a specific event and ritual for becoming a Christian or joining as a church member, is to insist that membership involves a range of moral responsibilities. The choice to be Christian is deemed so important that it should be made by the individual joining rather than by others, even family members. Only voluntary mature assent counts. Therefore, some denominations frown on infant baptism and insist that only "believer's baptism" will do.

The New Testament insists on the importance of conversion by insisting on a value transformation that is so radical as to deserve the description of "being born again." The Gospel according to John translates Jesus' term as "being born from above" (John 3:3). In effect, the individual becomes a new self, has new identity and may see much of life differently. That includes a transformed moral/ethical identity that takes its bearings from the commandment to love God, neighbors, and strangers. The assumption here is that liturgy (the structured elements of worship) creates identity in the sense of forming and transforming self-understanding in relationship with God and with the church.

CHRISTIAN ETHICS SOURCES

One way of learning biblical ethics is to gather biblical moral imperatives. That includes the Hebrew Bible as predecessor to the New Testament. There are the Ten Commandments and the summarizing double love commands, ancient Israel's prophetic warnings, practical advice in Proverbs, and letters to young churches. Jewish tradition names 613 commands (mitzvot) in the Torah, the first five books of the Bible. Such retrieval functions as *biblical case law*, the methods familiar from searching for precedents in order to make precedents speak in new contexts. The contrasting method, again, is theological rather than case-focused.

METHODS OF CHRISTIAN ETHICS: CASE LAW AND/OR THEOLOGICAL METHODS

While all inquiring Christians use, cite, and learn from the Bible, some search for precedents for a new particular moral problem. Others, preferring a theological method, search for how a moral issue might be illumined

Christian Worship and Ethics

by a theological concept, such as love or justice or the character of God. The search is for relevant theological themes, relevant to the problem or question they are facing. This second approach, followed and recommended here, is biblical theology. That resembles philosophical more than legal methods. It seeks metaethical understanding rather than searching for textual precedents. Theological ethics, again, asks how humans are related to God and how they should be related. Restated, theological Christian ethics focus on metaethics, mostly on the biblical God. Similarly, this method inquires about the meanings of being human and of the purposes of human lives (there are such!). One advantage of a theological metaethical (meaning of life) approach is that it can serve to identify biblical moral texts in terms of how they provide unifying themes between diverse texts and create some order or priority between them.

Another advantage is that a theological perspective opens more aspects of Christian faith than a morality-focused method. Considering the role of worship in ethics, for example, seems more promising than focusing on biblical moral case law texts. The triangular diagram (offered in chapter 2) seeks to describe the fundamental interrelationships between humans and God and probes their ethical/moral implications. That diagram implies a theological method by beginning with God's initiatives, revelation and character. A case-law approach begins with the triangular baseline searching for possible precedents. That implies a law-giving God and a record of relevant prior legal decisions. Finally, a theological biblical ethics looks to God for finding its way. Case law searches for precedents among God's prior revelation. Looking to God directly seems more promising than drawing inferences from precedents.

THE DISAPPEARANCE OF SIN

Communities of faith are not immune from being influenced by secular culture. The word "sin" may be incurably religious and is disappearing from use in a secular culture. Nevertheless, Christian faith must retain the term since sin describes human character and threatens to alienate relationships between humans and between humans and God. "Sin" is a religious term and means "a moral wrong" in a religious context.

The subjective effect of sin makes it difficult to face God and others whom one has offended. Adam and Eve seek to hide from God after eating the forbidden fruit (Gen 3:10). Christian worship begins with the resolve not to hide from God. The call to worship begins with confession and pleads for forgiveness. The effect of assurance of forgiveness of sin is akin to being healed, restored, reconciled, and enabled to begin again the life God intends for humans.

The waning cultural use of sin affects Christian self-understanding. "Sin" has become almost socially unmentionable. Sin has been *privatized*. It seems unlikely to be used in any political or social contexts. In the biblical past, sin was thought to manifested itself both individually and communally. Israel's ancient prophets denounced political sins. In the current century, the scope of sins seems to have shrunk. Sin no longer applies to the nation or national leaders, to culture, the administration of justice, national or military policies and actions. While congregations still pray for national leaders and for America, the conviction that public institutions or political leaders stand in need of repentance and forgiveness now seems odd. Religious criticism of public policy and practice mixes religion and politics, both risky and strange. Presidential national speeches invariably end with "may God bless America." No matter how perverse public policy or presidential conduct, the closing religious invocation will never plead, "may God have mercy on America."

NON-MORAL ALTERNATIVES FOR "SIN"

While it is difficult to be sure, communal church confessions name only personal sins. Sins of national size and importance fade out as offensive and wrong and become tragic instead: the malnutrition and plight of would-be immigrants at national borders, millions of Americans remaining without medical insurance, persistent major under- or unemployment and failure to pay a living wage no longer register as sins but as unavoidable or unfortunate complexities of modern life. They may elicit sympathetic regret but do not cry out as sins of indifference that require repentance, forgiveness, and remedy. The cultural residue of sin shrivels to national fascination with sexual sins of political leaders.

While sin has been individualized and privatized generally, in political discourse the word has disappeared altogether. American English lacks a secular translation or political equivalent. The popularity of "tragic" surely originates in its resistance to moral coloration. "Tragic" reaches beyond human doing in the sense that earthquakes and congenital diseases are tragic. Similarly, mistakes, as in "mistakes were made"—the passive voice without moral reproach—must do. Lamentable, unfortunate and tragic function similarly. Regret replaces remorse. If the word "sin" exists only in Christian worship, what sin used to designate in a wider context now requires renaming. But how to deal with what has no name? That would complicate confession as well. But national leaders remain unlikely ever to admit publicly that they or this country—what is the euphemism?—have become morally questionable.

As both sin and Christianity have been relegated culturally, politically, and legally to the private sphere, Christian ethics similarly contracts. This does not hold for the national leadership of mainline churches, who offer policy statements on such issues as abortion, euthanasia, poverty and who lobby politically for a wide range of social justice legislation. But it would simply not occur to many contemporary church members that their faith has anything to say about economic, political, and institutional injustice. And if that did occur, would it disturb the peace and test the conscience of the church?

POPULAR AMERICAN RELIGION

With the waning of awareness and perception of public and political sins, Christian loyalty and support of morally questionable politicians and of Congressional conduct becomes less problematic. The effect is numbing. In the 2020 presidential elections, almost as many million Americans voted for the re-election of the incumbent. That was a man whose lies were recorded literally in the thousands, who fomented national divisions for his own advantage, who denied losing re-election and incited an invasion of the Capitol; who never laughed and has no sense of humor! Who counted evangelical Christians as his strongest base and was not mistaken. Could American evangelicals be the avant-garde of political trends in a time when sins refer only to individual personal but not political conduct? If so, being Christian and being American no longer exacts a citizenship cost. Affirming both God and country then endorses a congenial patriotism. And if doubts remain, believers can be visually reassured by a presidential figure posing before a church with a Bible in raised hand.

REPENTING AND BEING FORGIVEN

In communal Christian worship and private prayer as well, worship begins with confession of sins. And that initial sequence is regarded as both necessary, normal and fitting. Is there any other cultural institution that begins with similar critical self-judgment? Repenting is a word with more bite than saying that one is sorry. Repenting means self-accusation. In a biblical context, self-judgment may well result from divine judgment, from being confronted and judged by God. The prefix "re-" means back or again.

Commentaries on the meaning of this word insist that repenting implies a turning-about or reversal of action. Repenting implies relationships with oneself, with God, and with those unjustly offended. As anyone married knows, repenting requires resolve and swallowing hard. But it makes being forgiven possible.

More ominously, repenting for murder deprives the murderer of the chance for forgiveness from the victim. Germany has repented for the Holocaust (the murder of six million European Jews during the Nazi years). It has memorialized that atrocity and has made Holocaust denials illegal. National repentance was addressed to the world. But from whom might that nation ask forgiveness? Lacking forgiveness may keep the memory unresolved and unforgotten. Painful though that is for those looking back, it should have a warning effect.

It is conceivable that the USA might repent for centuries of slavery and racism. Could that hold for repenting of American nuclear destruction of Japanese cities that violated just war limits? Judaism and Christianity have age-old traditions of repenting. But, to whom might secular nations confess repentance, and from whom might they seek forgiveness?

WHY SHOULD REPENTING BE IMPORTANT AND BE THE RIGHT THING TO DO?

Both political and personal repentance would recommend itself, despite the practical problems described, because it is the precondition for redeeming oneself, individually or nationally. Repentance may make it possible for individuals and nations to restore their integrity (the unanimity between avowed values and actual conduct). Still, repenting is humbling. And chances for denial are legion: "They all do it." "Washington is a swamp." "This is the time to unify America, not to look back."

Can there be forgiveness without repentance in Christianity? Christians assume that God takes an extraordinary personal interest in human conduct, remains aware not only of human acts but of their motives or reasons and has perfect memory. God's astonishing patience keeps offering forgiveness. Given the Christian meaning of the crucifixion of Jesus, Christians regard divine forgiveness as uniquely costly to Jesus and to his Father. The offer of forgiveness remains open: "Ask, and it will begiven to you; search, and you will find; knock, and the door will be opened for you" (Matt 7:7). Forgiveness is not earned. And one has no right to be forgiven. It remains a gift. But gifts, in turn, need to be accepted. Accepting the gift can restore the relationship. Being forgiven precedes being able to be blessed. Remaining unrepentant makes the person practically unblessable. Gifts, just as love, cannot be imposed. Therefore, no forgiveness without repentance! This logic may also hold for friendship and marriage.

WORSHIP AND ETHICS CONNECTIONS: GOD'S GOOD NAME

The thought that humans depend on God is both familiar and true for Jews and Christians. But the possibility that God might depend on humans is not only counter-intuitive but seems to violate the relationship between Creator and creation. Nevertheless, there is that unfamiliar petition in the Lord's Prayer, "hallowed be your name" (Matt 6:9). The expression reflects ancient convictions that a name is closely linked with the person named. Life-changing events could precipitate renaming the individual. Abram becomes Abraham (Gen 17:5) on the occasion of God's covenant with him to become the ancestor of a multitude of nations. Abraham's wife Sarai's name is changed to Sarah after giving birth to Isaac—who is the first link with that promised multitude. (US law permits naturalized citizens to change their name when becoming Americans. A new identity calls for a new name? Or is the point to prevent unpronounceable middle-eastern names?

GOD'S NAME REFLECTS ON GOD'S IDENTITY

The name is holy, set apart from all else, pronounced if at all only with deepest respect. God's name is not to be misused, abused or dishonored in a curse. The moral implication is that humans owe deep respect not just to God but to God's name and reputation. To hallow the name implies that God cares about God's reputation. Those who invoke God's name must respect it as well. More interesting, it follows that God takes a chance in identifying God-self (him-/herself) with human beings.

The prayer "hallowed be your name" asks that God's name be holy, set apart, sanctified. The petition in the same prayer, "your kingdom come"—when all humanity will praise and respect God's name—makes a similar point as the plea to hollow the name. Christian worship can, should, and does yield ethical bearings. "Your will be done" sums up the imperatives of the Christian life. It is generic, as it were, unspecified, all inclusive. It reminds one of wedding vows: it honors and promises love and loyalty in the most inclusive and general ways.

LITURGY

The worshiping congregation is also a community of moral discourse. Liturgies or structured worship express the very heart of faith. Here worshiping communities are formed and transformed by God's word and sacraments. Prof. Don Saliers, a scholar of liturgy, focuses on identity. Participation in Christian liturgical symbols is an act "of the people of God called by word and sacrament to become in the world who we are in God's sight."[1] More explicitly:

> Liturgy is a common art of the people of God in which the community brings the depth of emotion of our lives to the ethos of God. In these acts we discover who we are, but also and primarily, we discover who God is in this art. If understood fully, liturgy is doing God's will and work in the world while providing human beings with a time and a place for recalling who God is and who we are before God, and identifying the world to itself—what it is in God's eyes—the pathos of this terrifying and beautiful world.[2]

In turn worshipers cry, speak, sing out and reach out to God. This back and forth of receiving and responding deepens believers' understanding of their Lord and of themselves: who they are and should be. Analyzing ethics ultimately comes down to identities, to metaethics (the meaning of all that is real and worthwhile). One's responsibilities should prove coherent with who one is and is called to be. And that is revealed and effected within these trilateral relationships of the liturgy. Liturgy forms and reforms both Christian identity and therefore Christian ethics.

The point of identity formation bears repeating. Few hymns and liturgies offer specific action guides or explicit norms. But neither is Christian morality primarily a matter of action guides, principles, or revealed morality. Whether individual or communal, secular or religious, morality ultimately focuses on identity and relationships. Structured worship forms and expresses, expresses and forms the identity of its participants.

In terms of the trilateral relationship between God, the community and the individual, the diagram cited repeatedly in these chapters, God's responses to worship become imitable for human relationships. Being forgiven by God—one of the biblical God's greatest character traits—makes forgiving others not just reasonable but imperative. Failing to do so, holding on to one's grievance, becomes a retrospective judgment (Matt 18:21–35).

---

1. Saliers, *Worship as Theology*, 146.
2. Saliers, *Worship as Theology*, 27.

While humans are not gods, certain features of God's character become imitable and humanly achievable. Humans not only can but are expected to walk in the ways of God. Except, of course, for imitating divine judgment or condemnation.

WORSHIP INSTRUCTS ETHICS (THE THEORY) AND MORALITY (THE PRACTICE)

Given who believers and God are understood to be in worship reveals bearings for what the faithful are to be and to do. Being bound to this Lord alters character. But bringing ethical relationships into worshipful congruence with the relationship with God requires repetition, thought, and time. And it requires extra-human help: the Spirit of God moves not only when or where it will but at its own pace.

CAUTIONS

Coherence is key in relating worship to morality/ethics. What one believes should be consistent, congruent, coherent with what one says and does. That holds for both, the self and the community. The *we*, however, the worshiping community, may prove difficult to persuade to agree in controversial issues. Creating coherence between worship and controversial public policy can be divisive. Church members manifest convictions from Left to Right, from progressive to ultra-conservative. Congregations have been known to break up over how faith convictions should relate to ethical/moral issues. Protestants lack the cohesive discipline of institutional leadership characteristic of Roman Catholic traditions. To be sure, Protestant leadership propose new moral initiatives without institutional revolt. But when such changes actually affect and inflame local decisions, Protestants envy Catholic solidarity and stability.

Caution here concerns a certain realism about translating faith convictions into church policy and Christian practice. Church members must care for each other sufficiently to ensure that their loyalty to each other remains stronger than their political or social differences. To be specific, ordaining women now proves acceptable for most Protestant churches. Ordaining lesbian women or openly homosexual men, however, may precipitate an exit of tithing members. Yet it also may offer the opportunity to deepen Christian understanding of God and of love for the neighbor. My point is not to dwell on or to argue this issue. It is to insist that Christians have no choice but to relate and present their reflections and judgments to one another and to God. And to do so literally, verbally, singly and communally. Churches also need the courage and solidarity to confront controversial ethical issues in the name of Christ. The motto "peace at any price" may not only be rightly rejected militarily or politically but religiously, congregationally and morally.

When it comes to controversy over difficult moral/ethical choices, believers seek scriptural help. As they should. But caution proves necessary here as well. Where to look? In terms of the issue in the previous paragraph, is the fitting text Lev 18:22 (homosexuality as abomination) or 19:19 (love your neighbor as yourself) or Gal 3:28 (neither male nor female in Christ)? Linking worship with morality/ethics risks specificity. Just as every use of scripture presumes a selection and choice, so the linking of ethics or morality with worship must land somewhere in the biblical landscape. Appeals to Israel's Exodus traditions yield different bearings than focusing on texts coming to terms with its Exile. And to include the choice of hymns, Luther's "A Mighty Fortress is our God" offers a darker social realism than the sweet personal perspective of Amazing Grace. If the devil can quote scripture, he (surely he!) will not hesitate to mislead when it comes to linking worship with responsible consideration of moral issues.

SHOWING IT TO GOD

Linking worship and ethics constitutes a Christian responsibility. Believers, individually and communally, consult scripture, reason and aid each other in discerning what is right morally and faithfully. During and after that process of reaching agreement, they should show their efforts to God. This does not imply that God does not know what they are or have been doing. The point, rather, is to seek God's scrutiny, assistance and judgment of the process and result of their efforts. Showing it to God may be something of an acid test. That "higher consultation" must be more than a nod to God, pro forma, or an extended Amen.

While the prophet warns that human thoughts and ways are not God's thoughts and ways (Isa 55:8), showing moral/ethical reasoning to God remains obligatory. Whatever believers discern to be morally right and fitting must be presentable to the living God whom they worship. No example shall be offered here, lest the point be lost in the topic. The point is that showing it to God is not a one-way act. The biblical God responds to human invocations, needs, prayers, questions. However, confidence in this open and personal relationship with God, conversations with God familiar from biblical stories and major biblical figures, may be waning even among the faithful in contemporary secular America.

SECULAR OBJECTION: WHY SHOULD GOD CARE?

American secularism—the voice in this and the following paragraphs—is the soft rather than the aggressive and hard atheism of Marxists. Its primary objection to religion is not to the claim that God exists. Everyone indulges in harmless wishful thinking to some extent. The seriously objectionable quality to Judaism and its offshoot Christianity is the claim that this cosmic deity of infinite space would take an interest in—indeed cares for or even loves time-bound, perishable, pretentious, quarrelsome inhabitants of a minor planet. Such illusionary human self-magnification constitutes absurd vanity—so the secular objection. The author of the biblical book of Ecclesiastes got it right: "all is vanity" (Eccl 12:8).

HUMAN OPENNESS TO GOD

The reason for taking note of cultural secularism at this point is the importance of showing one's reflections, moral decisions to God. Transposing theological convictions to ethics and morality—and doing so publicly—is the sort of religious claim that alienates cultural secularists. A soft secularism is not primarily concerned with disproving or denying the existence of God, but in denying that a cosmic God would care about the likes of humankind. Why would a cosmic deity devote attention and care on momentary inhabitants of a mere speck in the grand cosmos? Have these worshipers of ancient myths not read the psychological and social explanations or reductions for these ancient myths? Religion manifests, so the secular perspective, the triumph of human need for meaning over the courage to confront an indifferent cosmos.

How to respond from a perspective of faith? In biblical traditions, God initiates the contacts and the conversations. The effect can surprise and often leads to a change of plans and of minds. "Now the LORD said to Abram, 'Go from your country and your kindred and your father's house to the land that I will show you'" (Gen 12:1). "So Abram went" (Gen 12:4). Moses, tending sheep, sees a burning bush and hears a voice, "Moses, Moses!" (Exod 3:4). The Voice sends him to Egypt to rescue Israelite slaves (Exod 3:7–12). And it takes almost two chapters of arguments between Moses and God to overcome Moses' refusals to go. The pattern of God's initiating contacts with humans repeats in the Hebrew Bible and holds for the New Testament as well. "God sent his only Son into the world so that we might live through him" (1 John 4:9). The secular skeptical objection to believers claiming that the cosmic deity should be aware or even care for them—religious cosmic presumptions, as it were—is that it indeed seems unreasonable. Nevertheless, God started it! Truer still, in the present tense: God starts it!

The reply of believers to the secular modern question/objection of how unreasonable! is simply that God, the God of Israel and the church, appears to them in person, is self-verifying, good, loving, joy-inducing, transforming. That Presence rescued an ancient slave people to initiate the redemption of a fallen world. Jews still wonder: how odd of God . . . ! And Christians join in wondering: how odd that God would do it again with the Jews in the ministry, life, death and resurrection of Jesus. God speaking, hearing, insisting, sending, judging, sustaining, calling prophets, judging and redeeming. God's seeking to save an alienated humankind continues. The Christian story repeats the pattern: An angel of the Lord—a messenger from God—appeared to Joseph to announce the birth of Jesus who "will save the people from their sins" (Matt 1:21), fulfilling a promise to Israel's prophets. God continues it.

The encounter with God transforms and redirects human lives individually and communally. The character of God, discerned in God's acts over time, offers morally imitable and imperative patterns. And the human ability to follow that pattern is provided by God's Spirit—God's gift of enabling power and presence. The answer to the secular question, how could a cosmic God care for the small creatures of a small planet, is a human question, not God's. Ancient and new believers join the crowd: Nobody knows but God. God's invitation holds: Taste and see that the LORD is good (Ps 34:8)! A believer's analogous afterthought: How unreasonable to question the lottery system when one has won first prize!

All expect that the directions believers find in worship will be consistent with the Lord's ways they have known and cite. Yet the past and the traditions will always remain analogical resources, noting resemblances despite differences. The process of doing that involves the faithful persuading one another as to what most needs doing and changing and how to achieve it. The presence of God and faithful reflection on what is good and right in God's eyes cannot be literally bound to the past. Culture, time, human problems and needs change. New occasions teach new duties. And the living God remains Lord even over tradition and text. The Lord of Israel and of the church has been known to do a new and surprising thing or two. And Christians face the responsibility to discern and affirm such surprising and obligating events.

The argument here is an appeal to be open to experience the presence of God. Such spiritual personal experience cannot be predicted or commanded. The biblical witness seems rather reassuring: "Ask, and it will be given you; search, and you will find; knock, and the door will be opened for you (Matt 7:7; cf. Ps 37:5–40). The Presence, the Person believers confess, love, and affirm in worship is the same Person who scrutinizes believers' moral reflections, decisions, and judgments. The biblical command to seek God's face—"Seek the LORD and his strength, seek his face continually" (Ps 105:4)—has both worship and ethics dimensions. Whatever Christians conclude to be morally faithful and fitting must be able to survive divine scrutiny without wilting. What is to count as faithful and right must be shown to God. What the church resolves morally/ethically should make glad the God whom Christians worship and know in Jesus Christ.

The sequence that argues from moral deliberation to divine scrutiny in worship may vary. Many Christians were raised in the faith. Christian faith may be as natural to them as breathing. Their ethics and moral reflections have always been faithful and, as it were, normal. The perspective may differ for converts. There the faith-relationship begins with God's self-revelation. In such encounters the living God becomes the center of human lives. The meaning of life transforms in being focused on God. Here theologians speak of the *transvaluation of all values*.

Lest an appeal to the living God before whom one and all must be able to justify moral decisions seems simplistic or esoteric, similar reasoning occurs in strictly human relationships. "Strictly human" here is code for "without awareness of God." Perhaps everyone who has loved or loves still understands scrutiny of moral decisions in the eyes of the beloved. Being loved and returning love not only alters the meaning of everything, transvalues values, it also makes one answerable. The perspective has changed from I/me to we/us. One no longer decides important issues alone. An actual counter-example: the refusal to share decisions, may be clearer in making the point that all is changed and we are mutually answerable in the most personal relationships. A young man engaged to be married, made the solo decision to buy a new car. In the context of lives pledged to sharing and planning together, that broke the engagement. Refusing to consult and to be answerable served notice that he was not sufficiently committed to the relationship, to her. One can say No without ever saying No. To a betrothed and to God.

While the Spirit of God moves where it will, ethics can derive specifics from a rich heritage of worship. What follows probes a few shared liturgical features for the moral light they may shed. Worship services usually begin with a confession of sins and a plea for forgiveness. Finding oneself in the presence of God, when that experience does not create self-forgetfulness, elicits an awareness of subjective unworthiness. "Woe is me! For I am lost; for I am a man of unclean lips, and I dwell in the midst of a people of unclean lips; for my eyes have seen the King, the LORD of hosts!" (Isa 6:5). To stand in need of forgiveness, as anyone married knows, expresses the very antithesis of the autonomous and self-reliant individual projected by our culture and therefore easily assumed. Yet believers acknowledge that their own standing and self-respect depend upon the grace of "significant others"—to use and to protest that bland phrase that avoids naming exactly what we are to each other. If "significant others" could reasonably be used for persons we love most, using it for God must reveal how depersonalizing and alienating that social science term actually is.

PRAYER

There is something self-contradictory about prayer. It may well be both natural and unnatural. Natural, because God creates, blesses, loves humans. Unnatural because individually and communally Christians acknowledge themselves to be sinners, who would rather avoid confronting God. Adam and Eve hide from God after eating forbidden fruit (Gen 3:10). That act breaks their immediacy and naturalness with God. And with each other. This sequence holds for all of their descendants. That is the logic for worship: resolving not to hide any longer and to resume worship with a confession of sins. Not just to God, who keeps secrets, but to those others inexcusably offended.

Why resume, why cling to this rocky relationship? The simple reason is human need. There are no other live options. The expression "So help me God" has more uses than the pledge of truthfulness. Theologians might explain why believers persist: Humans are created by God out of God's love. Human response and responsibility lie in returning God's love as well as to share that love with one another. Though that is true, it explains the present with the past. The sequence might well be reversed. It is the experience of God's love and presence in their own lives that converts and convinces humans. And it is out of their encounter with God that they then construe a theological past of the purpose and meaning of their creation and of their lives. The meaning of the past derives from the present. Both time sequences may be true.

Still, why hold on to God when one's grip remains so unreliable and God let's humans get away with so much? The reason is that experiencing God's love is life-transforming. Jesus insists on being born from above (John

3:1–21). Hiding from God did not work for Adam and Eve and it still does not work. Moreover, such avoidance can alienate hiders from each other: Adam blames Eve; Eve blames the snake. One resolution of this dilemma of saying both Yes and No to God in incompatible conduct is to distinguish between the old sinful and the new redeemed self. Conceiving personal identity as two conflicting selves is not reassuring, however, since it may be classified as a multiple personality disorder. Sticking to religious language of being both sinner and saint, being both the old self and the new, may be less alarming than psychological labels. But none of this seems helpful. Except perhaps it yields the conclusion that Christians need help.

Liturgy offers a built-in resolution to this ancient individual and communal experience of being loved and yet failing to reciprocate that love consistently and coherently. The confessional prayer invoking the Lord Jesus, "whose blood set us free to be people of God" repeats in word and in song, "Lord have mercy!" "Have mercy on us!" Faithful and confident in the divine response, the minister/priest declares forgiveness in the name of God. The effect of this assurance is to be healed, restored, reconciled, enabled to begin anew. Only time will tell whether or how long the Lord's gracious remedy lasts an eternity.

INTERCESSORY PRAYER

Commending others to God, and doing so in a communal setting, may be an inherited custom from religious and pre-modern times. But in a culture treasuring privacy, the practice has countercultural implications. Cultural individualism insists on privacy protections. But shared prayers can leave one exposed to questions. Congregational prayers traditionally share good news and bad. The more one cares for others—as members of one's individual family or the church family—the more difficult it becomes to stand back to protect privacy. By definition, intercessions presuppose interdependence and need for more than self-help. Such prayers express the communal nature of biblical faith. Biblical believers find themselves connected with each other in covenantal loyalty. Christians regard themselves as members of the one body of Christ. They pray for the persons they love as well as for those in need of practical love. And they may be surprised and grateful when others, too, pray for them.

Public prayers can compromise *privacy*—a liberal value and right that is strong enough in medicine and law to trump life itself. Standing in the need of prayer, as the spiritual puts it, assumes dependence on God and each other for our lives, health, and flourishing. But how to pray anonymously in the context of congregational worship? Prayers can be generic—"Comfort with the grace of your Holy Spirit all who are in sorrow or need, sickness or adversity." But urgency attaches to intercessions when it comes to specific persons. Those intercessory prayers require names. Moreover, it seems helpful to know what exactly to pray for: for recovery from a life-threatening accident? for an easy death? for an easy birth and a healthy child? Petitioners name names and offer reasons. Such specific intercessory prayers bespeak an ethics recognizing human need, vulnerability, interdependence, shared responsibility for the life and welfare of those in need of prayer. It assumes the willingness of others to be prayed for but may not risk asking for permission. Such prayers may modify one's self-understanding and self-reliance. Interdependence and need may be greater and more inclusive than one cares to admit, even in the most personal relationships. Keeping intercessory prayers private and silent in congregational contexts promises discretion. But what a great loss if that ancient tradition were to yield to modern privacy. Prayer when shared seems akin to shared singing. Something is gained that seems unavailable when reduced to lone singing and hearing.

Most of the text above focuses on personal relationships, where privacy may become problematic. But Christian faith includes moral responsibilities that reach beyond personal and individual relationships and call for social and political intercessions. Thus, spreading unemployment during an epidemic calls for more than individual citizen concern and generosity. Yet government emergency support of those who lost jobs or who have no medical health insurance increases the national debt. Such debt worries conservative Christians. Churches and congregations that do not have a tradition of strong leadership authority—as most Protestant denominations—risk alienating personally generous church members who support church charity but not "government handouts." I take it that the needs of those without the means to survive hard times outweigh conservative Christian objections and charity resources. Government assistance to the economically least among its citizens is included in government by the people and *for the people*. The injustices to workers relying on minimum or less than equitable wages lie beyond the resources of church charity.

The minimum wage must be raised to support adequately a family of four. And support for such legal reforms should be recognized as a Christian responsibility. Working politically and legally for a living wage for those who labor should be acknowledged as a Christian duty. There is something self-contradictory with Christians knowing the needs but resisting economic help for those who labor for too little. Obscuring essential human needs with a political ideology of individual self-reliance that condemns "government handouts" dehumanizes. How could one show such "grinch-ethics" to

God? How can one worship a generous God and reject government support for fellow citizens that is ever so much greater than church resources?

KNEELING?

Kneeling is one of the distinctions between "high church" and "low church," a characteristic of the role of ceremony in worship. Generally, only high church congregations supply kneelers, i.e., the cushions, not the worshipers who bend the knees. The fact that many churches make kneeling into a congregational tradition describes a practice, not a religious doctrine or belief. And in fact believers have prayed standing, prostrated, sitting or lying in bed, and who knows how else. Nevertheless, human beings are embodied minds and spirits. The body and mind are linked. For those in the habit of doing both, kneeling to pray seems just as natural as standing to sing. Kneeling is a tradition as ancient as Israel's biblical traditions. Daniel prayed three times daily "down on his knees" (Dan 6:10), a practice that risked his life.

Kneeling traditionally acknowledged distinctions of rank and of standing. Britain still honors that tradition when the monarch knights an outstanding citizen. Some suiters consider kneeling appropriate for marriage proposals. Others have had little patience with such old-fashioned honorifics. There is something submissive and reverential about kneeling. Kneeling acknowledges that humans are not gods, they are not self-made or self-created. All that they are is bestowed, at least initially. For Christians, gratitude is never out of season. And kneeling is a fitting posture for thanking and praising. In fact, that holds for petitioning as well. Perhaps even convinced no-kneelers kneel at home: closet-kneelers, when it is serious. Kneeling is an ancient practice and custom. And kneeling before God expresses physically who humans are in this God-relationship. The body knows that. The self knows that. And even low church scoffers know that.

GOD'S GOOD NAME

Jews and Christians call on God by invoking God's name. When Moses asks for God's name (Exod 3:14), God's reply is the enigmatic, "I am who I am." YHWH is translated as "the LORD." The fact that humans can call on God's name at any time and in any place becomes remarkable when one analyzes it. It appears that God's requirement for privacy may be minimal or non-existent. Believers seem convinced that God knows them, not just by name but intimately and in all aspects of their lives. One need not explain complications to God. In short, God is personal and near. "Closer is He than breathing and nearer than hands and feet."[3] If familiarity is said to breed contempt, that may explain why God's name is held so readily in contempt. That misuse is ancient and is forbidden: "You shall not make a wrongful use of the name of the LORD your God, for the LORD will not acquit anyone who misuses his name" (Exod 20:7).

Anyone who has served in the US Army is familiar with the fact that many in the lower ranks use vulgar and profane language as if it were a military requirement. The name of God forms a regular feature of such profanity. It is easy to dismiss such profane use of God's name as merely an esthetic matter of meager vocabulary. The practice seems primitive, an offense to good style lacking all originality and flair. Surely God would similarly dismiss any seriousness of vile speech. It was not until much later, discovering the weight that biblical texts ascribe to honoring God's name, that such easy responses mislead. Wrongful use of God's name is the *third commandment*. It is listed with such sins as idolatry, adultery, perjury, murder, theft. None of those wrongs could be mistaken as off-hand substitute for good style. In short, since God is to be respected and worshipped, holiness and dignity extend to the name.

There is more to this issue. The thought that humans depend on God is both familiar and true for Jews and Christians. The possibility that God might depend on humans is not only counter-intuitive but seems to violate the relationship between Creator and creature. Nevertheless, there is that strange commandment in the Lord's Prayer, "hallowed be your name" (Matt 6:9). The expression reflects ancient convictions that a name is closely linked with the person named. Life-changing events could precipitate renaming the individual. Abram becomes Abraham (Gen 17:5) on the occasion of God's covenant with him to become the ancestor of a multitude of nations. Abraham's wife Sarai's name is changed to Sarah after giving birth to Isaac—who is the first link with the promised multitude. US law permits naturalized citizens to change their name when becoming Americans. Would a new name prevent unpronounceable immigrant names? Or does a new identity call for a new name?

God's name reflects on God's identity. The name is holy. For Jews and Christians it is set apart from all else, pronounced if at all only with deepest respect. God's name is not to be misused, abused or dishonored in a curse. The moral implication is that humans owe deep respect not just to God but to God's name and reputation. The prayer's insistence to hallow the name implies that God cares about God's reputation. Those who invoke God's

---

3. Tennyson, "Higher Pantheism," para. 1.

name must respect it as well. More interesting, it follows that God takes a chance in identifying God-Self (him/herself) with human beings.

SINGING

Christians worship with song. Liturgically, they sing the Doxology together regularly. In "praise God from whom all blessings flow" worshipers offer univocal gratitude and praise God. Singing does more than reciting words in unison. With the help of a good musician, singing is more expressive and inducive to being joyful and grateful than speaking. One sings the national anthem and colleges' alma mater. If only the ancient creeds could be sung, perhaps they could become redeemable. Did God create the human ability to sing to enrich human lives? Does God sing? If so, how fitting that the body of Christ should sing its gratitude and love.

SERMONS

When it comes to the importance and effects of worship, most Protestants would consider the sermon more important than singing hymns or offering prayers.... Sermons, after all, can instruct and exhort morally. Sermons can offer a connection with morality (specific issues) and ethics (general rules and rationales of conduct). Hymns may do that only indirectly. Sermons are not sung. And normally only one person speaks while all others listen. Over time, however, it may well hold that hymns have a more penetrating and lasting effect on worshipers and Christian conduct than the spoken word. Hymns are remembered, while recalling last week's sermon or even its subject can challenge old and young. Hymns can and should be repeated; sermons require aging before reuse. Poor sermons can be redeemed in effect by good music and song. Singing can gladden the human heart, while that is a rare effect of sermons. Singing contributes to the joy of living and thereby lightens the seriousness of Christian ethics. But sermons come with high expectations of instructing and edifying hearers. Lectures tend to invite questions and engage hearers responding to lecture subjects. Sermons tend not to invite responses. Asking questions publicly during or after a sermon would startle the speaker and alert the congregation to pay closer attention. Congregational discretion remains the unspoken expectation during the sermon. Listener propriety, the cost of good order, has the last word.

CELEBRATING THE EUCHARIST

The church's Eucharist centers on Jesus' last meal with his disciples before his arrest, suffering and execution: "The body of Christ, given for you"; "the blood of Christ, shed for you." Blood is the biblical term for life itself. Jesus' life was in his blood. This is sacrificial language. In the distant past the lives of animals and of humans were sacrificed to atone for sin and restore right relationships with a deity. Jewish law prohibited human sacrifice (Lev 18:21; Jer 7:31; 32:35). The Christian meaning of sacrifice transformed its significance. The Christian conception is that the voluntary self-sacrifice of Jesus was not to appease an offended God with a blood sacrifice. It was rather to express and to embody, the unique redemptive love of God: "This is how much I love you (humankind), I give my only Son—and therein myself—so that you might be reconciled with me." The very heart of Christian worship centers on this bloody self-sacrificial and atoning gift. That makes the Eucharist into the preface to Easter, the celebration of Jesus' resurrection. Finally, if the sermon seems uninspired and the singing was too slow, the Eucharist' profound ritual will reliably save the day.

CHRISTIAN ECHOES IN SECULAR SETTINGS

Christian holidays or holy days have become recognized as special cultural events. That may be a holdover or echo of earlier, pre-secular times. Celebrating Easter, Christmas, births, weddings and death in religious settings may still hold for many. More interesting may be that dying and death may still evoke belief in some sort of life after death among the secular. Such is the impression when the secular speak of the dead in the present tense.

In pre-Christian times, it was reasonable to consider suffering and death as miserable and godforsaken. The events of Jesus' death and resurrection transform the meaning of Christian dying. In human suffering and dying God draws near to human beings. Human dying need not mean the God-forsaken plight of approaching the inevitable end of animated dust. Christian traditions declare that death is not The End but will be followed by a promised sequel—of which believers have already seen a preview in the resurrection of Jesus. God will raise the dead, Jesus will judge them and restore them to everlasting life.

To be more specific about human beginnings and endings, for Christians, being alive is a great good and a precious gift. "Gift" may mislead if it implies a transfer of ownership. A human life is not earned, self-caused or accidental but results from God's creative act in human procreation. That conviction explains God's ownership of human lives, even though everyone refers to "my life." That expression simply means "me." When persons misunderstand who owns whom, they may conceive of suicide, self-neglect or extreme risk-taking as legitimized by self-ownership. However, humans are the stewards of their lives, not owners. Human slavery, of course, assumes that humans can be owned by other humans. A more theological concept of who owns whom might have expedited the ending of slave ownership.

The story of God's love for human beings continues. God's creation of human lives repeats itself in the conviction of a future universal re-creation of the human dead. The Great Judgment that follows will involve Jesus, the only human who died and has already been recreated. Christ, returns as Lord and Judge (Rev 19:11–16).

A EUCHARISTIC SURPRISE

In my congregation the kneelers (cushions) for communion form a circle around the altar. That results in some of the communicants facing fellow worshipers during this ceremony. One realizes that "we are in this together." We are all members of the body of Christ. Each individual is someone for whom Christ has died and whom God loves. Unexpectedly, seeing a person across the way and remembering that person's awful political convictions gives one pause. Pause long enough to realize the generosity and love of God that unexpectedly shames one into self-reproach. The Eucharist can create a reality-adjustment as it were: Human standing does not depend on political convictions but on God's creation, love, and redemption. That recognition, occasioned by liturgy and the presence of God can be an antidote to resentment and condescension. Who knew!?

THE SHARING THE PEACE

"Peace be with you," is a blessing given and received. There is simply no way to retain one's resentments (always justified, of course) toward anyone with whom one shares the peace. Such sharing seems to be linked as a sort of postscript to the petition in the Lord's prayer to be forgiven as we forgive. It seals forgiveness with a blessing. Just as importantly, this affirmation of the person, the fellow or sister worshiper, makes it impossible to remain indifferent or inactive when such a member suffers illness or poverty. Just as it would mock the hungry to offer them peace without sharing food, so it seems incongruous to share the peace without—when able—responding to the needs of the poor and the sick. Being poor, being hungry, being out of work, being unable to pay bills for the necessities of life, such emergencies prevent being at peace. Sharing the peace may have unforeseen practical implications.

SUFFERING AND DYING ALONE

How hard to die alone! God's faithfulness to those who suffer and die not only transforms suffering through divine presence. It sets a moral pattern for human responsibility. Christians are to accompany, to be present to the dying. Which is no new thing, since in Jewish traditions one never abandons the dying. This transforms not only the meaning of suffering and dying but the manner of dying as well. One of the harshest implications of the coronavirus epidemic is that its infectious quality necessitates patient isolation. On hospital admission, such patients are prevented from visits by family, friends and clergy. Given the social nature of human beings, this poses a hardship. May one ask hospital clergy to take the same chances assumed by front-line medical professionals?

Believers know themselves and all humans to be enclosed within divine love even as they move into the shadow of death. The love that reaches into the grave and defeats death—celebrated at Easter and at every Eucharist—normally reaffirms trilateral relations in living while dying. Not that believers are spared the inevitable suffering that living and dying bring. It is God's, the family's and the churches' presence that expresses that the dying still belong to communities of faith.

CHRISTIAN AND PHILOSOPHICAL ETHICS

The task of comparing Christian with philosophical ethics is said to be a matter of different beliefs. While that may be true, it may not be right. The reason for such doubt is that growing up and growing older while trying to learn and keeping an open mind is surely a life-time calling for both philosophers and Christians. Getting things halfway right may be the best one can do. And if that holds for the human condition, then surely human certainties and truths are not preconditions for God's acceptance and presence. Divine forgiveness of sins includes human pride of human ideas. A more reasonable difference between Christians and philosophers may be worship. Worship is not essentially a head- but a heart-thing. It is a personal relationship of caring and loving—between humans and between God and humans.

Worship forms the birthplace and home of Christian ethics. The secular versions of philosophical ethics omit worship, by definition. But worship is intrinsic to Christian ethics, also by definition. Beginning with the respective similarities, philosophical and Christian ethics overlap in that both affirm the intrinsic value and standing of human beings. Philosophically one bases that conviction—named human dignity—on human abilities to think and to choose. Religiously such abilities and standing result from the creative generosity of God. Philosophical ethics looks to moral principles, human discipline, resolve and cooperation to create a good life for self and for others. Christian ethics remains more pessimistic about such goals since its judgment of human nature is darker or more pessimistic. While humans are created good in the image or in kinship with God, their standing or inherent worth lies not in their rationality or free will (less free and unreliable in practice, it turns out) but in the creative and redemptive love of God.

What went wrong, Christians confess, is that their loves are divided. At their best they indeed love God and others. But their love of themselves (singular and plural) distorts their closest relationships. Though rational, human volitions (their wills) are unreliable. This generic flaw, long ago named as "original sin," means loving oneself more than God. That creates the need for forgiveness by God and others wronged and for new beginnings. The main context for such confessing, forgiving, and starting again, is worship. Such is the pessimistic/realistic but still hopeful assessment of Christian self-understanding. The aspiration of philosophical ethics—a moral and just life with clear thinking and self-disciplined conduct in a tolerant and just communal context—in the experience of Christians, exceeds human abilities. Bootstrap self-salvation makes for memorable childhood stories but even children know them to be imaginary.

Given the flawed moral condition of Christians, when self- and God-acknowledged, hope lies in repentance and forgiveness. God's forgiveness, when invoked and granted, can restore the insight and experience that life is good. Christians confess that they can do better in becoming who they are meant to be. Not that worship creates all that much moral wisdom. But being on speaking and loving terms with God makes things whole, coherent, good. And, that hopeful plea, "with the help of God," offers hope for coming closer to God's hope for humankind.

Liturgically (in the order of worship), the links with God seem not primarily normative (what to do or refrain from doing) but metaethical (relating to the meaning and purpose of life). Focusing on God in worship includes moral implications because the biblical God is moral, just and helpful. Christian ethics takes its bearing from what it believes about the character of God. It is the presence and goodness of God linked with love of humans, more than ethical sophistication that can transform human beings morally.

SUMMARY

The task of this chapter has been to relate Christian worship with Christian ethics. Christian ethics originates in the context of worship and is an indirect response to God. Again, *indirect* because love of neighbor is the intent and direction. It is God's identification with neighbors in need that links such acts with God. Such response expresses not only gratitude but calls for imitation of the character of God who loves humans. Like Parent, like child!

There is another effect of the presence of God in worship that is not as such moral but pre-moral or metaethical. That is an assurance of the goodness of this world and of this life. This metaethical affirmation is fittingly expressed in the hymn, over a century old, "This is my Father's world." That assures Christians of the most basic confidence that this world and all human life is good. That makes the world into the human home and provides reassurance that human existence is not accidental but good and meaningful. The first stanza of that hymn concludes, "I rest me in the thought."

Christian worship responds to the presence of the parental God. In worship, God may use human openness to divine presence to offer a taste or foretaste, of who God is. That transforms human beings and how life makes sense. The celebratory meal in the name of Jesus, the heart of Christian worship, does not present norms or commandments. The Eucharist celebrates God's costly life-giving love for humankind. No strings attached. And yet everything is connected with it. Communicants in turn promise God their loyalty and, in a sense, themselves. As in the covenant of marriage, the covenant with God does not itemize responsibilities. When Christians or those married remember who they are, they will discern their responsibilities. They will also remember that God is faithful and will have the last word.

7

Human Rights

> We hold these truths to be self-evident, that all men are created equal, that they are endowed by their Creator with certain unalienable [inalienable] Rights, that among these are Life, Liberty, and the Pursuit of Happiness. That to secure these Rights, Governments are instituted among Men, deriving their just powers from the consent of the governed.
>
> —United States Declaration of Independence

THIS EXCERPT FROM THE 1776 Declaration of Independence expresses the very spirit of liberalism.[1] These liberating words, after being used by American founding fathers in their revolt against Britain, were applied initially only to free white men. Yet these words project a vision that has blossomed progressively. Applied to Jews, then to "Negroes," and of late to women, they beckon to all oppressed people. In its most universal affirmation, this vision reappears in the 1948 United Nations Universal Declaration of Human Rights. Its first paragraph affirms the "recognition of the inherent dignity

---

1. Liberalism is a political and social philosophy advocating individual opportunity, rights, equality and democracy. Liberalism holds political views that are socially progressive and promote social welfare. A caution: The features listed here may not include the earliest of human lives.

and of the equal and inalienable rights of all members of the human family" as "the foundation of freedom, justice and peace in the world."[2]

THE MEANING OF HUMAN RIGHTS

Rights are justifiable claims in either the context of law or of ethics. Eventually human rights became just claims raised for all humans, no matter their identity, gender, nationality, race, wealth or abilities. The unspoken assumption here is that all the conditions listed in the previous sentence have been used to exploit or harm human beings. Human rights, then, when effectively enforced, offer basic protections for everyone. The value assumption here is that being human counts, counts enough to be legally and/or morally protected. That also is the claim and assumption of democracy. Having universal human standing liberates and reassures. That rights exist for all humans in the USA was a gradual achievement. May it become a global achievement.

Legal rights, more diverse and complex than moral rights, are claims recognized and enforced by law. Moral rights are claims justified by moral reasoning but which might not be enforced by law. In both law and in ethics rights protect. Other forms of legal protection exist than the protection created by rights. Historic houses, rare plant and animal species, national parks, air, water and land can be protected without recourse to rights. But rights offer the strongest protection. In both legal and moral contexts rights are ascribed only to persons or citizens but not to animals or objects. Meat-eating has been morally challenged but will not normally cause conflicts over rights.

Legal rights may also be called *positive laws or entitlement* (as in due process, access to justice, ownership, voting, freedom of speech and of the press, worship). In legal contexts one invokes civil and constitutional rights; ethics and morality appeal to natural and moral rights. In effect, human rights constitute levelers among humans. Rich or poor, male or female, strong or weak, all count and count equally, at least in theory. Christian ethics can be a leveler as well in that all humans have standing in regard to God and all have responsibilities toward neighbors. And it is the one God who is Lord of all and who constitutes the ground or basis for unity of humankind. The conviction that God creates and loves all human beings is fundamental to biblical ethics. A certain difference from democratic egalitarianism arises from the biblical conviction that greater human need calls

---

2. See "Universal Declaration of Human Rights."

for greater responsibilities. Such priority care only *seems to* contradict the leveling effect since all the worst off should be included in prioritized care.

NEGATIVE RIGHTS

The right to say No!—protects defensively. As defensive walls around individuals, such rights secure persons from harm. Summarized in the Bill of Rights, they protect not only from overreaching by governments but from incursions into a person's life, liberty, and property. Rights assume the intrinsic worth of the individual who is protectable by rights. The democratic belief that everyone counts, counts enough not to be subsumed under some greater good or cause, forms the unspoken self-evident truth safeguarded by rights. Individual citizens have the status that assures them of due process and a fair trial, for example. The value conviction underlying human rights is that humans have intrinsic worth that must be protected from harm. In liberal philosophy such valuing and protecting arises from respect for persons as rational and volitional or thinking and deciding beings. The source for Christian ethics of such respect is that humans are creatures in the image of God. Human links with God constitute an external source of standing. Philosophically and secularly the source for standing and rights originate internally through mental and moral abilities unique to humans.

POSITIVE LEGAL RIGHTS

Legitimate claims on others known as *entitlements*, have evolved more slowly. Entitlements prove costly to finance and support. They require contributions by others and not just the non-interference granted by negative legal rights. Given the ubiquitous resentment of being taxed—the right to keep what one has earned (the negative right to property)—many resent and resist paying for entitlements or positive rights of others. If free speech were a positive right, someone would have to provide individuals with the means needed for expressing and disseminating speech: a bullhorn, a platform, a printing press, internet access. If abortion were designated a positive right, someone other than women seeking to end their pregnancy might have to pay for abortions.

Western nations have established the positive legal right to basic education regardless of ability to pay. The United States supports individuals with Social Security entitlements. But despite repeated efforts, this nation—to the amazement of Europeans—has not created an inclusive positive national right to basic health care. The major reason for denying such entitlements is the creed of political conservatives that treasures the right to property and the responsibility to provide for one's own needs. Individual moral responsibility for oneself, the correlative of individual rights, resists taxing all to pay for the medical care of some. Christian ethics, in contrast—except for ultra conservatives—considers financial assistance for those unable to afford medical insurance or medical treatment pragmatic expression of loving or caring for neighbors.

PERSONS AND RIGHTS

Only *persons,* more or less, have rights. The reason for hedging that claim requires a definition of "person." While "person" and "human being" overlap, they are not identical in meaning. Philosophically, "person" names an individual with the abilities to think and to decide. Alien earth visitors would be regarded as persons. Data, the sentient android officer in the fictional TV series Star Trek, was able to reason and make decisions. He was respected and had certain rights (such as to be reassembled in order to continue functioning).

Christian ethics looks elsewhere for person-status for human beings. Persons are human recipients of God's love. God's love for humans need not be based in rational-volitional capacities (self-generated standing). Humans count because God creates humans in God's image and loves them. This is not just a semantic or theoretical distinction. Legally, rational and volitional abilities can spell the difference between life and death. Human beings in their earliest developmental stages, as embryos, fetuses and neonates (newborns), are assumed *not* to have developed the ability to think and decide. Therefore, they have not yet developed the status of "person." (Even if liberals may not insist on newborns actually having the person-creating abilities.) That explains the "more or less" above.

The human unborn is not a person in the legal or philosophical sense. It (!) does not qualify as rights-bearer. "No rights" may imply no need for protections. Therefore, within certain restrictions, abortion may interrupt a woman's pregnancy. After all, a pregnant woman is not yet a mother. Or is she? As a national community, Americans have legally decided that the human unborn shall not count as the rest of us count. The human unborn, within certain limits, may be aborted. That expression avoids bloodier labels. The least troubling rendition avoids reference to the unborn completely and prefers "interruption of pregnancy"—a condition of the woman. (Abortion is the subject of a subsequent chapter.)

Newborn humans count legally as humans and are protectable with rights. One would think that such protections seem inconsistent with the human unborn lack of standing. The fact that birth legally begins human status protection may have a pragmatic or practical reason. Birth is identifiable in time and procedure. Human development of rational and volitional skills seems impossible to locate precisely and non-controversially. Those who insist on the ability to think and choose as establishing human intrinsic worth and inviolability may be willing to tolerate some compromise when it comes to human standing and rights of newborns. Pro-life advocates, reasoning in reverse, tend to use newborn rights protections as precedent for protecting the unborn.

PERSONHOOD

"Personhood" means the ability to think and to decide. It is a remarkably value-laden term. This and a few comparable words make persons into ends-in-themselves. In secular contexts, personhood capacities make persons precious and inviolable. These abilities elicit awe and respect, establish human dignity, and justify protective rights. *Personhood* is one of those special words that protect with rights and prevent reducing the value of humans to their usefulness. When liberals are religious, which is conceivable, their adjective for "persons" may well be "sacred." In liberal vocabulary *mind*, *self*, *person*, and *moral agency* enjoy similar status. All provide protection for those so described or named.

A PAUSE FOR PERSPECTIVE

These introductory pages introduce legal terms and concepts that create human and legal standing. "Standing" means that whoever so named counts. Here counting is not a matter of numbers but of status or intrinsic worth. Specifically, when and why do humans count enough to be protectable with rights, legal rights that acknowledge standing and offer protections? To be sure, both legal and moral rights can and do wax or wane over time. The focus here is on Western modern words and concepts (meaning of words) that justify the ascription of rights in modern Western American culture. Attention here considers a familiar secular and legal modern approach and relates that to a biblical Christian perspective. Both secular and Christian ethics offer metaethical or world-view visions and values. That is, they are deeply rooted in how to make sense of life inclusively and coherently. While human rights do not appear in biblical texts, contemporary religious ethicists can and do affirm rights as secular renditions of the infinite worth of each human being created in the divine image.

While secular protections invoke self-evidence—"we hold these truths to be self-evident"—biblical believers derive such status and protectability from God. Except, of course that historically Christians did not always "get it" when it came to protecting persons (as Turks, Jews, slaves). The sobering possibility suggests itself that Enlightenment humanists, in the centuries following the rise of Protestantism, acknowledged the preciousness of all human beings and insisted on their equal protection with rights. Meanwhile, Christians were killing each other in the name of God. Irony is not a biblical concept. But it suggests itself when Christians warred against each other and humanist secularists created lasting human protections with rights.

SECULAR/CHRISTIAN DIFFERENCES IN HUMAN STANDING

Secularists and Christians differ in reasons why humans deserve standing and protective rights. Secularists look to human abilities to think and to decide while Christians invoke God as Creator, Savior, and Lord. Both perspectives insist on protective human rights. There is, of course a major difference, namely the respective "take" regarding the human unborn. If the abilities that base intrinsic worth and standing for humans are reason and will, nothing is lost in abortion except human potential. Here Christian faith makes a decisive difference: God as the Creator of life endows all humans with worth and standing. That includes their beginning and ending. In effect, here conception counts as the beginning of a new human being. No rational capacity yet expected or required. No threshold of birth required either, for as genetics and the practice of medicine insist, an individual human comes into being at conception.

Despite the popular misleading phrase, the issue never has been, "when does human life begin?" That is a biological and medical question answered long ago. The actual critical and decisive question is: when is a human life worth valuing and protecting? Christians, when consistent, insist that the protection of human life should coincide with its existence—from beginning to end. Conception is the point at which one should acknowledge intrinsic worth, the image of God, a soul, human status—whatever value term will replace scientific labels for a new human life with human standing and protective rights.

Human Rights

ODDITIES OF WORDS OR WHO COUNTS AS A PERSON

The *human unborn* (forward looking and therefore protective) is not a legal person in the US. Human non-persons have no rights. Specifically, the human unborn lack the most basic human right, the right to life. From 1973 until 2022 (when *Roe v. Wade* was overturned), the human unborn had no legal protection against being killed at will (of course never so bluntly described). Such crass language will be avoided by advocates of liberal abortion laws. The act leading to fetal death will be described in terms of the woman unwilling to remain pregnant. That avoids the word *mother*. "Ending a pregnancy" refers to a condition of the woman and avoids reference to the subject at hand. When it comes to inflicting fetal death, non-offensive language requires a lawyer's verbal skill.

Distinguishing *persons* from living bodies, focusing primarily on rational and volitional qualities, has had universally liberating effects for Jews, for Blacks, and for women. In the Western world, liberalism as the heritage of the Enlightenment, triumphed in envisioning humans as persons rather than to conceive and define them in terms of their bodies, ethnicity, gender, race, or birth. Isolating and concentrating on rational and volitional abilities has had a liberating, equalizing, and humanizing effect. In medicine it humanizes not only through patient rights, but also by focusing on persons as moral and volitional beings with handicaps and afflicted by illnesses rather than defining persons in terms of their bodily limits as *the handicapped, the sick* or *the dying*. Such liberal focus on humans as *persons* has possibly had two contradictory effects. On the one hand, it contributed to a more genuine and more inclusive human standing. Being considered a person insists on justice and fairness for all humans born. Focusing on human rational and volitional abilities (mind and will) rather than on race, gender or age has had egalitarian and equalizing democratic effects.

For the human unborn, however, "person," still implying reason and will, cannot reasonably applied to the human unborn. That exposes the human unborn to unprotective status. They are not yet "persons." Without that key word they are deprived of the key term protecting persons from harm. Literally millions of human beings annually pay the price of being cut off from standing afforded by "person," liberally conceived.

THE IMPORTANCE OF "PERSON" STATUS

In liberal perspective, being able to think and to decide, the key features of personhood, makes humans protectable. If Descartes' cogito be true, "I think, therefore I am," then the *inability* to think may imply lack of personhood including its advantages. Liberal human standing is self-generated through thought and choice. For liberalism, non-rational human beings without an "I" or a mind, devoid of a self-aware self, lack the quality that establishes Western-liberal human dignity and worth. Non-persons, both human and non-human, therefore, remain without similar claim to rights. They count only insofar as others—persons individually or communally—value them. Whatever value such non-persons may have is derived from the rational choice of persons. And rational choice, at least in social theory, is not a phrase associated with generosity.[3] If the reader permits an imaginary "what if," if aliens made contact with humans, they would be immediately respected as persons, if only for their intelligence in mastering interstellar travel. As with the imaginary Data, they would enjoy non-human personhood status.

The liberal rights of persons, particularly the right to be free, trump any claims that might be raised on behalf of the human unborn, of future generations, or of non-human animals. In the liberal vision, human beings in their earliest stages—designated with the scientific words *embryo* and *fetus* and never with the forward-looking term *unborn*—do not merit rights. They remain identified and named as bodies only. And human bodies, just as nature generally, merit no rights. Pre- or non-rational human bodies fall short of being ends-in-themselves and remain means to the ends of others. While unborn small humans have been known to fight for life prenatally when treated for congenital diseases, their life or death depends upon the choice or whim of those with power or authority over them. Their lives lie literally in human hands. Unprotected by rights, they perish under the cloak of the right to privacy. The freeing and humanizing liberal vision also manifests this dark and bloody side.

Similarly, at the end of the human life span, when mental abilities may fail, when trauma and disease, senility and abuse can put an untimely end to the rational abilities that qualify humans for personhood, the person or mental self is said to be gone. Only the shell or *a living vegetable* remains. Such individuals are still legal persons. But the imperative of dehumanizing words and of the liberal belief that what is essential to persons and constitutes their value and dignity is mental ability—is to urge the law to be *flexible*. And indeed, PVS (persistent vegetative state) patients, may now be legally *allowed to die*. The legal rationale for killing such patients is that their dying is willed by the patient him- or herself. Who would want to be sustained in such an

---

3. Rational choice theory holds that humans are rational beings who seek to maximize their own gains and minimize their losses. That would imply non-persons and perhaps even other persons as means to one's own self-interest ends.

existence? After defining artificial feeding and hydrating as treatment and lacking a living will or other directive, the patient's appointed surrogate then exercises the well-established individual right to refuse treatment on behalf of the patient. And no one lives for long without fluids.

Legal reasoning that endorses such *killing*—a word that will, of course, never be used in this context—killing the patient in the name of patient rights, makes sense to courts and to the public: life in such an apparently non-conscious condition is not worth sustaining. And that may be true and right. The point here is not to evaluate but to clarify by distinguishing the liberal concept of "person" from the human body. Without anyone who cares for such individuals, a living patient devoid of detectable personhood qualities loses all dignity, worth, and standing. Aided by a legal fiction—the autonomous will exercised by proxy—such *bodily remainder* loses the most fundamental of all rights, the right to live. Moving farther along the spectrum of mere bodily existence without protective rights, it is possibly only emotional queasiness unsupported by good reasons and an outdated legal definition that finds death preferable to sustaining these living bodies as organ banks.

Defining *person* in terms of mental capacities excludes any essential role for the human body except as necessary support base. Nor does it reflect any vital role for the emotions or for personal relationships. The essential relationship in the liberal definition of person is that of the self with itself—as in holding oneself accountable, blaming or praising oneself, being self-aware. External evidence of such mental abilities is not always available. Is the person or personal self really absent in a patient in PVS (persistent vegetative state)? Or is the self simply unable to communicate its presence to anyone else? A medical condition referred to as a *locked-in state* prevents the patient from communicating in almost any form.[4] When friends or loved ones read or speak with such seemingly unconscious patients, as they are encouraged to do, this human contact may elicit tears from this silent . . . person. There is a personal presence after all! And that makes all the difference in the world.

Uncertainty about complete or permanent absence or death of a mental self even when there is no evidence of brain activity also worries critics of brain death. That definition relies on brain inactivity. Unwilling to link the mental self inseparably to detectable brain activity, such skeptics deem it safer to rely on the traditional criteria of death, the cessation of all vital functions, including heart beat and breathing, than to risk destroying the

---

4. "[A] paralytic condition in which a person may be conscious and alert but unable to communicate except by eye movement or blinking." Anderson et al., *Mosby's Medical Dictionary*, s.v. "locked-in syndrome."

inner self because the bodily self remains unresponsive. Reading medical literature about such carefulness to avoid killing patients on the edges or limits of life is reassuring—in regard to medical caution. But how remarkable it is that such care for human life is not self-evident in the practice of abortion. Would the difference be explained by the fact that mature humans have legal rights while the human unborn lack all rights? And would that imply that the unborn are not sufficiently human to merit equal protection?

THE INNER SELF/PERSON INACCESSIBILITY

When the self is defined in terms of its mental abilities only, and if presence of personhood can make the difference between life and death, one would need a robust and reliable indicator of whether "anyone is in there." But firsthand experience of personal presence or of the inner self remains limited to oneself. This limitation is named as the egocentric predicament. Perhaps that designation is only now coming into its own when a human being's life may depend upon detectable personal presence. One infers personhood in others. Yet when others become non-communicative, their "innards," their thoughts, motives, and always their self-awareness lie beyond the reach of anyone else. The liberal concept of person or personhood is self-referring rather than drawing others into this key concept. It is not birth, a beating heart or an infant's smile that will do for personhood. It is not kinship or living flesh-of-our-flesh that suffices for counting as a person. The liberal valuing of the person through detectable mental abilities may become one to die for.

This liberal concept of person or personhood may explain why there is so little attention paid to the body in bioethics literature. Liberalism focuses on rationalism in human nature, such as awareness, conscience, decision-making. Bodily existence is assumed but seems to play no decisive role in liberal versions of human existence. Perhaps such distancing from the body preserves personal dignity when the body is violated, when it ages and fails. And surely it is true that persons are more than their bodies. To be reduced to one's gender or sexuality, to be judged primarily in terms of one's bodily attractiveness or prowess, degrades the human person. But what are the implications for pain and suffering, for aging and failing mentally, for having children of one's own? The question would be whether one can live with this liberal distancing from the body when it comes to the human life span and the context of medicine. Clearly some human beings, beyond the human unborn, will not live if the liberal concept of personhood becomes/remains definitive.

PERSONS AND HUMAN BEINGS

In liberalism and in the law, not all human beings are persons. Neither liberalism nor the law agree with Dr. Seuss that a person's a person, no matter how small. The law withholds such status from human beings before birth. Becoming a legal person, having standing in a court of law, and enjoying the protection of legal rights begins with birth and ends with death. The 1973 US Supreme Court decisions, *Roe v. Wade* and *Doe v. Bolton* the Fourteenth Amendment due process clause guaranteed American women the fundamental right to medically safe abortions. (As noted, the 1973 court decision was overturned in 2022.) While those decisions do not establish the right to kill the fetus, very few fetuses survive abortion procedures. The legal right to life does not exist until the human unborn becomes a newborn and a legal person.

Because human physical and mental development offers no sharp distinguishing lines, liberal defenders of personhood may compromise by backdating personhood status and allowing the human newborn to count as a person or as one of us. But postponing the start of legal personhood to coincide with the development of rational abilities has been recommended in the case of seriously "defective" or handicapped newborns. The lack of mental abilities in newborns classifies them with fetuses, not persons. What some condemn as infanticide is then declared to be merely "postnatal abortion."[5]

Even where one is willing to let personhood or legal standing coincide with birth, careful definitions count. In American law, a human being becomes a person at birth. And it matters that the being emerging from the womb comes all the way out. If the head, foot, or some other body part has not emerged, the near-newborn has no rights yet. Before birth the law knows only "fetuses," not persons or unborn children. The state may have an "interest" in such fetuses as eventual citizens, but any protection of unborn children arises from the state's interests rather than from claims that might arise from this nascent living being itself or that might be raised on its behalf. When the right to life or to health of the pregnant woman is at stake, only birth itself will legally protect the new life. If the pregnant woman, the legal person with rights, is at risk, her rights trump state interest. Even as late as when the natural birth process has begun, it is not too late legally to abandon the almost-or partially-born. Through an incision in the back of the fetal neck a physician may evacuate the brain cavity. One hesitates to speak of "sucking its brains out" and names that a "partial birth abortion." If the procedure had been briefly delayed and the head had emerged, a legal

---

5. Fletcher, *Humanhood*, 144.

person with a right to life would have been destroyed. That might have been designated homicide or infanticide. The lessons lie near that becoming a legal person matters, that words and time count, and that the living should be grateful to survive long enough to have been blessed with legal rights.

PERSONS, RIGHTS, AND PRECEDENTS

American law grants personhood and rights only to born and living humans and excludes the human unborn and all other living creatures from legal personhood standing and rights. Liberalism excludes all creatures from standing and rights except rational humans (when conceptually consistent). Such exclusions result in grim prospects for the human unborn and does not bode well for future generations of humankind. If humans already on the way, conceived but unborn, lack all legal rights, how much less can one claim rights for future generations? Still, when this nation has the collective resolve, it can protect whatever needs protecting: historical sites, old houses, threatened species. It is conceivable that one might also legally protect the human species when it is threatened—as it is before birth and as it seems in regard to future generations. If one were to invoke the strongest protections, namely rights, one might cite corporate precedent. American corporations have standing in courts of law and enjoy limited legal personhood. Such options could be created for the human unborn. If only this nation stood in awe of the human unborn as it does of corporations!

Exploring such options requires legal expertise lacking here. But American law has been shaped by and resonates with liberal traditions. One can appeal to values within liberalism and within contemporary practices and beliefs that may mitigate the current deadly implications of personal rights in regard to the lives of non-persons. Moral arguments and plain common sense can create strong reasons for changing minds and altering laws and practices. The following paragraphs offer such reasons. The goal is not to abrogate existing rights but to counterbalance them by protecting other important values. Making such a case counters the flow of contemporary culture and law. Moreover, such countercultural recommendations involve the most basic of all value questions and confront such ultimate issues as the worth of a human life and what humans owe and should owe each other.

Three cautions preface that effort. First, when too many human lives are lost by current road design, reconstruction can alter hazardous stretches of the road. If that holds for traffic, it may hold as well for communal thinking patterns. The following pages attempt reconstruction. Secondly, highway signs warn of new traffic patterns: Proceed with caution! Such warnings seem helpful here not only in regard to what will be said but to how it is said. Value-neutral language might apply as a precondition of academic objectivity and fairness. Actual analysis of any word or term for pre- or non-rational human lives, however, reveals that no value-neutral language exists. Whatever the key word, it points or leads somewhere. That certainly holds true for scientific terms—sometimes recommended as objective or value neutral. The wording of what follows, then, just as much of what preceded, remains leading. As in all bioethics controversies, the reader does well here to be on guard. And lastly, there follows an appeal to secular liberalism from within. It suggests that liberals themselves may not want to go all the way on the liberal road.

INTERGENERATIONAL SOLIDARITY

The liberal logic so fatal to human lives when they are not yet or no longer able to reason dismisses timeless civilizing continuities between generations. Parental and grandparental links with children, including those on the way, has always been seen as natural and fitting. Children in turn acknowledge such continuity with dedicated responsibility to parents and to grandparents. Exceptions startle us. That in the third world the poorest of the poor may sell their children alarms Western readers. American historical practices and laws that tore apart slave families strike contemporaries as barbarous. In a context in which pro-family slogans recommend political candidates, the startling liberal logic of the US Supreme Court dismissed the role of the male progenitor. The inseminator, or any other word replacing "father" and any hint of parenthood, has no say when it comes to the legal right to abort. That proves awkward subsequently, when that other party is held legally responsible for the care of a child whose mother decided to affirm its life.

The current liberal logic and laws ignore and violate continuities between generations that not only link lives but also nurture and protect human beings in their most vulnerable stages. Legal individualism, fortified by the new right to privacy, disregards and violates ancient, humanizing, and protective intergenerational solidarity with the human unborn. United States abortion rights establish absolute individual personal power over nascent human lives. Neither the human unborn nor the rest of us may be able to live with that. Even liberal humanists might agree: We must not kill our children. Not even before they are born.

Intergenerational solidarity may also be weakening at the end of the human life span. Both American law and culture insist on adult children's responsibility for aging and ill parents. Legislation protects the lives of the elderly as it does the lives of the young against neglect and abuse. The state intervenes to protect those who cannot protect themselves. Nevertheless, the logic of individual self-reliance insists that aging and dependent persons should avoid becoming a burden on their children or grandchildren. Imposing on the persons one loves must be avoided. Better to choose a voluntary exit, as in Oregon's physician-assisted suicide law.[6] Liberal humanists might agree that we must not hasten to usher ourselves out in an individualistic and self-reliant rendition of what it means to love our children and to be loved by them.

CONSISTENCY

If fairness and resistance to human oppression be hallmarks of liberalism, even the firmest defenders of individual liberty and privacy may be troubled by the wholesale destruction of children before they are born. Because every person was once pre-personal and would not want to have been deprived of all prospects then or later, fairness counsels us to live and let live. If no right is absolute and if protecting children becomes a self-evident responsibility at birth, it ought to make sense in the liberal worldview to protect children while they are on the way—regardless of whether or not they are wanted. We were as they—the unborn—are now. If the thought of coherence and consistency be a virtue of a humanitarian ethics, any human community owes loyalty to its children prospectively not only not only when they are born.

Currently in all but the context of elective abortion, it seems reasonable and right to care for our children even before they are born. Prenatal care is only the most persuasive example. Offering prenatal care to low-income pregnant women through federal or state funds can seem like designating the human unborn as patients. They can become patients when wanted by their mothers ("mothers" when the child is wanted, "pregnant women" when it is not). And patients have rights (at least once they are born). No wonder advocates of federal support for prenatal care must defend themselves: "This is not a debate about abortion, and those who seek to advocate for children should stop making it so. It is about our undeniable health needs throughout the life cycle."[7] The point remains: one cannot consistently respect and care for children when born and dismiss them before birth.

---

6. Oregon's Death with Dignity Act (1997) allowed terminally ill individuals to end their lives through the voluntary self-administration of lethal medication. See "Oregon's Death with Dignity Act."

7. Thompson, "Benefits for the Unborn," A30.

RIGHTS AND CARE

Not only prenatal care, but also taking care not to conceive when both partners carry or express the same genetic disease would be prospective *caring* even before a new life comes into being. Offering early health care, communal support of women with dependent children, universal access to quality schooling, all express reasonable care for children. The word "care" differs from "rights." And one may well buttress practical care for children with children's rights. But caring reaches farther and includes more than rights can ever attain. Surely liberalism offers a place for such caring. And the continuity and consistency of such caring always prohibits killing unwanted children. Both before and after birth. It seems unreasonable and inconsistent to destroy or legally justify the destruction of human lives before birth and then advocate respect for the survivors.

LIBERTY *AND* DEATH?

Letting a human life depend simply on being wanted by one of its progenitors when children's bodies and lives are incontestably precious and protectable once born must seem odd even to liberal reason. Such oddity may be masked by euphemisms, as the invocation of "a woman's right to control her own body." Yet in fact there are two living bodies. And except for killing in self-defense, liberal rights ordinarily end when it comes to touching or harming other bodies. But killing is what the *legal right to privacy* implicitly legitimates when it comes to the human unborn! The right to abort literally means the right to expel "the uterine contents" and does not include the right to kill or destroy. But in the absence of artificial placentas, that right can and does decree the death of nascent human lives. Though the legal and liberal case only invokes liberty and privacy, death constitutes the unspoken but anticipated consequence. These deaths lack any of the justifying reasons with which law or morality normally permit killing. Destroying such dependent and defenseless lives and justifying doing so in the name of liberty seems perverse, even cruel. Choosing between liberty or death seems noble for patriots and for soldiers willing to sacrifice themselves for the rescue of comrades or the freedom of all. But in the abortion context, the frequent choice is for liberty *and* death. There, liberty refers to one life and death to another. That sacrifice remains involuntary and devoid of all nobility. A nation will not memorialize those deaths. The nation simply records them by the numbers. In the millions.

POTENTIAL

One protective value link between such developing human bodies and the full-fledged human community that merits consideration within liberalism lies in human potential. The continuities of biological, developmental, and personal potential of beginning human lives are both incontestable and astounding. In amazingly rapid progression, one thing leads to another. If one were simply to let this small human life be, it would become one of us amazingly quickly yet in its own normal and good time. Of course, pro-choice advocates will not let potential count here. For acorns are not oak trees,[8] and blue prints are not houses. Such denials make pragmatic and perhaps emotional sense. If one intends to take a human life, it makes sense to dismiss its future. By contrast, if one were to look at fetal sonograms, were to give this new life a name or project hopes for what it might become, offer prenatal care or treatment, one has reached out. When fatally insisting on one's own rights here, it is better not to look or to reach, to use only dehumanizing scientific words, and to refer only to what was rather than what would and might be.

Normally untimely death elicits deep mourning for the loss of what might have been. Existentialists insist that persons—liberally defined—need a future. Potential is another word for having a future. We all need time. If potential counts for rational selves, should it not count for beings engendered by persons, for new lives who are on the way to becoming legal persons? Perhaps one can be casual about potential personhood only in an overpopulated world. If fertility were to become universally problematic and difficult, actual conceptions would be cause for celebration. In fact, normally that is true already. Successful pregnancies would reassure everyone that humankind has a future. Even in an overpopulated world, however, there can be no oak trees without acorns (except for cloning). Even in a crowded world and a as a parent how can one dismiss potential? As a teacher? As a humanist?

BODY CONSIDERATIONS

Reflections on the human body belong into an ethics chapter on rights because liberalism defines the essential human self as person or mind and thereby dismisses the importance of the body. Rights can protect human lives even before personhood comes into its own (as in the case of newborns). It would simply require beginning human protection earlier than

---

8. Thomson, "Defense of Abortion," 25–26.

birth. The justifying value would simply be that human living bodily existence counts. Personhood not required—as it is not required for newborns. The liberal mind/body dualism, with priority for mind, has other drawbacks than to expose the human unborn to premature death. Defining human nature with emphasis on mind creates liberal problems with accounting for the effects of illness, aging, handicaps. More importantly, what does body/mind dualism imply for human bodies who do not yet or no longer qualify for what liberals mean by *person*? If the inherent value and dignity of human beings consists only in their personhood and not also in the body, liberal ethics will dismiss the living human body when it does not "contain" personhood or mind. Implications for the human unborn generally, for non-treatment of handicapped newborns, for the lives of patients in a persistent vegetative state or in a coma seem obvious.

METAPHYSICAL DUALISM

Deeply influenced by Greek traditional thought, Western culture has long been exposed to metaphysical dualism—the technical term for dividing all reality into two irreducible substances. The cleavage of human identity into mind and body seems most striking in contemporary notions of death. The mental self is assumed to be immune to death, a version of life after death that seems culturally pervasive and is not unique to religion. Judging from American obituaries, there is a prevailing conviction that the mind, the bodiless self, "the real me," continues to exist in some way after death. The spate of *afterlife movies* also attests to the popular belief that the essential self, the person as mind, does not die.

American culture is not univocal on this score. A contrasting contemporary approach to death that seems to link rather than to bifurcate body and mind manifests itself in the amazing loyalty that soldiers, especially elite troops, show toward the bodies of their fallen comrades. No Marine, no Ranger, no Seal leaves the dead body of a comrade on the field of battle—despite the serious danger that such dedication will cost more casualties. The body of the fallen comrade is so linked to the identity of that slain soldier that to recover the body is to honor the former comrade. The German military ode for honoring a fallen soldier—"Ich hat' einen Kameraden" or "I had a comrade"—speaks of the fallen body at one's feet "als wär's ein Stück von mir"—"as if it were a part of myself." We are our bodies. And loyalty binds us not just to inner selves but to bodies, even in death. At least for soldiers. Perhaps also for those devoted to each other. The recovery of bodies from the ruins of the New York World Trade Center similarly suggested that the preciousness we ascribe to human beings extends to their bodies, even to their corpses.

The English language aids and abets the dualistic tendency of the liberal worldview. The expression, "I have a body," implies metaphysical dualism. The "I" functions as the mind, the volitional agent who uses, controls, and directs the body. It would surely be more correct, however, to say that one both has and is a body. And if that is true, then valuing and respecting and protecting the self with rights must include the body, just as it normally does in requiring consent for medical and experimental interventions. Indeed, when it comes to illness generally, the body/mind dualism is hard to retain consistently.[9] "I am sick," or "I hurt" can refer to either mental-emotional or physical illness and pain. Though fierce and lasting pain can estrange the self from its own body, there is nothing like physical pain to remind us of the bodies we are.

BIBLICAL AFFIRMATIONS OF THE HUMAN BODY AND MORTALITY

To resume Christian ethics—that were excluded in the preceding paragraphs, biblical anthropology or view of human nature insists on a more unified vision than that of dualistic liberalism. Biblically, humans are earthlings, animated by God's breath, mortal creatures of dust. Created in the divine image, that kinship applies to the whole creature, not just to its spiritual or mental aspects. The human mind or will, the rational and volitional self, is not filtered out as the location of special status or worth or of clearer affinity with God. It is the whole human creature that God judges to be "very good" (Gen 1:31). The whole human being reflects and is charged with reflecting the divine image in a life lived in imitating the ways—or the character—of the Lord.

It is the whole human being that perishes at death. Death ends it all, body and mind. Biblical texts know no immortality except that of God and of Jesus. Despite the medieval notion of Purgatory—the intermediate state between death and resurrection so promising for non-venial sinners and for the income of the church—the biblical universal epitaph remains: "from dust to dust" (Gen 3:19). Hope for an individual future beyond death lies in a divine act of resurrection: God's creative word will re-create or restore the dead. The word of God evokes a new creation and new (and eternal)

---

9. But pain can also alienate the self from itself and can be depicted as the experience of psychophysical dualism. "The painful body emerges as an estranged, alien, 'thing-like' presence, separate from the self." Williams and Bendelow, *Lived Body*, 160.

life not out of a supposed spiritual remainder that never died but out of the loving memory and will of God. That resurrected human being is conceivable biblically only as wholly new: a new body and a new spirit. The cultural inclination to believe in immortal human souls does not arise out of biblical traditions, in which nothing remains but dust. The concept of eternal souls probably has Hellenistic (Greek) sources. There is, of course, the New Testament and Christian conviction that at some point in the future, or beyond all time, God will raise the dead and judge both the living and the (raised) dead. Until then, the dead are dead and remain dead. In both body and soul.

The biblical recognition of the importance of the body to human identity also creates a morally significant awareness of time, of generations, and of interdependence not found in contemporary liberalism. The biblical 'begats,' so tedious for modern readers, affirm bodily descent, link identity to ancestors, imply hope of being continued—both in name and descendants—with the birth of new generations. God opens Sarah's womb and fulfills an old promise. Pregnancy is never a private affair here but expresses divine blessing and providential care not just for a couple but for a family, a community, a people. Though the Bible does not forbid abortion, it would never occur to biblical communities that such a prohibition was needed. For contrast, the liberal logic defines identity in terms of the self as individual moral agent. It lacks a sense of self in terms of ongoing generations and of belonging to a community. It searches for meaning in terms of its own projects rather than in the peopled past and in a promised future for offspring and community. The assumption that children must be wanted before they become acceptable probably arises from secular individualism. Contemporary Americans create their own identity with their own choices. That can make the unforeseen and the unplanned problematic. An *accidental* pregnancy can ruin the best laid plans and necessitates corrective measures.

As a postscript to these reflections on cultural individualism and a relative indifference to the past, to ancestors, to those who passed on the name one bears, there is at the time of this writing a television program on PBS, "Finding Your Roots." That this program should draw sustained popularity surprises. The theme reflects the title by interviewing well known individuals, inquiring about their past and researching their past with birth, marriage, census figures, immigration data, old letters and by retracing their genes to past generations. What surprises the viewers is how little such bright and forthcoming individuals actually know about their roots. Memories do not extend beyond one or two grandparents. The effects of revealing more about the past of those interviewed can be not just surprise and laughter but can be deeply moving. Even for viewers. Humans are communal creatures with a personal past and a mortal future. Our family past may have formed us more than our individualism suggests.

Not only a biblical anthropology but central Christian theological beliefs insist on the importance of the human body. The Gospel of John claims that the divine Word became flesh, became human with saving purpose (1:14–18). The Incarnation, the embodiment of God, and the sacrifice of that body on the cross constitute the heart of the Gospel. It is celebrated in the Eucharist: "The body of Christ broken for you; the blood of Christ shed for you." Believers find redemption not in some new insight, in divine enlightenment, in heavenly wisdom. Rather they acknowledge the redeeming love of God manifested in the agonized bodily suffering of a Son of Man dying so that humankind may be reconciled with God. Biblical believers cannot consistently dismiss the unborn human bodies now being turned away from community and continued life. In the name of God, they are called to protest the current rejection of unborn unwanted human bodies. Devalued and degraded by liberalism's insistence on mind and will as essentials and sufficient for human dignity, standing or rights, these early human lives perish for imposing.

SOCIOLOGY OF THE BODY

The reader may wonder how sociology of the body might relate to Christian ethics. Sociology of the body reacts against the liberal dualism of mind/body that still permeates American culture with its emphasis on mind as uniquely human and body as shared with all animals. The study of the living human body, so sociological reformers argue, merits its own distinct discipline: that is sociology of the body or embodied sociology. That re-direction forms a reconceptualization of sociology that seeks to avoid the dualistic features of current perspectives. The philosopher René Descartes (1596–1650), honored as the father of modern philosophy, who made famous the claim "I think, therefore I am," has become a favorite scapegoat of those who call for greater attention to human embodiment. While liberal ethics looks to the rational and volitional abilities to establish human status, rights, and ethics, sociological embodiment advocates call for bodily emphasis revisions. Embodiment should be central rather than peripheral in sociology. Such reform "put minds back in bodies, bodies back in society, and society back into bodes."[10] They expect that such refocusing will do greater justice to ethics and politics and conclude with the confidence that embodiment, . . . "a

---

10. Williams and Bendelow, *Lived Body*, 209.

common carnal bond, becomes both our hope and our salvation."[11] When it rains, it pours.

Bryan S. Turner, in his *The Body and Society*, proposes that the concept of embodiment must be placed at the core of any adequate picture of social life. He considers embodiment as a matter of vulnerability and frailty. Human beings are frail and their natural environment remains uncertain. In order to protect themselves from vagaries and afflictions, humans must build social institutions (especially political, familial, and ecclesiastical institutions) that come to constitute what we call *society*. And humans must be protected with general human rights. Turner summarizes the general argument of his book thus: "the social sciences have often neglected the most obvious 'fact' about human beings, namely that they have bodies and that they are embodied."[12] The importance of the sociology of the body is a necessary component of any genuine sociology.[13]

VALUES OF BODY AND MIND

What follows here will attempt to focus on a few ethical implications of rethinking the importance of human bodily nature in Christian ethics. The body is not merely a physical vehicle for personhood and identity. It is the active basis of being in the world, and the foundation of self, meaning, culture, and society. The thesis of the social construction of human bodies,[14] the claim that the meaning, value, and status of human bodies are social creations, seem both true and helpful. Implications include the recognition that humans are responsible for human standing, treatment, and respect, not only for their own bodies and persons but for those whose bodies and selves that differ from their own. The human inclination, however, may well be to rank human differences in favor of one's own kind.

Resisting bias in favor of one's own identity may require care about our choice of words. As in recognizing that "Black is beautiful," as in seeing the "handicapped" rather than the "crippled," as in "the unborn" rather than "embryos/fetuses." Scientific terms when referring to human bodies *outside a scientific context* prove to be particular troublesome. The sciences avoid value judgments and assertions. That discourages making use of them in celebrating human life. But humanistic and Christian ethics should begin with a sense of gratitude for human beings, their diversity, their abilities,

---

11. Williams and Bendelow, *Lived Body*, 213.
12. Turner, *Body and Society*, 215.
13. Turner, *Body and Society*, 232.
14. Shilling, *Body and Social Theory*, 11, 12, 70.

their character and skills; their physicality, generosity, beauty, intelligence, kindness. Our joy in meeting and welcoming newborn children focuses on their bodies. Mental and spiritual growth would be natural. But that comes later. As is, the newborn delight us in their bodiliness.

CELEBRATING HUMAN EXISTENCE

In Christian perspective, human bodily life remains precious across the age span, whether before birth or in its ending stages. Lest human existence and its goodness be taken for granted, may the reader permit a celebratory acknowledgment of human life: The birth of children, the rapid change of children in growing up, the amazing achievements of athletes, the skill of performers, attractive models; the discipline and confidence of recovering patients; the generosity of victims of disasters in helping others to recover; the nod and smile of a stranger in passing; the strength, patience and endurance of laborers; generous, helpful, beautiful persons: all masterpieces created by God! Simply seeing and remaining aware of the diverse characteristics of being human reassures and retains perspective. Lacking awareness of such blessed dimensions of being alive impoverishes and distorts being alive.

The liberal focus on human abilities to think and to decide is of course also worth celebrating. But not just personhood is worth praising. Human embodiment, regrettably both easily taken for granted or disregarded, is worth honoring as well. To be human is also always to be embodied. That immeasurable good rises to awareness when in pain, when wounded, when handicapped, when aged and no longer able to climb stairs two at a time. Beauty contests and muscle men may lie beyond reach of most, but how striking and awesome! How impressive the agility and endurance of runners! Pole vaulters, swimmers, gymnasts! And, more modestly, how good to be touched and to touch! How happy to embrace and to be embraced! To see and to be seen; to hear and to be heard; to breathe after the rain; to catch a smile and to return it!

SELECTIVELY ENDING HUMAN LIVES

All that and everything else is being denied to many of us who have just begun to live. They remain unable to escape, unnamed, unmissed. All in the name of human rights. Such literal dehumanization of humans in their earliest stages of growth is neither liberal nor biblical nor moral. Rather it resembles a communal aberration, a cultural moral schizophrenia. US laws permit the selective annihilation of the human unborn. This leading phrasing describes the mass destruction of unwanted unborn children. Less than a century ago millions of unwanted human lives faced *selection* for mass death, retrospectively named as the Holocaust. The current practice of fatal selection, also in the millions, has not yet been named or recognized as an atrocity. Abortion deaths remain nameless—unnamed in regard to both individuals selected as well as their mass elimination. Perhaps fetal anonymity will ease remembering, regretting and repenting. Such mass killing, again those millions, makes killing unborn humans a legal practice rather than a criminal and immoral aberration. Harmful general practices can be slow in changing, as held true in slavery and continues in racism.

RIGHTS AS A LAST RESORT

The fact that in an American context almost any pervasive public issue will be discussed in terms of rights implies that this word is suitable, fitting, and right. As discreet signs in foreign shops welcome visitors with, "English spoken here," so "rights spoken here" is the American promise for public policy, politics, law, and ethics. But just as such English may not be spoken well, so rights may not be used well. The ubiquity of rights in its public uses becomes apparent and worrisome if one transfers that word into the context of personal and private relationships or contexts, where recourse to rights is not normal. A married couple's invoking rights against each other hints of serious marital difficulties. The advocacy of a child's right to whatever just claim it might have, suggests that normal parental or adult responsibilities have failed. Even the appeal to rights by roommates against each other implies the lack of normal courtesies and civilities. Invoking that powerful word, *rights*, in a personal context, alarms: "So that's what it has come to?!"

Rights can be a popular recourse when ordinary responsibilities and relationships have failed. Rights belong to the threatening limits of human lives, not at the center of normal living. They are the last moral and legal defense against injustice, the step before open hostilities. Rights not only suggest a certain defensiveness, they are *adversarial*. That explains rights' natural fit into the American legal system. The invocation of patient rights may express a protest against medical paternalism. Patients now have a greater responsibility to be informed, to consult, to decide. This is a healthy change from reliance on tightlipped and authoritarian physicians.

But invoking rights also extracts a price, often unanticipated. The patient-physician relationship and health care have not necessarily improved by recourse to rights. Physicians now feel compelled to practice defensive medicine, face increased litigation, and rising insurance rates. A relationship at arm's length lessens trust, trust that may prove indispensable for therapy and healing. Physicians may be less willing to conceive of their profession in a covenant model in which responsibilities remain inclusive and unconditional. Because rights are self-protective, they incline to focus on the self rather than on the needs of others. Self-protection, by physicians, may not make for good medicine. To its own credit, the American Medical Association reaffirmed classical medical dedication to the patient when it decided that no patient may be turned away because a doctor fears contracting what often is a fatal disease, HIV, AIDS, Coronavirus. And patients themselves, no matter how well informed and insistent on rights, finally have no choice but to entrust themselves and their children into the hands of their doctors.

Not only mutual trust and covenantal responsibilities can be threatened by recourse to rights; rights-language cannot capture and foster the richness of life. Michael Ignatieff describes that inability in the following critique (with British spelling):

> Rights are not a language of the good at all. They're just a language of the right. Codes of rights cannot be expected to define what the good life is, what love and faithfulness and honour are. Codes of rights are about defining the minimum conditions for any life at all. So in the case of the family they are about defining the negatives: abuse and violence. Rights can't define the positives: love, forbearance, humour, charity, endurance. We need other words to do that, and we need to make sure that rights talk doesn't end up crowding out all the other ways we express our deepest and most enduring needs.[15]

Emergency brakes, safety nets, or rights imply the possibility of failure. Better if they were never actually needed. Yet rights also embody genuine realism about human nature: individual persons need powerful defenses against others—protections that are morally authoritative and legally enforceable. While the Enlightenment inclined to general optimism about human goodness and the human prospect, it proved realistic enough to know that human beings tend not to do right naturally, spontaneously or reliably. Humankind, especially those with only minimal resources and support, need powerful protections. Rights, perhaps our best protections, can save lives. Normally. Rights can also become massively destructive when misused, as for those unable to help or to protect themselves.

---

15. Ignatieff, *Rights Revolution*, 22–23.

RIGHTS ADVOCATES NEEDED

As legitimate protections and claims in adversarial relationships, rights need to be invoked or activated in order to function. But who will help the helpless to invoke rights? If violation or neglect of due responsibilities seems assumed in a situation that calls for rights, such neglect will not self-correct by passing judgment on itself. Rather, aggrieved persons or their advocates must appeal to rights. That process creates practical burdens or barriers for those too poor, too ignorant, too weak, too sick, too old, or too young to be able to do that. Advocates must do so on behalf of those unable to fend for themselves. Voluntary defenders of the rights of those unable to defend themselves may qualify as moral heroes. Because they can be hard to find, the American legal system has created the positive right, the entitlement to legal counsel for those who cannot afford it. While public defenders are not well-funded, the presence of such defenders speaks well for the American legal system. Yet the human unborn have few defenders.

Before birth, human rights either do not exist or function destructively. Beginning human lives before birth have no rights and no public authorized defender. They lack legal and liberal standing and rights to defend against injury and death not only through abortion but through experimentation and novel "reproductive" methods such as cloning. Medical researchers will seek to avoid the results of possible harm by eliminating compromised and possibly compromised embryos and fetuses. Litigable harm will not be provable till birth when newborns become legal persons, have standing in court, and can sue everyone in sight who might have harmed them prenatally. But by then it is too late for them. They had no advocates while on the way who might have persuaded their progenitors and technological experts not to take chances with children's lives under the banners of reproductive and research liberty.[16]

WHEREIN LIES THE PROBLEM?

Focusing on unborn children, who lack both moral and legal rights, may imply that abortion issues originate with them: If only they were not lacking the qualities our culture values most! If only they were the persons we are, they, too, would have rights. But, of course, the problem does not lie with them. Their lives and growths are as natural and proceed as fast as can be.

---

16. Experimenting with human embryos and human clones cannot be known to be harmless to their subjects before being tried. If one affirms the rule that human lives should never be used involuntarily as means only, then these practices become procedures that should never be done.

The human unborn have always been what or who they are. Their legalized massive destruction is a recent phenomenon. Who would have thought that the liberal vision, so respectful, liberating, and protective, could prove so deadly in this modern and enlightened age?

The fatal flaw does not lie in the human unborn. Reversing perspective locates the problem where it belongs: in a culture that disavows its children before they are born. The missing qualities are intergenerational solidarity and care for children-on-the-way. It is we, the people refusing to welcome unwanted unborn, who deny them life. And we, the people, are not grieved by their ruin. The reason we are not grieved is metaethical: American secular culture bases human standing on the human capacity to think and to choose. The *potential* to think and choose does not count sufficiently to create protective rights. Except for those newly born—since certifying the presence of actual rational abilities for them seems practically impossible to predict or to ratify.

ENRICHING MORAL VOCABULARY BEYOND RIGHTS

Because rights serve as protections and appeals in emergencies or when things go wrong, since they form safety nets to keep the worst from happening, they normally belong only at the margins of ethical consideration and controversy. The wide-ranging and diverse relationships that constitute and sustain the richness of human lives require more. What humans owe each other normally and consistently rarely even mentions rights. Marriage vows promising loyalty, and unconditional lifelong devotion never include rights—except perhaps for pre-nuptial agreements—that many consider incompatible with mutual commitments required by marriage. The need for insisting on human rights should never even arise. Parental love of children looks to their needs and does not make care depend on rational abilities, smarts, or personhood—and never lets it come to the need for invoking rights. Our children belong to us. And we belong to them. Parents belong to their children. But before birth US law refuses to recognize "the product of conception" as children. As do those who seek to prevent the birth of unwanted children. No enriching of moral vocabulary here!

Using emergency brakes, safety nets, or rights implies the prospect of failures. Better if such were never actually needed. Yet rights also embody genuine realism about human nature: individual persons need powerful defenses against others—protections that are morally authoritative and legally enforced. While the Enlightenment inclined to general optimism about human goodness and the human prospect, it proved realistic enough to know that human beings tend not to do right naturally, spontaneously or reliably. Humankind, especially those with only minimal resources and support, need powerful protections. Rights, perhaps our best protections, can save lives. Normally. Rights can also become massively destructive, as with those unable to help or to protect themselves, the human unborn.

Care has become a key word in the self-understanding of medicine and nursing. Care forms a key word in certain forms of feminism. Even the word *love* survives sentimentalizing, not just in marriage and intergenerational responsibilities but in friendship and in love of country. Indeed, all relationships except those at arms-length require more than rights. Such words—service, responsibility, care, loyalty, love—reach beyond the individualistic self-protective quality of rights. However, rights invoked for others practiced by reformers, intercessors, public servants, or the kindhearted can be life-savers. Advocacy rights may be able to transcend individualism and become community-friendly. But once rights are invoked, they may well trump more caring and humanizing words. Even in a community-affirming context rights prove adversarial. The appeal to rights forecloses other concepts with which to interpret an ethical issue, as those offered in this paragraph.

To tell the truth, I used to be surer of what love requires in tragic situations where the medical phrase "incompatible with life" is used. That phrase leads and may recommend death, sooner rather than later. But parental love considers what is best for this child. Preventing a child's future suffering weighs against shortening the precious few days that that child will ever have. From the letter of a mother of a baby girl with Trisomy 18 who agonized over the inevitable loss of her baby girl but still thought that brief life to be good and refused to abort:

> She experienced my love, the love of my husband and so many other people. She was held, sung to, read to, danced with. She gave every indication of enjoying it all. She also had the opportunity to touch many, many people. She taught everyone who met her how little the word "handicapped" tells us about the totality of a person. She left love wherever she went.[17]

The letter writer also insists that the doctors were wrong when they said that Trisomy 18 is incompatible with life. "Obviously, they couldn't tell us that as we held our very live baby." How did the couple make it through such trying times? "We kept focused on things we had to be grateful for: Maggie was alive, Maggie was home, Maggie was beautiful. We had each other. We had wonderful families. We had good insurance."

17. From a 1997 letter of a former student quoted here with permission.

RIGHTS *AND* RELIGION

Rights are a modern invention, wholly absent from biblical traditions. Moreover, the Enlightenment heritage of human rights was forged in opposition to religious wars and as a civilizing alternative to decades of devastation when believers killed each other in God's name. Leaving religion out of it made good sense then in order to protect individuals with rights—all persons, regardless of religion, no matter what faith. It continues to make good sense against religious fanatics who terrorize nations and intentionally kill innocents in holy war.

In American culture the intentional killing of human beings now occurs under different auspices. It now takes place under the authority and protection of federal law. The right of a woman's privacy trumps the value of the life of a beginning human being. In effect that Court decision dismissed parental responsibilities, any relevance of child protections laws to the child-on-the-way, any hint that an incipient human being might be or would become one of us. Moreover, not even the father or the father-to-be (when does fatherhood begin?) is permitted to intervene on behalf of a life engendered by that man. There may be those who would celebrate this law as the liberation of women. Others deplore such abandoning of all protections for the human unborn as a bloody and grotesque abomination.

By way of pausing, this critique invoked intergenerational solidarity, consistency in caring and nurture for children, and valuing and welcoming new human lives. Moreover, this text advocated recognizing the limits of liberty and of rights generally and made a case for taking human embodiment and physical potential seriously. The point has not been to deny rights but to curb their current fatal expressions, their unjustified, routinized and legal deadly effects. The intent as well was to question the assumptions, logic, and consequences of the liberal worldview that so accentuate human thought and will as to dismiss respect for human bodily existence. Literally, the human unborn cannot live with that. And it is not self-evident that thoughtful liberals can. Liberal reliance on individual personhood, on human reason and will, has obscured the importance and role of communal and bodily human existence. These conclusions are not explicitly religious. But they are compatible with biblical perspectives.

A DEFENSE OF HUMAN RIGHTS

Leaving religion out of it is not an option for Christians. And it is not an option for Christian ethics either. Abrahamic religions—Judaism, Christianity, and Islam—relate everything to God. Such faith permeates all aspects of their lives. More correctly, it should so permeate. But that requires a life time. That goal is recognition of God as Lord over everything. Just as secular philosophies of life seek inclusive and coherent renditions of all reality, so do these faiths. The recommendations of liberals to restrict the venue of religion to religion and to stay out of public policy strikes believers as depriving persons of faith of a public, legal, and political voice and role. Christians and Jews are also citizens. May only the secular speak in politics? Neither church, synagogue, nor mosque has the option of a merely private and personal faith that remains silent on matters of public policy, values, and ethics. Abrahamic faith communities are called to see all of reality in the light of faith and to attest to that faith in thought and in practice. They owe God and humans a public and political moral witness in word and life.

That such religiosity is no guarantee against inhumanity is beyond dispute. Believers can and have used God and religion destructively—not unlike liberal rights being used with fatal intent and effect. Such violent misuses of religion or of liberalism make rights indispensable. Not that rights offer a cure-all for human indifference, abuse or aggression. But rights can limit the damage. To be specific, the protection of children within the institutional church, equal opportunity for ecclesiastic leadership roles for women, advocacy for the equal rights of LGBTQ persons exemplify the current religious need for the liberal tradition of individual rights.[18]

The Christian theologian Stanley Hauerwas offers an insistent and coherent critique of American liberalism and of its tradition of human rights. The view implied in this chapter of a constructive relationship between American liberalism and Christian faith must seem to him like leading American Christians, already seduced by a liberal culture, further down the garden path. He brands the notion of inalienable rights a philosophical mistake.[19] Rights express Enlightenment individualism. But Christians cannot believe that they have inalienable rights. And they do not have a right to do whatever they want with their bodies. As Christians "[w]e do not believe that we have a right to our bodies because when we are baptized we become members of one another; then we can tell one another what it is that we

---

18. The ordination of women to priestly or ministerial roles has worked its way through mainline Protestant churches and through all but Orthodox Judaism. Blessing homosexual unions and ordaining homosexuals is a theme of current struggles in those congregations. The invocation of economic rights is a feature of the Pastoral Letter on Catholic Social Teaching in which human rights "are bestowed on human beings by God and grounded in the nature and dignity of human persons" and become the minimum conditions for life in community (National Conference of Catholic Bishops, *Economic Justice for All*, 41). For a Jewish affirmation of rights, see Novak, *Covenantal Rights*.

19. Hauerwas, "Abortion Theologically Understood," 608.

should and should not do with our bodies."[20] This claim may well be true. But here the context does not refer to any Christian rights. The reference here is to the right to life of the human unborn. The right to life itself was denied to such children-on-their-way by the US Supreme Court in 1973. And that is where those rights must be restored. Christians and persons of conscience are called to be advocates for those yet unable to speak for themselves.

Hauerwas may be correct when it comes to Christian rights. What have Christians to do with individualistic rights when they are baptized into a community that is redeemed and bonded by God's love and called to reflect that love in word and deed? In families and in the family of faith, appeal to rights indicate alienation, self-defensiveness, and failure of responsible and caring love. It should not have come to that! But of course, it does come to that. And in such failures, in such emergencies, in such crises rights keep the worst from happening. Rights are cultural reserves against moral failure, exploitation, abuse and oppression. Enlightenment insistence on human rights mitigated European religious hostilities and now constitutes the only universally recognized secular language to protect human beings. Though rights may not be listed in the index of prayer or worship books, human rights are one of the universal blessings for which believers should give thanks and which they should defend on behalf of the voiceless. While deliberately secular, who knows where Enlightenment values of human worth and protectability have their roots? And who is to say where the limits of providence lie? If a pagan Cyrus can become God's anointed (Isa 45:1), do modern pagans lie beyond God's reach and use? The least among us—whom God considers members of God's family (Matt 25:45)—need rights to protect them. Liberalism has been the modern advocate of such humanism and does so by insisting on human rights. The objection throughout this text is that liberalism is not consistent when it comes to the human unborn.

LIBERALISM *AND* RELIGION?

Liberalism needs better grounding than personhood based on rational abilities. It needs reliable and solid grounding for the liberal assumption that humans count and count simply as human beings. Specifically, it should include an account of human embodiment and its implications, such as aging, pain, disability, mortality. Positively, that might include the joy of living, in all its manifestations. Christianity accounts for all of that. Relying on rational awareness and moral decisions for human standing proves to

---

20. Hauerwas, "Abortion Theologically Understood," 609.

be insufficient when confidence of the Age of Reason is overshadowed by modern skepticism and secular irrationalism.

Enlightenment awe and respect for human rationality has been contested by non-rational and irrational cultural forces. Marxism declared economic interests, not universalizing rationality, to be the driving force of civilizations. Freudianism and Behaviorism see human reason as subservient to lower drives and needs. Two World Wars in one century cast their shadows over a human rationality that might have prevented such fruitless bloodletting. The Holocaust bespeaks inexplicable human evil that nevertheless was rational in its cunning and efficiency. The policy of nuclear deterrence, with which not only the most powerful but progressive nations seek to establish their security, threatens mutual and final obliteration of humankind. Ethnic cleansing reverts to tribalism and regards with contempt any universal reason that acknowledges the status of every person.

Pervasive cultural doubts about why human beings count intrinsically and should be protected with rights include the postmodernist challenge that value absolutes lack objective foundation and authority and express merely cultural preferences. Michael J. Perry concludes "that there is, finally, no intelligible (much less persuasive) secular version of the conviction that every human being is sacred; the only intelligible versions are religious."[21] Perry explains that "sacred," refers to inviolability, human standing, being regarded as an end-in-oneself, human preciousness. After the death of God (Nietzsche) or after metaphysics has collapsed (Habermas) sacredness cannot possibly be ascribed to human beings on secular grounds.[22] Could it be that secular renditions of human nature not only dismissed the biblical God, they may also have lost the only true source of objective valuing of human life?

Human standing, in Christian convictions, is not derived from human nature but is endowed, externally bestowed, by the creative and redemptive love of God. While Christendom, if that term may still be used, has diminished in modern times—just as liberal rational-volitional personhood—where else to look for grounding the sacred value of a human life? For any biblical ethics human beings are God's creation of both body and mind. The body is not just the support base of the more significant human mind and will. Humans are created as, exist as, inseparable body and mind. Developmentally, body precedes mind. Normally human couples hoping for children celebrate success and may well thank God when pregnancy results:

---

21. Perry, *Idea of Human Rights*, 5.
22. Perry, *Idea of Human Rights*, 58.

"She is with child!" Not just any child, but the parents' flesh and blood. From their very inceptions, humans are living bodies, no matter how small.

Any Christian affirmation of liberalism in defense of human rights will have to take the human body seriously. It will have to extend protective rights to human beings from the beginning of a human life until its end. One might even cite precedent in that past extensions of rights to human beings previously deemed undeserved are now recognized as moral progress. And even the fiercest advocates of the most recent human liberation may suspect that there is something illiberal, unnatural, inhumane, self-contradictory, and unconscionable about invoking rights to destroy children before they are born.

LIBERALISM AND WHO OR WHAT COUNTS

Today American secularism has the upper hand in regard to what counts and who is protectable with human rights. While "medicine and ethics" had its beginnings in theological literature, bioethics now seems dominated by secular assumptions to such an extent that even some Christian ethicists write incognito, competing with liberal ethicists and using liberal assumptions and language. The Christian faith, much as in its origins, is a minor voice. And there is no emperor waiting in the wings to establish Christianity as the right or established religion. If anyone needs the compassion and intercessions of Christians it is the threatened human unborn: voiceless, without legal rights, unable to help themselves.

In the conflict over the standing and protection of the human unborn, Christian ethics is called to work for a cultural conversion that recognizes and acknowledges the goodness and importance of human physical existence. It does seem odd for Christian ethics—expected to function in spiritual dimensions—to advocate the intrinsic importance of human flesh and blood. It may be similarly unexpected to fault a materialistic national culture for not being materialistic enough when it comes to human bodies in their earliest form. Neither of these charges is intended to detract from the importance of personhood, the banner of liberalism celebrating the human abilities to reason and to choose. But there will be no reasoning or choosing by those whose bodies are destroyed before they are old enough to grieve over what they are about to lose.

HUMAN LIFE COUNTS. OR DOES IT?

Those who legally decide on human rights, the US Supreme Court, decreed in 1973 that unwelcome human unborn lack personhood and all legal standing and rights. If pregnant women decide that these newcomers on the way threaten to become too burdensome or simply remain unwelcome, these new human lives may be jettisoned. What might be comparable to this legal dismissive practice with the human unborn? Is that similar to war in which defense justifies killing the enemy? National self-defense so decrees. But female self-defense is not ordinarily preventing loss of adult lives. If it were, the matter might well be moot. Capital punishment is receding in Western nations. But for what crime might the human unborn be prosecuted and killed? Looking for parallels or precedents simply does not work.

One could simply invoke an ethical principle, as "do not kill." Or, "do not kill humans." But morality and ethics are not fundamentally about rules or do's and don'ts. Ethics takes on depth when it comes to metaethics or worldviews, including the meaning of a human life. For Christians metaethics this issue is a matter of how to make the world meaningful in a way that Christians can show to God. God's character reveals implications. If God is considered to be the personal Lord who creates and blesses all human lives, justifying taking human innocent life becomes ever so problematic or even impossible.

Human rights, constituting almost absolute claims, seem not easily divisible or compromisingly shared. In the words of Michael Ignatieff, "'Give me my rights' is not an invitation to compromise. It's a demand for unconditional surrender."[23] A procedural or supposedly value-neutral liberalism is not always neutral in effect. A liberal Court has had the last and fatal word, no matter what democratic legislatures, state laws, or religious voices may say. Liberalism owes us more. Liberals owe us more. That holds not only for the importance of human bodies or for who deserves the protection of rights but for rules in creating public policy. When it comes to people living together in difference, Charles Taylor recommends a robust version of liberalism. I refer to it as *liberalism with courage* because Taylor does not shy away from public discussion of conflicting versions of the good.

> The crucial idea is that people can also bond not in spite of but because of difference. They can sense, that is, that the difference enriches each party, that their lives are narrower and less full

---

23. Ignatieff, *Rights Revolution*, 17.

alone than in association with each other. In this sense, the difference defines a complementarity.[24]

Referring to the communal or civic humanism of Humboldt, Goethe, and Herder, this form of liberalism expects to benefit from close association with people who have taken other paths. Appealing to the musical metaphor of an orchestra in which the whole offers more than the sum of the parts, personal lives can be enriched from the exchange and communion between differently minded individuals. Taylor's vision is inclusive: "What I am pleading for is a more complex and many-stranded version of liberalism."[25]

Although Taylor does not challenge his own metaphor by worrying about cacophony and the need for an orchestra conductor, he is not unrealistic about the barriers obstructing genuine openness in considering the views of others. "Indeed, it may sometimes seem that the less we know, the easier it may be to treat people equitably, because their actual views are so offensive to us that it is hard to ignore these once known in all their repulsive detail."[26] And yet actually understanding another view may change one's understanding of oneself. Taylor rightly takes that to be a good thing. "We are meant to understand each other. This mutual understanding is growth, completion."[27]

Yet mutual understanding can also create resentment and objection. Biblical realism notes human overreaching: brothers become fratricides and even the best of kings commits adultery and murder. Taylor's liberal humanism appears too benign. While the popular song claims that to know you is to love you, to know you may be to despise you for good reason. That goes both ways; it holds for knowing oneself and for knowing others. Thus, Christians continue to be amazed over being understood by God and yet still loved by God. That holds not only for character but for one's views and values. But whether fellow citizens turn out to be despicable or decent, the biblical command is to love them. Regardless. For that it surely helps to be open about the most basic convictions and to seek mutual understanding. Therefore, even if one cannot share the confidence that different voices will blend into harmony, Taylor's recommendation seems more promising than remaining silent about what counts most and making do with mere procedural justice.

Taylor's liberalism, with courage to insist on reasoned public debate over diverging visions of civic good, offers additional grounds to recommend

---

24. Taylor, "Democracy, Inclusive and Exclusive," 191.
25. Taylor, "Democracy, Inclusive and Exclusive," 192.
26. Taylor, "Democracy, Inclusive and Exclusive," 192.
27. Taylor, "Democracy, Inclusive and Exclusive," 193.

it. It acknowledges that citizens, including citizen-believers, have a stake in each others' well-being here and now. Whether secular or religious, citizens owe one another the commitment and trust required to explain, to persuade, and to compromise. Taylor's courageous liberalism advocating public argument over the human good also deserves credit for improving prospects for a human future. Given the fierce, selfish, and short-range human inclinations coupled with devices of nuclear-Armageddon, genetic germ line technology, and an all-devouring global economy, an actual human future requires clear and convincing yesses and nos. Both now and then, we are all in this together. To be sure, otherworldly and separatist religious visions look elsewhere than to such shared future and common cause. But those for whom this world is home and who still sing that now gendered hymn, "This is my Father's world," Charles Taylor offers a version of liberalism open to most visions of the good.

Liberal humanism and Christian humanism may share the common cause of politically protecting and supporting persons most in need of help. The liberal rights heritage is most needed to protect those who lack the voice or will or ability to protect themselves. Furthermore, the liberal invocation of equal process and equal rights presupposes a vision of the good: Each person counts, is precious and protectable. Liberalism does not just yield sound procedure but presupposes a humanism with considerable depth. Although Christians look elsewhere than to liberal intuition or self-evidence or self-generated rational abilities for justifying human status, they also support such humanistic values. To be sure, they point elsewhere for the source of that valuing and for its range. But converging convictions about the preciousness of human beings, though justified on different grounds, should be grounds for gratitude and cooperation. In an age of ethical and moral uncertainty we need public, explicit, coherent reasons, both religious and secular.

Finally, Taylor's counsel of public debate over pluralistic claims for the good may prevent the current recourse to rights as a conversation stopper. A right is a trump that requires no explanation; that is how the game of rights is played. Winners take all when it comes to Constitutional rights. Taylor writes that "by having their demand declared unconstitutional, the loser's program is delegitimated in a way that has deep resonance in American society. Not only can we not give you what you want, but you are primitive and un-American to want it."[28] There must be more civil ways of acknowledging and resolving our differences.

---

28. Taylor, "Democracy, Inclusive and Exclusive," 193.

8

Abortion in America

THE PREVIOUS CHAPTER, IN dealing with human rights, used the American practice of abortion to analyze the nature and function of rights in both legal and moral contexts. This chapter considers abortion in wider and metaethical (worldview) context. Abortion issues involve matters of life and death, and this nation seems no closer to resolving this issue than when the law made the topic a matter of legal rights in 1973 This chapter was written in 2022 before revisions of the US abortion law in which the Supreme Court overturned *Roe v. Wade* and turned the legality of abortions over to state laws. Abortions in America continue and remain among the most practiced surgical procedures nationally. The goal here, as in other chapters, is to consider abortion in both secular and Christian perspectives.

CAUTION RECOMMENDED

If there is any moral issue in America that has remained divisive over decades, it is disagreement over the morality of abortion. This chapter attempts a Christian perspective on abortion. Assuming that everyone knows the key facts of human fetal development, this text avoids that topic. Since abortion arguments arouse deep concerns they elicit leading and perhaps misleading arguments that rely on self-evident wording or other shortcuts. For example, "taking human life is immoral," bumps against "individual privacy must be respected." "The unborn are children on their way" elicits "the unborn are not yet persons whether in the law or in any sense." The arguments function largely in terms of metaethics (worldviews), as in the topic of personhood. The moral clarity of "Taking a human life is wrong" confronts the reply that "the fetus is not a person and has no rights." Since the issue of abortion invokes metaethical or worldview claims, the moral arguments involve depth. Beginning human lives may be small but the issues are not.

Christian ethics of abortion relies on religious assumptions. But abortion laws rely on the law, and the law insists on separation of religion and law. That may create a handicap or a challenge for Christian arguments and values. The legal separation of law and religion may require reliance on secular arguments and mute religious assumptions. Understanding abortion issues, much less than resolving them, requires competence in the law, lacking here. But the issues—matters of life and death—remains not only important but raise ethical questions.

ANALYZING ABORTION WORDING

Given that abortion involves a matter of human life and death, popular abortion-wording—in contrast to medical and scientific language—tends to be leading. That is, wording tends to reflect the views and moral judgments of the speaker/writer. Whether one agrees or disagrees with what one reads or hears about abortion, abortion-language is rarely value-neutral or objective. Abortion discussions focus on the status, worth, and rights of the *human unborn*. Note that the previous word "unborn" leads. The term is forward-looking, anticipating birth and thereby implies opposition to abortion. Moreover, the term "human" creates the similar effect of reminding the reader that the unborn is one of us. Probing specific words for their assumptions, implications, origin, uses, contexts, etc. is called *word analysis* and is an indispensable ability for professionals focusing on words, com munication and persuasion.

Continuing the examples, *abortion* focuses on the pregnant woman, not on what is being aborted. Other medical procedures, as appendectomy or tonsillectomy, name what is being removed. *Abortion* focuses on the woman and avoids attention to what is being aborted. The term *abortion* is woman-focused and leads or misleads by omitting naming or even noting whatever it is that is controversially at stake. Whoever coined or popularized the word *abortion* in effect advantaged a pro-choice perspective. The earlier *human unborn* was said to imply pro-life cues.

Objective writing should avoid leading or misleading words. Yet when it comes to abortion, it appears that most or maybe even all terms lead or mislead. For example, the language of the natural sciences is often assumed to be objective and non-leading. Yet when it comes to describing human beings, strictly descriptive or scientific terms dehumanize. That explains why scientific terms prove to be a godsend for pro-abortion advocates. When scientific terms are used in *non-scientific contexts*—such as law, public policy or ethics—the use of scientific words also import their dehumanizing quality. Scientific words must avoid personal and valuating words. Those who disagree, should try to write a love letter with scientific words.

The practice of medicine, in contrast to research biologists, must become bilingual. Speaking with patients requires words expressing medical care—as explaining the ultrasound image of a pregnancy with "your child" or "your baby" that moments earlier was named as "fetus" in conversation with a colleague. "Human unborn"—the preferred term in these chapters—leads as well by referring to what "it" could be or would normally become. Even the term "human" in a patient-doctor context means something different than the scientific use of that word classifying it as non-animal. In patient care "human" means "one of us." And one more caution of leading or misleading terms: "fundamentalists" for advocates of early standing of the unborn or "godless liberals" for granting human standing only at birth prove less than helpful for mutual understanding. Linguistic fairness recommends itself all around.

Much of the abortion debates proceeds by means of development analysis of the stages of human pregnancy: Should the fetus/unborn count as a human being from the moment of conception, from the embryonic or the fetal stage? Before birth, at birth or after birth, when there is awareness of pain, viability, self-awareness? Such "stage of fetal development" arguments and counter-arguments are omitted here. That has been done but remains inconclusive—in the sense of failing to advance or resolve the issues.[1]

A PRO-CHOICE VERSION OF ABORTION

In ethical controversies, basic fairness dictates that one strives to present the views that one opposes in its strongest version. The pragmatic test whether that has been achieved would be that its advocate would consider the result to be fair or reasonable. The following paragraphs attempt such a summary.

It is risky to generalize about secular renditions of human worth or standing in the context of abortion. Given that abortions are so numerous,

---

1. Gillon, "'New Ethics of Abortion?'"

motivating reasons may be multiple as well. But there is a pattern of justifying abortion in terms of prevailing concepts of human nature. Secularists initially tend to offer what is *not* decisive for their pro-choice stand, namely the physical existence of the human embryo or fetus. Bodily existence is shared by all animals. There is nothing special about humans there! Rather, the unique quality of human existence originates from the human mind, usually defined as the *ability to reason and to choose*. Early human lives, conceived but unborn, may be aborted within a certain time frame by pregnant women in medically secure settings with the prospect that the fetus will not survive. Pregnancy is a very personal experience that can impose considerable burdens on the pregnant woman and on families. Since there is no need in this nation or in this world for more people, and since embryos and fetuses are merely the physical beginning of what may become human beings, abortion is morally justifiable.

Continuing the pro-choice perspective, before birth humans remain mindless. And that makes them more akin to animals than to thinking and acting humans. While human biologically, the earliest versions of humans (embryos, fetuses)—unable to think or to decide—are not yet persons. But "person" is the key word of respect and status for humans. And "person" is the trump word, the human being able to think and to choose. In contemporary America bodily existence deserves no equal rating with mental abilities or the mind. The human embryo and fetus cannot reasonably be said to have minds. Mere physical existence proves to be insufficient to elicit human respect or legal personhood standing. The human fetus in effect lacks any mental or legal standing, remains devoid of all rights and is no match for the rights-bearing pregnant woman, who would rather not be pregnant.

Such description of the human non-standing of unborn human lives may also account for the 1973 Supreme Court that so readily dismissed the life and worth of a human unborn. The human unborn lacks that which is most important in a liberal worldview, namely a mind. That assumes secular dualism of body/mind with a clear preference and respect for the mind. The pregnant woman, who does have a mind, simply makes a decision about herself, namely to abort. This is a matter of her own rights. She does not impose on the rights of anyone else, since the fetus is literally not *anyone* and is certainly not a person. "Pregnancy" describes a condition, not a person. While the woman's decision affects (!) the body of fetus, the fetus does not have a mind and therefore is not a person with rights. The fetus does not count as "anyone" or as a legal or moral person. The human unborn, being mindless also remains rights-less.

BODY, MIND, POTENTIAL

The 1973 Supreme Court decision surprised many. Who would have expected that the repeated past humanizing effects of liberalism for diverse "minorities" such as Blacks, Jews, women, who had been devalued for their physical identities, would have such a deadly effect on the human unborn? The lesson: in contrast to the human body, in Western secularism the mind makes all the difference in the world. The mere prospect of a mind does not count protectively. Human potential does not count in this context and remains disregarded. Since human beginnings normally deserve respect, given that human status is generally respected, I have not been able to find justification for disregarding human potential in abortion logic. One would think that any parent, any teacher, or any humanist would find that puzzling.

In pro-choice arguments, whatever value a human fetus may have morally or legally shrinks to private preference of the female *progenitor*. That stilted term attempts to avoid personalizing words, such as *mother* or *father*. Linguistic dehumanization avoiding references to family connections dehumanizes the human unborn. That precedes and eases the disposal of *the products of conception*. To include a wider context, American traditions honor individual liberty and personal rights, qualities reasonable ascribed only to the pregnant woman, not to her pregnancy. The human unborn constitutes a condition of the pregnant woman and remains her concern rather than having any justifiable claims of its own. The human unborn in effect disappears as a human being in its own right. Besides, if the woman's legal privacy were to be rescinded, women would again take any measure to liberate themselves from such imposition, even with all the risks that involves. So it is said.

By way of objecting to the Supreme Court's 1973 decision, that ruling in effect reduces the human unborn to the property of the pregnant woman. That property can be disposed, within certain time constraints, at the discretion of the owner. One hesitates to refer to "mother" here because motherhood is what the pregnant woman may seek to avoid. Unborn human lives—without whom there can be no later protectable human persons—may be regarded and treated as disposable.

HUMANS MAKE REALITY SPEAK

Where, then, to look for understanding and for probing abortion issues? The unborn have always been there and have normally been welcomed, nurtured and protected when born. In modern times that cannot be assumed.

The moral meaning of pregnancy has changed. And we, the decision-makers and judges of the worth and standing of unborn human beings, have changed with it. In contemporary secular perspectives, the human unborn are now sufficiently *unlike us* to be regarded as human persons or even as human beings. In effect, the legal status and future of the human unborn appears to be that of personal property—property of the pregnant woman. And property can be disposed at the owner's discretion. Announcements of pregnancy used to be good news. Congratulations were in order. Now one may not know whether to congratulate or to sympathize. It is we who have changed. The human unborn, reduced to property, have no rights, have no standing in the law, and have no moral claims. One is reminded of slavery's reduction of humans into property.

The dehumanization of the human unborn described in the previous paragraph describes one secular version of abortion. Christian ethics includes an additional person in reflections about abortion—or in any other issue. That, of course, is the living God. Christians look to God for understanding themselves and for making responsible decisions. Human life is not a human possession but belongs to God. One's own life is not one's own. God is the Creator and Owner of human lives, lives of which humans are stewards. Such ownership includes human lives before birth. Whether the human unborn lives or dies must not be understood as a human option. That judgment is part of a more inclusive claim: humans must not own other humans. They don't even own their own lives since all lives belong to God.

Where, then, to turn? We should look to *ourselves* by creating suitable words for the values, relationships, priorities and morality involved. Humans make the world speak. That includes the world of abortion. Creating meaning begins with naming. It can be done emotionally with leading or misleading words. It can be done individually and/or communally (as in the abortion controversy). It would be reassuring if one could claim that humans can discover how the world can be explained and understood *as it really is*, or *is in itself*. But empirical scientists no longer claim that even their best discoveries describe the true nature of things forever and ever. The natural sciences and probably any academic discipline will never be done, complete or final, having answered all the questions. Each discovery brings new questions. Probably that holds for the formal sciences as well, given that we invent new concepts and new relationships of numbers and symbols.

Knowing "the thing in itself" (Kant's "Ding an sich") lies beyond human reach. That makes naming, relating and knowing aspects of our world essential, flexible and unavoidable. Naming our world is a bit like taking possession of it. Explorers named the land conquered when reaching a new part of our world and thereby intended to own it. Human limited knowledge of reality might be called a *modesty principle*. It holds not just for empirical knowledge (sense data) but for how humans make sense of our world philosophically, religiously, metaethically, morally, etc. Humans make the world speak. As time changes, so do the meanings ascribed to our world.

Humans are the namers, meaning-givers, discoverers. To cite a helpful philosophical metaphor, humans see or perceive the world only with the help of eye glasses. The prescription for such glasses are written by humans—researchers, scientists, theologians, philosophers, artists—by all who create and offer new insights of how to see, ascribe sense, meaning and value to the world. Without such glasses we would remain blind and could not make sense of what we face. We tend to take our glasses for granted and may remain unaware of them. We become aware of them when immersed in other cultures or when historians make us aware of change over time. Even old love letters reread can make one aware of change over time. For example, a husband reading his letter saved by his wife and realizing, "She married me anyway!" or preachers reading old sermons a decade or two later, finding them to be unrepeatable. So also in dead-end abortion debates. We need new prescription glasses. That focuses on ourselves rather than on the human unborn, aka the fetus.

As an aside, the Kantian modesty proviso also applies to religion, to understand God and God's will. Believers only know the texts they inherit and their shared experiences of divine Presence. Key terms such as "holy," "mysterious, "other" describing their religious experiences implicitly also confess lack of satisfactory knowing. "It is impossible to see God" is also an expression of modesty regarding knowing or understanding God. That sobering insight might give Bible-thumpers pause. Recognizing the limits of human understanding of God might make our rock-bottom convictions and certainties somewhat more flexible.

HISTORICAL CHANGE IN RESPECT FOR PREGNANCY

The past may well differ depending on who remembers it. But there was a time when pregnancy was unquestionably protectable. That communal respect for pregnancy has disappeared. We, the people, see, speak, value and vote differently. What then is it about Americans that changed in the last century or two that affected respect for the human unborn? The chapter on rights suggested that modernity—our own time—was deeply influenced by the Western Enlightenment in the eighteenth century. That era also redefined American politics, declared human rights to be self-evident and established democracy—derived from the will of individual citizens—as the foundation of government authority. Monarchy became questionable. The status of individuals and their reasonable interests, defined as rights, began to come into their own. As American historians noted, the European Enlightenment and early American beginnings changed the axis of the world from vertical to horizontal. The rise of secularism was a part of that horizontal transformation.

The light of reason rather than religious superstition and dark authoritarian traditions promised improvements and raised hopes. New natural and formal sciences were born and flourished. Slavery became outlawed. The liberating effects of human rights transformed the status of women and Blacks. American liberalism made human rights its cause and now pervades American politics in both its conservative (property) and its progressive (civil rights) versions. Liberalism's secularity now forms the self-evident cultural default position. The roles and authority of women, liberally conceived individually with human rights, may well explain women's enhanced status—while human embryos and fetuses, yet unable to think or decide, lack the key qualities—the mind and will—that make *persons* respectable.

ROE V. WADE

The 1973 Supreme Court decision to establish a woman's right to privacy as a legal right was coupled with the absence of *any* rights or legal personhood standing for the human unborn. Under *Roe v. Wade*, American males, whether responsible for the pregnancy or not, had no legal say about abortion. Yet they could be held legally responsible for the child who survives the gauntlet of female life-or-death authority over the unborn. The unborn was legally declared as falling short of being a protectable person. In effect, in regard to abortion, only women had the legal right to let live or to end an unborn human life.

WORDING COUNTS

There is a venerable tradition that academic writing should be objective, non-leading, and impartial. When it comes to matters of life or death, such impartial language actually may advantage inflicting death. While the professional study of medicine remains strictly descriptive, when it comes to patient-care, value judgments become unavoidable. Scientific research retains descriptive language. Medical patient care devotes itself to helping the sick. One would expect that pediatricians use words for the human unborn that differ from the vocabulary of physicians offering elective abortions.

Context explains word usage. "The human unborn" and "the products of conception" can refer to the same being but differ in context and use. Abortions are medical procedures. If abortion constitutes a medical procedure, does it heal the pregnant woman of an unwanted but curable condition? That would be a feat of linguistic legederdemain.

Caution about words is a theme running throughout these chapters. In an abortion contexts one is not dealing with "your unborn child" but "a condition." Again, this is not "a child on the way" but a "troubling fetus or organism." Medical professional commitment pledges, "First, do no harm!" How to end the existence of an unwanted unborn without committing harm requires linguistic dexterity for professionals who have pledged themselves to do no harm.

MIND-BODY DUALISM

American thinking has changed from historical protectability of pregnancy to individual female options of sustaining or ending human life in its earliest stages. Certain aspects of American secular liberalism include growing individualism and increasing human rights, lessening of the influence of the past in favor of the modern present. It should have included fewer children per family and de-emphasis of citizenship responsibilities. That avoided what may be the most telling reason for an abort-at-will legal policy: contemporary Americans regard abortion issues as *metaphysical dualists*. And not just equal opportunity dualists but clearly rating one side of human nature over the other. Such dualism is less discussed and more demanding to explain.

The dualism here conceives a twofold human nature as both body and mind. That includes a definite preference for mind over body. René Descartes' "I think, therefore I am" makes the mind crucial for human identity and existence. Of course he could have reasoned that he hurts (a toothache?) with more compelling force for his conclusion. Despite the appeal of *The Body Beautiful* and a host of supermen, American metaphysics prioritize the mental over the physical dimensions of human life.

How does such popular mental-physical dualism manifest itself? Most simply one can notice it in speech patterns or in the form of common expressions. We say, "I have a body" or "I have a mind." There is an I with two properties. A unitary expression might be "I am body/mind." More telling may be the experience of aging. The mind seems ever young, except for a bit of forgetfulness. But the body might leave the self behind, only to rudely remind us who we are when ill, losing hair, gaining wrinkles and weight. Yet such bodily unreliability worries us less than when our minds disappoint. The prospect of Alzheimer disease, a type of dementia that affects memory, thinking and behaving, might unnerve anyone. It seems that Americans (humans?) regard their minds as more important than their body.

American popular conceptions of death or of human mortality express a dualistic feature as well. Everyone knows that the body dies. But the mental self, the self as mind or soul may not share mortality in popular belief. Instead of dying, the bodiless soul relocates. Attempts to console mourners suggest "he is in a better place now." "He is now with God." Long-married couples "are now together again in heaven" (invariably upward). Even Christian believers can talk like that. And who would question their sincerity? Perhaps such expressions of the dualism of human nature and the preference for mind may be echoes of Neo-Platonism by way of the Enlightenment. As a postscript to such expressions of belief in a mental afterlife, perhaps because the context is consolation, none of these expressions of survival of the mind include any hint of moral accountability or judgment. We are all OK.

Lest such after-death claims express or imply biblical texts or Hebrew traditions, the biblical view is brief and realistic: from dust to dust (Gen 3:19). The New Testament reflects the same realism. Except that God's resurrection of Jesus was understood as precedent: Jesus was the firstborn from the dead (Col 1:18). Death was inclusive and real, without spiritual or mental left-overs. Jesus' resurrection from the dead was God's doing, not that of Jesus, who really died on the cross, body and soul. More inclusively still in terms of the New Testament, eventually God will raise all humans and hold them accountable for what they did with "their" lives. The re-creation of all humans who died is understood biblically as God's doing. The resurrected or re-created humans are not considered to be spirits but are seen as new or transformed body and soul: a recreated holistic and unitary being in the image of God.

Descriptions of human nature as body/soul creatures in which mental factors outweigh the physical, also manifests itself in responses to human disabilities. Americans seem more forbearing over physical disabilities than over mental incapacities. A prenatal diagnosis of Down Syndrome—a genetic disorder that causes both physical symptoms and lifelong learning disabilities of varying severity can be *avoided* with early interventions (abortion). Abortion seems indicated, even though children with this handicap can lead surprisingly happy and loving lives. "Surprisingly" to us, not to them. For how could we be content if we or our children were deficient in the unique humanizing quality that our culture and we treasure most, our mind, our personhood, our moral agency and dignity?

The twofold aspects of human nature in body and mind manifests themselves at different paces. It turns out that the time lag between human physical and mental developments proves to be relevant for the popular moral logic of abortion liberty. The fetus cannot reasonably be said to have developed even a minimal mind, self-awareness or any mental ability that might qualify it as sharing the mental existence that counts as uniquely human. The mind counts decisively in endowing status or unique value to humans. The *Roe v. Wade* Supreme Court decision similarly denied legal personhood to the human fetus. Culturally, the mind is the most important human ability. No mind, no human standing. To be sure, given time, the mind will emerge. But prior to at least rudimentary rational abilities, an abortion ends only the physical aspect of a human life, not a person. Of course that is only a difference in timing. One would expect that if mind were to precede physical development, abortion would be less frequent. The mind/body metaphysical dualism with an unequal or slower growth of mental abilities compared with physical growth may partially explain the popularity of abortions. If a functioning mind were lost in abortion, it would be a more grievous than loss of the body. As is, cultural self-understanding finds the loss of physical existence less troublesome than loss of the mind. If it is true that culturally we understand ourselves primarily as mind, what is lost in abortion is not really one of us. For we have or are minds. But the fetus is assumed to be mindless.

And there we are, mitigating our destruction of the earliest human lives. Creatures of our bone and flesh; humans we have caused to begin and to be; not strangers or interlopers but ours, our children! Our laws offer permission and fellow citizens offer "understanding."

Without ever scrutinizing the stages of human fetal growth. The dualistic distinctions with mind outranking bodily standing can justify even the non-treatment of seriously ill newborns. *Postnatal abortions,* delayed because fetal problems remained undiagnosed till birth, invoke the same secular logic as abortion.[2] Only rational life counts as humanizing, precious and protectable. Only actually existing mental abilities and not the potential for minds count decisively. After all, acorns are not oak trees and blueprints are not buildings.

THE IMPORTANCE OF TIME

Time for human development is important for abortion issues. That was reflected in the many responses to the 1973 law. Longer fetal development

2. Fletcher, *Humanhood*, 144.

results in greater growth and possible fetal survival. The logic of pro-abortion advocates insists on importance of time. The pro-choice advocacy notes not how much has developed in fetuses but points to how much is still missing of what it takes to count as a human person. Specifically, pro-choice advocates tend to assume that to be a human *person*—the key value term in both ethics and law—it takes both a body and a mind. And the human fetus cannot reasonably be said to have a mind.

Bodily and mental development proceed at different rates. Human fetuses have a body but still lack a mind. Pro-choice advocates reason that human fetuses prove to be similar to animals, who also are said to lack a mind. (If certain animals began to speak coherently, their standing would rise and perhaps call for protective rights.) As is, abortion intervenes early, before it can be reasonably claimed that human fetuses have mental abilities. That is, they still lack a mind. Human potential for mental abilities is dismissed as irrelevant. Since fetuses still lack a mind, they cannot even be said *to mind* premature death. These non-persons will be gone before they know anything or could apprehend their fate.

BIBLICAL COUNTERPOINTS

Biblical traditions do not see humans as the originators of human standing or their inherent worth. The creation and meanings of human life arise from God. The biblical creation stories are not dualistic. Human life is created by God. And all of it is good. Genesis, in the initial chapter of the Bible, closes each creative act of God with God judging that to be good. On the sixth day, God creates the first human couple. And the biblical author sums it all up with "very good" (Gen 1:31). Humankind is special in regard to living beings in that men and women are created in God's image. That relates them to God in a unique but unspecified way (Gen 1:27). The unitary quality of human nature lies in the fact that they are declared blessed and very good, body and mind, inner and outer, male and female. Being created in the image of God sets them apart from all other creatures. What makes humans unique is not rational ability or mental distinctions, as in modern liberalism. Rather what distinguishes humans is the conviction that God relates them to God-self. Humans are kin of God in some sense. Only humans reflect the image of God who creates, blesses and loves them and places the rest of creation into their hands. And, as best we know, only humans and God are on speaking terms.

Biblically, human nature is not dualistic but unitary—dust formed and animated by the breath of God. As all creation, God regards humans as very good (Gen 1:31). Humans, as all living beings, are mortal. There is no clue that one dimension of their life, spirit or mind, survives death. Centuries later, in New Testament times, there are speculations and controversies that the dead might live again. God will restore the dead to life from divine memory, not reanimate bodies or re-embody eternal minds. Since humans are actually dead—dead in both body and mind—they can only live again by being re-created (not re-animated with immortal souls). Resurrection from the dead—achieved by God—is the only option. And that is how God resurrected Jesus after he died on the cross. And God will raise or recreate humanity bodily and spiritually in a time to come or beyond time. God will then hold humans accountable for the life with which God initially entrusted them.

Human standing originating in God's creative and sustaining love extends to children. "Be fruitful and multiply" (Gen 1:28)—perhaps the only divine command humans have consistently obeyed. The link with God continues to be direct. While contemporaries refer to their lives and to their children's lives as *theirs,* that misleads theologically, as mentioned earlier. God creates and owns all creation and entrusts it to humans. Humans do not own themselves; parents do not own their children. God creates, owns and entrusts humans to humans. Humans are not owners of themselves or of their children. For better and for worse. Humans are called to be stewards serving God. God retains ownership. And in a time to come, or perhaps beyond all time, humans will have to give an account of their stewardship.

The biblical meaning of human standing relates to the scriptural concept of human purpose. What are we made for? What is the meaning of life for Christians? "[Y]ou have been created to praise and glorify God—all moral life derives from that truth."[3] That holds not just for Christians but for all humans. It holds as well for children and for the human unborn. To abort the unborn not only deprives them of life but of their relationship with God and of God's relationship with them! Who would have thought that humans can and do rob God?! God has placed human life into human hands. Parents and parents-to-be are entrusted with such lives. Since they do not own their children, they may not dispose of them (even when beginning humans are denied legal protection).

Abortion is not only a matter of who owns whom. God takes sides. The biblical God does not wear a blindfold, the human symbol of egalitarian justice. Analogous to parents, God sides with children in trouble, afflicted by disease, handicap, hunger, poverty, weakness, mistreatment. Actually, not just standing with children but with all of humankind mistreated or

---

3. Hauerwas, "Christianity," 52.

deprived. This divine self-identification makes everything personal. Whether hungry or thirsty, unwelcome strangers, the poorest of the poor, the sick or the imprisoned—"Truly I tell you, just as you did it to one of the least of these *who are members of my family, you did it to me*" (Matt 25:40; italics added). The human unborn is already a member of that family. This unborn member is not only the most vulnerable, it is also mute, cannot cry or complain, cannot care for itself, depends for its life on the care and support of its family. Not listed by name or condition in biblical texts, to be sure, but what Israelite or Jew could have conceived of rejecting God's greatest gift?

ARRIVAL OF A NEWBORN

The title of this chapter is abortion. And the moral judgment of Christian ethics about abortion, as argued here, is that, except for certain very limited exceptions, abortion is morally wrong. A major reason for why it is wrong is that abortion prevents a human child from being born. Human birth may seriously alter existing plans. And the presence of a newborn may be foreseen as a preventable imposition. As a counterpoint to the advantages lost and responsibilities imposed, the next paragraph offers a father's perspective of a planned birth. That forms a personal and subjective account, devoid of academic objectivity.

Knowing what is on the way and witnessing its arrival are not the same. Seeing, hearing, smelling, touching this new creature proves that it is real. How awesome that we, my wife and I, were instrumental in giving life to this creature, that we may kiss, name, feed, hold—ever so cautiously. One marvels that this handful, this armful, comes from us. It alarms us with its cries, charms us with its smiles. The experience has a sacred aspect: God did it through us! With us! The occasion commands not only awe but gratitude. It reminds one of that text when God completed creation, looked at it and saw that it was very good (Gen 1:31). Here, in this birth, God does it again—with minor human assistance. And much later an insight: It is a long-standing maxim that *humans* give, ascribe, impose meaning on reality. I defend the claim that humans make the world speak. But remembering that birth, the conviction was undeniable that the preciousness derived from this child, perhaps as well as from God the Creator and Witness, but not from me. And not from my wife and me! *The newborn commanded gratitude.*

PERSONS AND HUMAN BEINGS

In liberalism and in the law, not all human beings are persons. Neither liberalism nor the law agree with Dr. Seuss that a person's a person, no matter how small. The law withholds person status from human beings before birth. Becoming a legal person, having standing in a court of law, and enjoying the protection of legal rights begins with birth and ends at death. Since the 1973 US Supreme Court decisions *Roe v. Wade* and *Doe v. Bolton* and since the "flexibility" of the Fourteenth Amendment (1868) the due process clause guarantees American women the fundamental right to privacy and medically safe abortions. While those decisions do not establish the right to kill the fetus, very few fetuses survive abortion procedures. A legal right to life does not exist until the human unborn becomes a newborn and a legal person. Countless humans never get there.

TECHNICALITIES

The following two paragraphs consider two other situations relating to the timing of abortion. The first deals with some variations of when human personhood begins. That term is bound to mental abilities and the importance of legal personhood. However, since human development offers no sharp distinguishing lines, liberal defenders of personhood tend to permit back-dating personhood status and allowing *newborns* to count as persons or as one of us. That would make birth into the start of personhood and would make liberal agreement into a concession. Yet postponing the start of legal personhood to coincide with the development of rational abilities has been recommended in the case of seriously "defective" or handicapped newborns. The lack of mental abilities in newborns tempts pro-choice advocates to classify such compromised newborn as fetus, not newborn or person. What some condemn as infanticide is then declared to be "postnatal abortion."

When health of the pregnant woman is at stake, only birth itself will legally protect a near-term fetus. As to the emerging fetus, even as late as when the natural birth process has begun, it is not too late to abort. Before the head has fully emerged, the physician may cut an incision in the back of the fetal neck "to evacuate the brain cavity." One hesitates to refer to "sucking its brain out" and names that a "partial birth abortion." If that procedure had been briefly delayed and the head had emerged intact, a legal person with the right to life would have been killed. That would have constituted homicide. The lesson lies near that becoming a legal person matters, that words and time count, and that the living should be grateful to survive long enough to be secured with legal rights.

PERSONS, RIGHTS, AND PRECEDENTS

American law grants personhood and rights only to humans born and living. The human unborn and all other living creatures remain excluded from legal standing and individual rights. These exclusions result in grim prospects for the human fetus/unborn. If humans already conceived lack all rights, how much less can one claim rights on behalf of future or not-yet conceived generations? One has the impression that considering the needs of future generations may elicit general respect and considerations. But existing persons trump possible rights of not-yet-existing generations. Nevertheless, when this nation assumes communal resolve, it can protect whatever needs protecting: historical sites, old houses, threatened species. It is conceivable that one might also legally protect the human species when it is threatened—as it is before birth and as it might be in regard to future generations. If that were the strongest protection, namely human rights, one might cite corporate precedent rather than future generations. American corporations have standing in a court of law and enjoy limited legal personhood. Such options could be created for the human unborn and for future generations. If only this nation stood in awe of the human unborn and of future Americans as it does of corporations.

PROTECTING THE UNBORN

The human unborn—conceived but not yet born—should be included in the human family. In terms of rights, of which the unborn are deprived until the moment of birth, these earliest versions of ourselves deserve as a minimum, the right to survive. The reasons, again, do not focus on the unborn but look to ourselves. Human beings are the namers and deciders who make reality speak. The issue is not out there but within—within communal metaethics, the meaning of life and conscience. What does denial of the protection for the earliest version of ourselves say about us, the judges of who counts and who lives?

Pro-life arguments are not directed to Christians. For biblical believers—if they understand what they believe—the question of human standing never seriously arises. Human lives are God's handiwork, entrusted into human bodies and hands. But only as a trust, not as property. God retains ownership and holds human accountable for what is entrusted to them. These human beginners, aka embryos and fetuses, are members of God's family. God does not let them out of God's sight. What we do to these children of God—in effect we do to God (Matt 25:45)! For Christians, enough said.

A PRO-CHOICE VERSION OF ABORTION

When it comes to ethical controversies, basic fairness dictates that one strives to present the view with which one disagrees in its strongest version. The pragmatic test whether that has been achieved would be that its advocates consider the result to be fair or reasonable. What follows is such an effort at fairness by a pro-life advocate in two paragraphs. Again, for clarity's sake, what follows is an effort to describe fairly a pro-choice version of abortion by a pro-life advocate:

Early human lives, conceived but unborn, may be legally aborted within a certain time frame by pregnant women in medically secure settings with the prospect that the fetus will not survive. This process, legal in the USA, is moral and progressive for the following reasons: Pregnancy is a very personal experience that can impose considerable burdens not just on the pregnant woman but on families. There is no need in this nation for more people. Also there is no inconsistency or conflict of abortion with respect to persons. Embryos and fetuses are merely the physical beginning of what may become human persons. Exclusively physical, such organisms are literally mindless. Whether in terms of law or in terms of ethical personhood, the human unborn are not persons, defined as rational and volitional humans.

Not only are the human unborn not persons, they lack and should continue to lack legal and moral rights. Human beings do not have legal standing until birth. And even birth may be premature, since a mind or a will are still out of reach of the human unborn. Unwanted by the pregnant woman, the continued existence of the embryo/fetus must not be imposed on the pregnant woman, fully human, with life plans of her own and with the right to her own autonomy. American traditions honor individual liberty and personal rights—both qualities reasonably ascribed only to the pregnant woman, not to her pregnancy. The unborn product of conception constitutes a condition of the woman, remains part of her body and her concern. The right to privacy makes explicit that her decisions of what to do in regard to herself trumps any interference with what she judges to be necessary and right. Besides, if such legal privacy were to be rescinded, women would again take any measure to liberate themselves from such imposition. That has led to countless deaths and serious illness of pregnant women. And no one wants to return to that.

PRO-LIFE RESPONSES

The following several pages analyze pro-life arguments. Several personal vignettes are included to provide a sense of the personal nature unavoidable in issues of abortion.

ACKNOWLEDGING THE STANDING OF UNBORN HUMAN LIFE

Apart from religious justification of human standing of the human unborn, how might secularists argue against the denigration, abuse and destruction of pre-personal humans, i.e., of human embryos and fetuses? One option would be to follow the precedent which identifies animal species. The lives of animal species begin with fertilization. That biological beginning extends to human animals. The ethical adjustment for pro-life advocates lies in extending human respect for persons to their physical beginnings. Precedent for that exists in the legal protection of newborns, creatures who cannot reasonably be said to have abilities of thought or choice. Consistency and coherence lie in advancing human person-status to conception. Conception is where we all begin and where human status should originate.

One difficulty with such reasoning is that conception might not be detectable for some time. Nevertheless, conception is where new lives begin. If that holds for animals, it should hold for the human animal. To be human counts in terms of values and especially in terms of protection. The second paragraph of the Declaration of Independence declares, "We hold these truths to be self-evident." Backed up with the resolve to defend that Declaration with human lives and civil war, the Declaration now has become a founding national document. In that context, declaring so, made it so. And revolution is not the only context where declaring had real legal effects. The pronouncements of judges, of explorers and namers of new continents, by naming in the right contexts, make it so. Even individual couples, in saying the right words in fitting contexts, create a marriage. Decisive for abortion issues, polititions, legislators, judges, voters make abortion legal. They decree and transform the human unborn into non-persons without standing or legal protections.

AN EARLIER EXAMPLE OF DEPRIVING HUMANS OF LEGAL STANDING

Having been born and raised in Germany, for long years National Socialists (Nazis) declared and enforced that Jews, including Jewish citizens, did not have a right to live. The slogan was "life unworthy of living" (*lebensunwürdiges Leben*). American abortion laws seem ominously similar. Of course, before the Nazis deprived them of citizenship, these Germans were persons in every sense of the word and had human and legal standing. Becoming unwelcome can be a prelude to extinction. So the human unborn in the age of abortion. Might the Holocaust be a prelude to the elimination of unwanted unborns?

How to discern and resist the sequence of dehumanization—loss of rights—ending in death? Shakespeare asked the question in the *Merchant of Venice*, when Shylock implores his enemies with, "Hath not a Jew eyes? . . . If you prick us, do we not bleed?" If they could, would not the human unborn ask analogous questions? America as a national community has not yet looked and shuddered.

THE PLEDGE OF ALLEGIANS

The point of citing this Pledge in this context is that it may foster a more humane vision of the human unborn and of ourselves This pledge speaks to all Americans. In my case, reciting the Pledge was linked to becoming an American citizen, expedited by serving in the US Army. The text: "I pledge allegiance to the Flag of the United States of America, and to the Republic for which it stands, one Nation under God, indivisible, with liberty and justice for all."

This Pledge has long appealed to me, not just because it accompanied the gift of US citizenship. It is aspirational in the sense that it projects who or what we, the citizens, intend to become. Authors of the Pledge probably did not give the human unborn a second thought. But that is neither here nor there. The question raised by the Pledge is whether its affirmation relates to the practice of abortion. Does liberty and justic include the human unborn? Is the Pledge compatible with ending the lives of the unborn for any or no reason? The human unborn literally cannot live with that. The dissonance between justice and liberty for all and limitless abortions may not even be audible to many. Yet abortion on demand violates key words of the Pledge. Liberty and justice for all? Not for the many unborn who would join us but remain unwelcome and unborn.

The closing words of the Pledge refer to "all." Does "all" include the human unborn? Certainly these humans-on-the-way need justice, since they lack protection from being killed at will. It does seem odd to insist on protections for all, except for those most defenseless and unwelcome lives and most at risk. Since the context of these chapters is Christian ethics, the Pledge invokes "under God." That is a generic rather than a Christian appeal. It gives the impression that God endorses or blesses this Pledge. That one would invoke God's affirmation in a nation that jettisons unwelcome human unborn leaves only the plea, "God help us!"

LOST CHILDREN?

There is another link between the care for children and the practice of abortion. When a child is lost, that becomes an alarming communal problem. Everybody knows and pays attention, perhaps even joining one of the search parties. Radio tells the up-to-date story; the next day's paper offers pictures of the missing child. All remain on edge. And then, thank God! the child is found. In America a lost child counts. Fittingly so. May one relate that assumption to lost unborn children-on-the-way? To children without names and faces and, before birth, without legal protection? Is there not a social and moral disconnect or inconsistency when we are alarmed by a child lost but remain untroubled and unmoved by uncounted unborn children also lost—"lost" irretrievably?

AMERICAN GENEROSITY

American generosity was memorably demonstrated in the years following World War II. Lack of food in Germany was felt more after than during that war. A package from America, with special foods (almost forgotten) was a godsend. The Marshall Plan was the grand version of such help. Generosity within this nation is exemplified in helping those at the margins of society. Support for persons unemployed, free food for the hungry, medical care for those without insurance. At our best, Americans look out for and help each other. That sense of generous national solidarity does not extend to unborn children lost deliberately and irretrievably.

INTERGENERATIONAL SOLIDARITY

Family relations and mutual care should resist resorting to abortion. Parental and grandparental links with children, including those on the way, have always been seen as natural and fitting. Children, when grown, in turn acknowledge such continuity of care with dedicated responsibility to parents and grandparents. Exceptions startle us. Being subject to harm and death without humanizing protective laws dehumanizes. The pro-choice refrain centers on autonomy and a woman's rights to her own body, with never a word about another body at stake. In effect, that other body has no legal or moral standing. It resembles property that can be disposed at will. Yet it ought to make moral sense—even in the liberal worldview—to protect children while they are on their way to us. Here it is "on their way to us," lest "mother" or "family" may mislead.

AN ANECDOTE

A true story to interrupt these grim sentences. While a student in divinity school, those of us who were married ordinarily took measures to prevent pregnancy. We seemed all to be short of funds, and children would have to wait. A surprise note from a fellow student, a friend's invitation to a conception party: "Despite the best defenses of the Gentiles, the Lord is blessing us with a child!" It would not have occurred to the writer or to his wife to abort, accident or not. Aborting would have been inconsistent with their identity as well as their calling.

CONTRACEPTION AND ITS CONSERVATIVE CRITICS

If one engages in sexual activity and does not intend to engender a child, one must take steps to prevent conception! The sophistication of that rule is as profound as the rule to look both ways before crossing a street. Here trusting luck or prayer is frivolous. And trusting in traditional natural law rejection of artificial contraception proves to be similarly careless. Conservative scruples based on natural law remind one of Protestant fundamentalism: ancient truths may not be a fail-safe. The natural end of sexual intercourse is said to be making babies. If that is all that God had in mind in creating humans, did God bless us with loving passion, sexual joy and exuberance simply to assure fruitfulness in begetting children? What a miserly, diminutive and joyless concept of the Creator! Making nature speak involves risk that nature says what we want to hear. One may ask, where are these joyless "natural rules about sex" originating? It's enough to give natural law a bad name!

Contraception does not violate the ordained nature of things. Rather, contraception can be an expression of responsible care and love. Lack of contraception when fertile and sexually active is simply irresponsible. If a child is unwanted and unwelcome, it can be an act of love—of all involved—to take effective but non-abortive measures through preventive forethought.

God places human procreation into human hands. That assumes that humans have at least a modicum of common sense and foresight. Humans make nature (and reality) speak. What is natural or unnatural proves to be malleable or pliable. Those who offer guidance in things sexual, might at least consult female perspectives. Lest that risks ad hominem logic, women tend to be more perceptive on this score of contraception since they have more at risk.

The role of males in regard to abortion may be distorted when federal or state laws focus primarily on women. While woman have abortions, men who impregnate women share responsibility for abortions. And, of course, they share responsibilities when a child is born. An anecdote about male responsibility to avoid recourse to abortion: A close departmental colleague confided that he and his wife had long agreed to limit their children to two, citing a "replacement" justification in an overcrowded world. This occurred in the 1970s, when the risks of overpopulation were very much on everyone's mind. He and his wife had just experienced the birth of their second child. How then to enact their resolve? Additional decades of relying on birth control pills seemed neither safe nor certain and placed all responsibilities on the wife. Knowing that male infertility was easier to attain than female interventions, the husband volunteered, and his wife agreed, that he would undergo a vasectomy. The brief outpatient procedure followed. The only complaint was that the surgeon did not have to certify the procedure by presenting the severed vas.

ETHICS OF THE BODY?

The widespread use of abortion in America has been analyzed and opposed here. But how to explain the pattern of abortion decade after decade in a society that, when asked, understands itself as loving its children? We are alarmed by a child lost. Yet we remain untroubled and unmoved by countless unborn children being lost to abortion. Such discontinuity may have a metaethical explanation. Metaethics, again, refers to ethical aspects or implications of inclusive views of life. And views of life are interpretations of how things (everything) make sense. The metaethics implied in American abortion practices seem to be that aborted unborns fall short of human standing. It is not self-contradictory to note that humans develop more quickly physically than mentally and that the human unborn exist only bodily. Here *potential* for personhood status, the abilities to think and to choose, is simply dismissed as irrelevant. An abortion, then, is taken to be different—in the sense of less troubling—than depriving a child of life. In fact, to use medical professional designations, what is lost in abortion are not children but embryos, fetuses, the products of conception. And such "products," existing only physically but without ability to reason or choose, are trumped by the needs and choices of actual rational and volitional persons. So the dehumanizing popular reasoning supporting abortion!

A CHRISTIAN ETHICS OF THE BODY

Christian faith may overlap with many features of a secular ethics, but when it comes to the importance and value of the human body, it radically differs from the previous paragraph. Human existence, body, soul, and mind exist as God's good creation. The body is God's initial good creation and so is the more gradual emergence of the mind, of speech, of abilities to choose and to love. To be sure, God places the creation of humans into human hands and care. But children have their own links with God as well as God's links with them. Bodily parental care gradually shifts toward the growing child. And, when living long enough, the care relationships may reverse.

Abortion justifications differ in meaning from a faith perspective. Recalling previous faith assumptions here, human life does not belong to humans but to God. The human unborn, just as all human life, is God-created and God-owned. When, in 2022, the US Supreme Court struck down the 1973 abortion decisions, demonstrators protested with signs declaring their bodies as their own. That and the appeal to rights—in this contexts the right to abort—expressed the popular spread of secularism and the alienation from Christian faith and Christian ethics.

SECULAR ABORTION LOGIC

The secular abortion logic in American culture reflects metaethical assumptions. Metaethics, again, refers to a worldview or a philosophy of life that offers a vision of how everything interconnects and makes sense. In an earlier chapter metaethics was described analogously to *eyeglasses*. Eyeglasses serve to create focus and meaning for what we encounter or behold. Without such focus-creating ability, our "experiences" would remain as a buzzing, blooming confusion. A mild experience of lacking such ordering or sense-making vision can occur in entering a culture whose language is alien to oneself. Being lost, one cannot even ask for directions. Even simpler, waking from sleep in a strange place without knowing how one got there or where one is, can be unnerving. It is not till the place suddenly reassumes identity, that one can thankfully relax. Metaethics, created gradually from experience, language, memory, forms our orientation, assumptions and bearings. Ethics (rules of conduct) and morality (actual moral problems) grow out of metaethical assumptions (when we are being reasonable).

To connect with abortion, I had suggested that a major reason for widespread popular national support for abortions was the general metaetical assumption that the human unborn simply exist as bodies, devoid of mind or personhood. Such lack of human standing—though normal in every sense—can deprive embryos and fetuses of human standing and worth. Being a-rational or pre-rational can deprive the human unborn of human standing and respect. The expression (not advocated here) "when mindless, one might as well be dead!" remains reasonable, if a-moral, nonmoral or immoral. Note that the quoted text in the previous sentence usually assumes a context of the end of life. But it seems applicable to beginning and unborn life as well.

SOCIOLOGY OF THE BODY

Sociology of the body seeks to re-emphasize the importance of the human body. That has ethical implications in that the human body is not just the physical vehicle for personhood. Christian ethics has a similar interest in restoring the bodily nature of humans as an intrinsic unitary feature of human beings through the creative love of God. While liberal ethics looks to rational and volitional abilities to establish standing, rights and ethics, this relatively recent innovation in sociology focuses attention on the human body in larger than ancillary perspectives than mind and its reasoning and choosing abilities. Sociology searches for new ways to do justice to human embodiment from an empirical perspective. Christian ethics seeks a new appreciation of the human body from theological assumptions. Both seek a more profound understanding of the human body than the dualist (body/mind) perspective.

The body is not merely a physical vehicle for personhood and identity. It is the active basis of being in the world, and the foundation of self, meaning, culture, and society. Two authors who unfurl the sociological banner of the body in opposing Cartesianism (the latinized version of Descartes' name and the father of modern philosophy), propose a truly embodied sociology that makes embodiment central rather than peripheral, and puts "minds back into bodies, bodies back into society, and society back into the body."[4] These authors expect that such refocusing will do greater justice to ethics and politics. They conclude their book with the confidence that "[e]mbodiment, a common carnal bond, becomes both our hope and our salvation."[5] When it rains, it pours.

Bryan S. Turner, also in a sociological text, proposes that the concept of embodiment must be placed at the core of any adequate picture of social life. He considers embodiment as a matter of vulnerability and frailty. Though he is writing about the human condition, his description fits the exposure of the human unborn (perhaps better than he intended). "Human beings are ontologically frail and their natural environment uncertain. In order to protect themselves from vagaries and afflictions, they must build social institutions (especially political, familial, and ecclesiastical institutions) that come to constitute what we call 'society.'"[6] Humans must be protected with rights. To acknowledge the "frailty and the precarious nature of social reality, human beings require the protective security of general human rights."[7] The biological nature of human frailty requires human rights as a protective canopy. Taking the body into account, Turner defines the self in bodily terms and does greater justice than dualistic perspectives to human fragility, aging and disease.

> Both sociology and anthropology have demonstrated that identity is fundamentally embodied, because subjective and objective identity cannot be easily separated from embodiment. It follows that "self" is not an enduring or stable fact, but changes with aging, the life-course. And the disruptions of illness.[8]

If frailty and precariousness of human life be the human condition that calls for protection of rights, one would not have to go far to recognize such exposure at the earliest stages of human life. The often invoked thesis of the social construction of human bodies,[9] the claim that the meaning, value and status of human bodies are social creations, could be helpful not

---

4. Williams and Bendelow, *Lived Body*, 3.
5. Williams and Bendelow, *Lived Body*, 213.
6. Turner, "End(s) of Humanity," 10.
7. Turner, "End(s) of Humanity," 19.
8. Turner, "End(s) of Humanity," 28.
9. Shilling, *Body and Social Theory*, 11, 12, 70.

just to feminists and racial justice claims *but to voiceless human bodies at life's beginnings*. It is not the case that pre- or post-personal human bodies merit no protection. It is the liberal vision that remains blind to their preciousness. That blind spot in liberal eyes—excluding the human unborn from protection with rights—might be correctable with such sociological revisions. In any case, Christian support of liberal human rights must not stop short of protecting those human lives now at greatest risk in a culture that defines "person" dualistically and one-sidedly. "Mind over body" expresses resolve. It does not endorse metaethical dualism, a metaethics with which the human unborn cannot live. Literally.

"CARE" INSTEAD OF "RIGHTS"

The language of the abortion controversy has become defensive and constrained. Since human lives are at stake, it is easy to suspect one's opposition of bad faith. The abortion controversy, extending over half a century, has created deep roots in its adversaries. To return to the metaphor of eye glasses, adversaries see this issue with very different prescriptions. And taking a look through the other's glasses—if one dares—proves alien, distorting, unnerving and unnatural. So one falls back into a defensive stance and wording. And that is the language of rights, the adversarial nomenclature of lawyers.

In a sense, the language of rights is an emergency concept. Rights should protect humans from abuse, neglect, threats. That presupposes the risk of harm and injustice. Rights are both negative and positive. Negative rights protect from harm. Positive right are legitimate claims that should assure benefits. As the right to a fair wage, to a free basic education, the right to police protection.

What people owe one another normally and consistently rarely involves rights. When it comes to children, parental care anticipates needs and problems and never lets it come to reaching for rights. Our children belong and are entrusted to us. A similar reliance on trust can be found in what are called the serving professions. Rights seem alien to the loyalties of soldiers, fire fighters, public servants, teachers, professors, doctors. As if rational choice theory had never been invented, the meaning of the professions place serving others over serving self. Resolving our differences requires a language other than rights. A more promising term would be "care." Caring reaches farther and includes more than rights can ever attain. Caring has an affinity with love. The abortion controversy may become less adversarial—or at least seem to do so—if it construes itself with a softer and more personal vocabulary than rights.

ABORTION AND CARE

When pregnant women resort to repeated abortions, that may imply that abortion is used for failed birth control. If that is the function of abortion, those who conceived the human life at stake seem alienated from it. The unborn may be reduced to an inconvenience. If the unborn is diagnosed with a serious or possibly fatal or disabling disease, an abortion takes on a different moral meaning. Anencephaly (a missing upper brain), Tay Sachs, trisomy and other serious threats to the life of the unborn may call for an induced death before birth. So I had assumed. And yet the lives shortened by disease would be all that such afflicted children would ever have. The aim of the medical profession is to save lives. Christian ethics, almost by definition, seeks the same end. I learned from a former student who became the mother of a child with trisomy 18. She and her husband did not abort and regarded even a brief life of their daughter as good.

> She experienced my love, the love of my husband and so many other people. She was held, sung to, read to, danced with. She gave every indication of enjoying it all. She also had the opportunity to touch many, many people. She taught everyone who met her how little the word "handicapped" tells us about the totality of a person. She left love wherever she went.... We kept focused on things to be grateful for: Maggie was alive. Maggie was home, Maggie was beautiful. We had each other. We had wonderful families. We had good insurance. (From a 1997 letter of a former student)

This letter persuaded me to widen my notion of human need and of parental caring and devotion.

ABORTION POLITICS AND POLITICAL DILEMMAS

The two major American political parties have aligned themselves in different directions in regard to abortion issues. While no political party can claim unanimity for its members, the Left, the progressively inclined Democratic Party, is pro-choice. The Right and more conservative Republican Party stands for the right to life. Such cleavage on abortion issues creates difficulties for voters who do not fit these options. There are Democrats for

Life and Republicans for Choice. It would seem that there has not been a national election from 1973 till 2022 that such "outliers" could celebrate, no matter what the election results.

Abortion laws have changed in June of 2022 in that the US Supreme Court reversed the privacy and pro-choice 1973 laws and turned abortion laws over to individual states. While some state laws were already waiting in the wings, state legislators are likely to battle over abortion and appointments to appeal courts in the coming years. Legislators continue to have a vital but indirect role in laws over who shall live, that is, over whether the human unborn remain unprotected and at risk or whether they may be included with us all in being important enough to live.

NAMING ISSUES AND MORALLY JUDGING ABORTION

When it comes to ethics, it matters how one names the issues at hand and identifies what is at stake. The liberal versions of abortion issues define abortion in terms of women's rights: women should have the legal right to abort without consulting men or the law for permission. Such rights constitute a civil liberty or freedom. A Christian ethics perspective, advocated here, identifies the issues differently. One difference turns to *human* rights rather than focusing on *women's* rights. And human rights include men and should include the human unborn. Specifically, the key issue is to save the lives of the human unborn. That turns abortion into a matter of human life and/or human death, even though abortion rights do not include the right to kill.

American prevailing cultural winds seem to be liberal and secular, even if the 1973 Supreme Court decisions legally permitting abortion has been overturned in 2022. If that is correct, an American metaphysical dualism or worldview of body/mind, with mind outranking body, favors the pro-choice perspective. If the human unborn still lacks a mind or self-awareness—and it seems unreasonable to contest that—abortion *cannot be said to kill a person.* To be sure, it will almost certainly kill a human being before birth, a human being with moral and Christian but not yet legal standing.

Again, if humans before birth do *not* count as legal persons, what would be lost by abortion is literally not anyone, not a legal person, or a person in any sense, not a rights-bearer, not a citizen. That defines the human fetus/unborn in terms of what it was, not as what it will be if left alive. The unborn are human lives but not yet persons. Just as animals have no standing in court, so the human unborn. That exposes them to the women who conceived but will not welcome or let them live. One reads of animals devouring their young and shudders. Legalizing abortion in effect constitutes the national decision to create a Damocles' sword, suspended over every human unborn.

THEFT FROM GOD?

If Christian faith here lapses into the prevailing moral dualism of body and mind, it risks losing its Christian identity. God creates humans in the divine image. While the meaning of that is not clear, it does at least mean that humans are related to and in some sense similar to God. If that is true, such likeness or relationship might hold from the very beginnings of human lives, that is, from conception. God is the Creator, owner and Lord of humans from their very start. That makes elective abortion into theft from God. Actually, theft and homicide! In a secular culture, stealing from God may not trouble those secure in their atheism. But for those who thank the biblical God for their own existence or for the blessing of children, the pragmatic rejection of unborn human lives is grievous. Unborn human lives, as we all, exist at risk from inherited diseases, malnutrition, accident, warfare, violence. But the human unborn live under the additional threat of being unacceptable and deprived of life. For any or no reason. In effect, such lives are disposable. And we, as a people, are not aggrieved.

ABORTION EXCEPTIONS

There may be complications of pregnancy that endanger the life of the pregnant woman. If that becomes a matter of saving one or neither, it is the woman whose life should take precedence. Both lives are precious. But others are dependent on the woman, while no one yet depends on the existence of the unborn. Given that human relationships can be complicated, it is unwise to multiply examples of what lives should take precedence in unavoidable conflicts. The law should intend to serve human beings. And those who have to make difficult decisions should be aware of what they bring to hard choices. Christian ethics has no ready solutions for genuinely difficult cases. Christians, however, have to give an account to their Creator. Taking the life of an unborn human being is not a trivial thing. Assuming the standing of human lives yet unborn as created, owned, and loved by God, just how might one justify an abortion to God?

CHRISTIAN ETHICS AND "IMPOSING RELIGION"

Christian ethics in the American abortion controversy may elicit the accusation that Christians are seeking to impose religion on everyone else, especially when Christians make unpopular judgments. Given that abortion has been legal and popular since 1973, Christian respect for the human unborn becomes countercultural. "To impose" implies synonyms as "to inflict," or "to foist upon." That crude charge implies that religion, specifically pro-life Christian convictions, should remain private or restricted to religious communities and contexts. The claim of privacy in this context is legal but not moral or Christian. If privacy were to apply to God's Judgment, the term "judgment" could no longer be capitalized. Perhaps less is more when it comes to a Final Judgment. But for those who respect humans across the lifespan, the deliberate annihilation of unwanted human lives is distressing.

Christians get involved in politics because they are citizens. Democracy assures individual standing: to speak, to vote, to participate in public issues—and to pay taxes to make all that function. Christians owe God and humans a public, political and moral witness in word and deed. Indeed, Christians consider themselves called to public responsibilities because God points and sends them there. Public controversy over life and death will be inevitable. And democratic responsibilities include us all in reasoned arguments over what and what does not count.

ABRAHAMIC RELIGIONS

The faith vision of Judaism, Christianity and Islam—relate all of life to God. At least that is the goal, though always contested by prevailing secular worldviews. The biblical expression, "God is LORD" (Ps 100:3; someone has counted 34 such expressions) is a unitary rather than a dualistic expression. God's lordship extends to politics. Politics has been defined as the realm of who gets what, when and how (Harold Laswell). Politics may be the sphere in which the most important economic-financial-political decisions are made, affecting all citizens. The biblical God not only attends to politics but identifies with those denied opportunity or justice. Biblically, God described these losers as members of God's family. What one does to or for them one does to or for God (Matt 25:40)! The Bible is also a political text. That makes anti-abortion politics into a Christian duty.

CONTROVERSY AND CHRISTIAN RELUCTANCE

Christian ethics takes its bearings from biblical texts and Christian traditions and from what it considers to be the will of God revealed in the life and teachings of Jesus. Such bearings, however, leave God standing in the wings. "Praying about it" is a notorious cliché. Yet those who worship the living God should do precisely that. And do so, if possible, in company of those with whom they differ? A key feature of Christian ethics is the act of showing an issue (a disagreement) to God and probing whether one can do that without being dissuaded. Dissuaded by opposing voices and/or by the presence of God. Lest that sounds unacceptably subjective, serious moral issues should have already been deliberated by all willing to think and to debate a problem. The issue of abortion is long-standing and incendiary in American culture. Church leaders will create position papers on abortion. But raising this issue in sermons or conferences may be incendiary. Should pastors who risk this topic first insist on tenure?

American liberalism is noted for its emphasis on individual rights, as in freedom of speech, civil liberty and equality. The liberal vision of the functions of government is to protect those who are least advantaged by providing aid for education, universal health care, protecting the environment, affirming women's rights (including abortion?), affirmative action for minority groups. Liberalism was rightly named in that its logic liberated slaves, and guards the standing of citizens threatened by prejudice and poverty. American liberalism supported the Social Security System, opposes segregation, honors civil rights. Such activism extended to support for the New Deal (in the 1930s) and The Great Society (1960s).

Except for the advocacy of abortion, this affirmative action program could be and was endorsed by Christian activists as practical expression of the commandment to love the neighbor. But what of endorsing abortion? In American liberalism, the human unborn do not count as neighbors. American law as well certainly denies the unborn human personhood and rights-bearer standing. How remarkable that liberalism and Christian faith should now be at such odds over abortion!

Stanley Hauerwas, a leading American Protestant theological ethicist, offers a coherent critique of American liberalism and of its tradition of human rights. He brands the notion of inalienable rights as a philosophical mistake. For Hauerwas, rights express Enlightenment individualism. Christians cannot believe that they have inalienable individual rights. And they do not have the right to do whatever they want with their bodies. As Christians "[w]e do not believe that we have a right to our bodies because when we are baptized we become members of one another; then we can tell one another what it is that we should and should not do with our bodies."[10]

Hauerwas is right: Christians do not own their bodies. And I have made the point that Christians are stewards, not owners, of their bodies and their lives. Moreover, rights should be a protective. When responsibilities and love fail, rights should keep the worst from happening. That makes rights into our cultural and legal reserves against moral failure, exploitation and oppression. Enlightenment insistence on human rights mitigated European religious hostilities and now constitute the only universally recognized language to protect human beings. The current use of rights, women's rights, to end the lives of countless human unborns is an egregious misuse of rights.

Though rights may not be listed in the index of prayer books, human rights are one of the blessings for which believers should give thanks and support. While deliberately secular, who knows where Enlightenment values and protectability have their roots? And who is to say where the source and limits of providence lie? If a pagan Cyrus can become God's anointed (Isa 45:1), do modern pagans lie beyond God's reach?

Professor Hauerwas, a born Texan, has his own unique directness when it comes to abortion. In the context of Catholic immigrants to the US asking themselves, is it possible to be American and Catholic, he writes:

> But then what happened? Abortion happened. Catholics were forced to ask themselves, "What is this society that we just bought into?" It turned out to be a society that is going to kill its kids. Abortion is not just some little mistake. Abortion is a reflection of who Americans are: people in the United States are supposed to concentrate on themselves and pursue happiness; thus they ask themselves, "Why should we bother having children?"[11]

Killing kids before their birth remains underwritten with legal rights—easily mistaken for moral rights. In fact, such killing is a horrendous abuse of rights. The purpose of rights is to defend the most vulnerable and helpless among us. In abortion the use of rights is reversed and perverse. The cure is to amend rights. Given that the 1973 womens' rights decision have been overturned in 2022, one hopes that the human unborn now no longer are exposed to survive the gauntlet of abortion. May we, the citizens, now welcome and protect our human unborn rather than to abandon them when their lives have just begun.

---

10. Hauerwas, "Abortion Theologically Understood," 608.
11. Hauerwas, "Christianity," 526.

RIGHTS AND LIBERALISM HUMANIZED

Though rights may not be listed in prayer books, human rights offer protections for humans when kindness, respect, or compassion for humans at risk fail. While deliberately secular, who knows where Enlightenment worth and protection of rights had their roots? And who is to say where the sources of providence lie. Human rights have a long history of protecting humans abused, exploited, deemed less than useless. The irony of American abortion rights lies in the reversed power imbalance that rights ordinarily establish or re-establish. Human rights traditionally protect the weak from the strong, the poor from the rich. In American abortion law, that has been reversed. Pregnant women have held human lives—the most powerless humans can be—in their hands. Human nature may well take self-focused advantage when opportunity arises. Biblically, human aggression is familiar. Rights humanized would be to extend legal rights to the human unborn. At a minimum that should be the right to life. Liberalism humanized would acknowledge the human unborn as legal if not moral persons.

The current conflict between the human unborn and pregnant women choosing abortion is not a conflict of which Americans should be proud. Nor should one dismiss such ferocity as a matter solely for pregnant women. How can Americans not be troubled by what turns out to be mass destruction of the unborn? Americans have rightly been deemed generous. Yet, is there any generosity or even fairness when we dismiss the human unborn for anything or for nothing?

9

Judgment

THE WORD "JUDGMENT" HAS at least two meanings, namely "good judgment" as in *discernment/perceptiveness* or in "The Judgment," that will be the Final Judgment of all humans by God, anticipated in biblical texts at the end of time and after God's raising of the dead. The New Testament Second Letter of Paul to the Thessalonians warns and reassures believers of the near Judgment of God in its second chapter:

> (5) This [steadfastness and faith during persecution and afflictions] is evidence of the righteous judgment of God, and is intended to make you worthy of the kingdom of God, for which you are also suffering. (6) For it is indeed just of God to repay with affliction those who afflict you, (7) and to give relief to the afflicted as well as to us, when the Lord Jesus is revealed from heaven with his mighty angels (8) in flaming fire, inflicting vengeance on those who do not obey the gospel of our Lord Jesus. These will suffer the punishment of eternal destruction, separated from the presence of the Lord and from the glory of his might, (10) when he comes to be glorified by his saints and to be marveled at on that day among all who have believed.

The footnote to the above verse 8 assures the reader that *vengeance* is not used in the sense of revenge, but of just recompense. And the clarification for verse 9 *eternal destruction* does not mean annihilation but "endless ruin in separation of Christ." Still, one might ask whether "recompense" and "eternal ruin" are not close cousins. More importantly, the text cited remains alien to Jesus' insistence on loving enemies (Matt 5:44).

The ability to make discerning and sound judgments in human relationships is a sound and possibly moral ability. Faculty judge student achievements. Students evaluate faculty with serious implications for faculty tenure and salary decisions. Consumers seek assurance of the quality of costly purchases and look for professionally qualified judgments in politics, medicine, justice, art, law enforcement. The lack of individual judgment can justify caution and personal distance in human relationships. The evidence of good judgment reassures and invokes trust. Such are among the virtues of good human judgment. Yet, when the word Judgment applies to God, that word takes on ominous connotations and invokes apprehension.

Given the dual meanings of the word "judgment," the way to distinguish them in this text is to use a capital J for God's Judgment and the lowercase judgment for human discernment and perceptiveness good judgment). Books in Christian ethics tend to avoid the subject of biblical Judgment, of the universal Judgment of God. That event is thought to follow the end of historical time or time as we know it. That is, the normal passage of time, the usual day following day, will be ended by God's resurrection of all the human dead. Then all humans alive and raised will be judged by God/Jesus for an eternal fate. The word *Judgment* here means being held to account for what one has done or failed to do and includes a verdict. The ability of judging justly, of discretion and good sense, is presupposed, given that God/Christ do the Judging.

There are certainly biblical texts that remain outdated in modern times. And being judged morally by God easily disappears along with *God* in secular contexts. But even in Christian churches the Judgment of God may be all but forgotten. It is retained in traditional creeds but in many churches—except for fundamentalist congregations—Judgment seems all but forgotten.

The thought of being judged morally is not attractive, especially in an individualistic culture that admires personal self-reliance and autonomy. Obituaries do take a look back, but proper style limits judgments to praise—in effect implying a *post-mortem moral metamorphosis*. The fact that the topic appears here in chapter-length *assumes* that biblical divine Judgment is not hyperbole, remains coherent within biblical religion, and should constitute a serious warning and elicit caution. The claim that God makes humans, all humans, accountable for how they live—or have lived—holds. One imagines that any actual Judgment and its results—not only final but eternal—will not lack in surprises.

Judgment

Biblical religion has always proclaimed the importance of religious confession of sins and the plea for forgiveness. The sequence of the liturgy begins with confession for good reason. Assuming that human sinfulness perennially describes the human condition, sinners have little choice but to begin worship with personal confession of sins. Akin to having wronged or ignored an old friend, meeting God in a post-resurrection context requires truth-telling and truth-facing. That functions as a precondition for seeking the merciful presence of God. Divine Judgment at the end of time therefore is nothing new in principle, except that it extends moral responsibilities across a lifetime and ends what one might call ordinary times (one day following the next). Moreover, the Judgment will not only involve individuals but communities. Personal pronouns, as "we" and "us" will be unavoidable. No one knows when ordinary time, time as we know it or day-after-day, will end. But when it does end, confession of sins and the plea for forgiveness will be initial, fitting and inclusive human responses. This assumes that in the God-human relationship in the end-time will resemble the God-human relationship familiar forever. But not in everything. The end-times focus on a familiar past, a weighing of the past. and the prospects of an eternal Judgment. But now, the end-times have begun

Divine Judgment of all humans assumes human accountability and is part of a larger coherent sequence in a theologically coherent context. From among all people the biblical God has chosen a people or nation (Israel) to serve God as living witness to the character and purposes of God. Biblical law, expressing the will and purpose of God, became imperative not just for Israel and the Christian church but for all of humankind. Israel's biblical prophets became advocates of God's will and purpose. "Thus says the Lord" is the prophetic call for Israel, the chosen people of God, to repent and to reform. The Last Judgment forms the reckoning of accountability of humankind to its Lord. It now takes on a conclusive and near or present sense. A universal Judgment forms both the conclusion of humankind held answerable to its Creator and Lord and the beginning of eternal life in the presence of God or endless suffering away from God.

APOCALYPTIC TEXTS

Daniel, the only apocalyptic (revealing, disclosing) text in the Hebrew Scriptures, offers the first clear biblical reference to the resurrection that initiates Judgment (Dan 12:1–4, 13). Those who are resurrected, will be raised to everlasting reward or punishment, with Daniel among the saved. In the New Testament, the Gospel according to Matthew announces the Great

Judgment in 25:31–46. This Judgment will proceed on moral grounds: on whether persons have aided the poor and needy—with whom God identifies—or whether they have disregarded such needs and persons—and thereby ignored God. The Son of Man, speaking in his resurrected return: "'Truly I tell you, just as you did not do it to one of the least of these, you did not do it to me. And these will go away into eternal punishment, but the righteous into eternal life" (Matt 25:45–46).

Though the New Testament texts refer to divine Judgment repeatedly (Rev 20:11–15; 2 Thess 1–5, 12), it seems that mainline churches now avoid such texts as sermon topics. Judgment tends not to feature in Christian ethics texts either. Ordinarily, of course, one not only remembers, anticipates and prepares for an appointed court appearance.

A CONCEPT TO BE AVOIDED?

Modern cultures have modern convictions. The claim that humans will be held accountable for the conduct of their lives in a Last Judgment is as ancient as biblical records. Its survival into modern times is a remarkable. Secularism or disavowing faith in God ordinarily makes faith in divine Judgment moot. In contrast, medieval drawings featured pictorial versions of the Last Judgment, with devils waiting in the wings, hoping to snatch the souls condemned. Now it seems as if the topic has been forgotten or banned. Except for fundamentalist churches and street corner preachers, sermons avoid the topic of a Last Judgment. Preaching Judgment seems outdated from a bygone era when people still believed in God and in biblical texts. While Judgment sermons would now scare children and alienate church members, it used to scare everybody, young and old. Some of the New Testament texts predict fierce futures for the damned, sentenced to everlasting punishment, in contrast to the happy eternal future of the redeemed who end safely, secure in the sheltering and loving presence of God.

A secular world assume that the dead will remain dead. And without faith and the expectation of resurrection, the Last Judgment also becomes incredible. A godless culture lacks a Judge and a Savior. It knows nothing of a Creator or a Redeemer. Contemporary secular assumption simply expect that time will continue as it always has, with the exception of human nuclear self-destruction or ecological ruin of the world. The modern sense of historical time includes the confidence that time will continue, unless cut off by human self-inflicted catastrophe. "Once dead, always dead" is a modern truism. And in retrospect, the texts of Jesus' resurrection and return as Judge of humankind become less credible and less troubling.

ANALYZING "JUDGMENT"

(As reminder, analyzing a text examines and probes that text in its contexts for meanings and implications that were not apparent at first sight.) The assumption in Judgment is that God is LORD, as in the Revised Standard Version (RSV) translation of the Bible. God outranks God's creation. That includes human beings, whom God creates in God's image. The fact that humans can know right from wrong, are aware that they are not self-created, can say both Yes and No to God and to their fellow-humans is God-created and God-intended. Such an option to affirm or reject God makes freely affirming, loving and serving God possible. Yet such freedom can be misused. All that is God-given and God-blessed can be turned inward and misused in self-serving and self-affirming ways. And God does not strike them dead on the spot! Instead God offers forgiving love and invites sinners to repent and to turn back to God and toward fellow humans. Assuming that all this was predictable, God would have concluded that these creatures were and remain worth the risk and the trouble. The right human response should have remembered their origin and dependence—indeed, their identity as creatures and as created in God's image.

The subjects of Judgment are all humankind, the living and—in due time—the resurrected dead. This Judgment evaluates thoughts, words and deeds and focuses on human conduct over a lifetime. It forms a Last Judgment in the sense that it is conclusive and without appeal, as far as the biblical texts go. In the sequence of events the New Testament Judgment precedes the destruction of the existing heaven and earth, corrupted by sin, and the subsequent renewal of both a redeemed earth and heaven for all eternity. At some point in the future the seemingly endless sequence of creation, loving, sinning, redeeming will cease—with humankind eternally divided between heaven and hell. And humans in effect have created their own judgment by lifelong choices. That means that God has given up on those who made the wrong existential choices. To conceive of the character of God as willing to leave unforgiven sinners in eternal hell (2 Thess 1:9) may reflect the suffering of those early Christians more than the character and Judgment of God.

PREPARATIONS?

There was a time when the prospect of divine Judgment was a very serious matter and called for forethought and preparation. It was important to be reconciled with one's adversaries lest the lack of forgiveness endangered one's own salvation. The Lord's Prayer links divine and human forgiveness:

"And forgive us our sins, for we ourselves forgive everyone indebted to us" (Luke 11:4). Soldiers faced special risks in regard to Judgment, since sudden death could deprive them of time to prepare, to repent of sins, to forgive and to receive forgiveness. Traditional prayers include the account humankind will have to render: "O merciful Creator.... Make us, we beseech thee, ever thankful for thy loving providence; and grant that we, remembering the account that we must one day give, may be faithful stewards of thy bounty."[1]

One speculates why divine Judgment has faded from Christian awareness and concern. Pervasive secularism plays a role. Avoiding religion would certainly exclude the worrisome aspects of religion. While God is still invoked on serious occasions, as in presidential addresses to the nation, the appeal will always be for God's favor and protection: "may God bless America." "May God forgive our national sins" or "may God have mercy on America" would be unforgivable politically. While the confession of sins is a regular feature of Christian worship, keeping sins non-personal, generic or nonspecific remains a prudent political practice.

CHRISTIAN AND PHILOSOPHICAL ETHICS

Assuming that philosophical ethics in a secular context remains a-religious, there are still similarities between Christian and philosophical perspectives. Both views insist on respect and person-standing for human beings. But the respective reasons differ. Philosophically, humans count as rational (thinking) and volitional (deciding) beings with a nod of appreciation to human evolution. Biblical or Christian approaches ascribe value to humans as creatures of God, related to and in the image of God. Indeed, all that exists and is good is initially from God. Human rationality, celebrated in philosophical ethics is God's blessings more than a human achievement for Christian eyes. Indeed, the awareness of being created and blessed by God in all aspects of life suffuses Christian self-awareness. Philosophical appreciation of being alive, talented and making a success of things would be a matter of having good genes, responsible parents, and the best of luck.

ANALOGOUS COVENANTS?

An analogy describes similarities between different things. Where to find a fitting analogy with the covenant between God and humans? The *covenant of marriage* recommends itself. The intent here is to gain insights

---

1. Episcopal Church, *Book of Common Prayer*, 208.

into the personal nature of God. Both relationships involve changes and adjustments from being single to function in relationship to another person (or Person). The relationship does not just bind but transforms former self-understanding. It enriches and delights through the presence and love of the other person. Marriage expands responsibilities: being answerable to another person to whom one is committed obligates a person to being faithful and answerable. Indeed, taking the other person (Person) into account becomes second nature. And when one has failed to do that, there is nothing to be done but to confess and ask to be forgiven. Being covenanted to God may become a source of encouragement and an incentive to mature. One is not alone and can reason and manage together. Analyzing Christian marriage and covenanting with God offers not just simple addition but may yield unexpected life-sustaining and—transforming implications

GOD IS PERSONAL

The God-created personal link between God and humans is God's self-manifestation to humans. It is this God-human encounter and relationship that atheism denies. To repeat, it is this personal and transforming relationship that is at stake between theists and atheists, not some theoretical issue of whether God exists. It is the surprising encounter with God—a transforming experience rather than an argument or series of reasons that attests to the reality of God. God attests to God-Self. The living reality and presence of God, not the best of human arguments, transforms seekers into finders. The biblical God is personal, creating, blessing, loving human beings. Prayers use personal pronouns, as "my God," "our Lord" and "our Father." The fact that one can pray and reasonably expect God to hear and to respond reflects God's personal nature. Biblically, God not only creates, loves, and blesses humans but expects love, worship, a transformed life from those so blessed. The popular notion that God is looking for believers in God actually misleads. God seeks disciples, servants, worshipers, lovers of God, qualities that passed belief long ago! "Believer" is simply too head-focused, too neutral and tame a word. What "lover" worth that designation could ever be adequately described as "believer"?

By way of contrast, impersonal concepts of God would be "a creative and guiding force in the universe," "the power that sustains all existence" or "an inaccessible Being that created and sustains our universe. Christian ethics seeks transformed responsible seeing and doing in all human relationships—with God in mind. That makes all relationships and living itself religious. Christian faith and ethics form triangular connections between

God, self, and others. The triangular logic of Christian existence, visualized in the triangle diagram in chapter 2, all signify personal relationships.

The personal quality of the interrelationship between God and believers distinguishes Christian ethics from all secular ethics, whether deontological ethics (universal rule-based) or utilitarian ethics (greatest good for the greatest number). Christian ethics is God-relational; it looks to the character and will of God to discern what is fitting, right and good. And, of course, it looks to God for the vision, courage, and strength to enact what is right and good.

THE LAST JUDGMENT

The Last Judgment is the ultimate but not final feature of this moral and personal relational affinity with God. The review in that Judgment is retrospective and personal as well as being communal and social-political. The review includes public and political dimensions of life, despite the modern tendency to conceive the God-relationship as merely individualistic, personal, one on one. In contrast to humans, God has flawless sight and perfect memory. The Last Judgment is God's review of how humans lived their lives, individually and communally. And in that review Christians (and all humans) will witness how they have lived: *as seen through God's eyes!* Christian ethics includes word of such Judgment—as due notice.[2]

NEW TESTAMENT ASPIRATIONS

Historical secular aspirations have been remarkably different from Christian visions. Empire banners celebrated the "Glory of Rome." The Nazis envisioned a "Thousand-Year Reich." The Marxist "Classless Society" was to be the hope of the oppressed. "Making America Great Again" still appeals as a political banner. By contrast, New Testament visions relinquish hopes for communal self-redemptive success. The New Testament focus on hope and source of moral direction is God, offered in the transforming return of Jesus. Preparations for such saving events focus not on movers and shakers but on helping the least of God's children. Feeding the hungry, offering water to the thirsty, welcoming strangers, clothing the naked, visiting the sick and imprisoned—these exemplify Christian responsibilities. And the

---

2. *Due notice* is a legal term. It means information that must be given or made available to a particular person or to the public within a legally mandated period of time so that its recipient will have the opportunity to respond to a situation or to allegations that affect the individual's or public's legal rights or duties—and sins.

reason for such acts is God's identification with the likes of these. "Truly I tell you, just as you did it to one of the least of these who are members of my family, you did it to me" (Matt 25:40). This text expresses the heart of Christian ethics. Prospectively it offers clues to what might count when it comes to the Judgment of God, as argued below.

The logic or nature of the charitable acts summarized above for helping the helpless is God's identification with humans who are living on the margins of community. Their standing or social status remains minimal. They are the persons with whom God identifies, singles out, worries about, points to. God is not an egalitarian here. In contrast to the image of justice, the blindfolded statue holding the scales of justice, God *sees* these marginal humans and points others to them. These are not images to which one is drawn naturally nor do they normally invite a second look. God's concerns express the logic of parental love. The child who is sick, handicapped, troubled takes precedence in attention and care. To enlarge the dimensions of such divine parental care, the poor, the meek, the merciful, the peacemakers, the wrongly maligned, the generous are at the center of God's focus and attention. Such are the apple of God's eye. Such is the character of God. Peacemakers, non-resisters, non-judgers, good fruit bearers, hearers and doers of Jesus's words, debt forgivers, non-worriers—such are the salt of the earth.

JUDGMENT AND THE MEANINGS OF DEATH

While the biblical God is said to be near to humans (Ps 145:18), aware even of their inmost thoughts, humans may do their own thing unimpeded. Biblical convictions insist that since humans owe their life to God, they owe God an account or judgment of their life-conduct. Judging the quality of a human life is a serious matter. One must resist using the popular neologism *lifestyle* here. That term invokes an esthetic context (matters of style) and reduces morality to esthetic taste. In the context of Judgment, morality is not a matter of style but becomes ultimately serious, a matter of life or death.

In the Judgment, both the living and those raised from the dead will be held to account. God's Judgment includes raising the dead. God, who, having created life initially, can and will do so again. But since the topics of eternal life and final death are involved, and since all humans will find themselves summoned, popular meanings of death may merit review.

MEANINGS OF DEATH

Secular perspectives of death divide into a monistic and a dualist concept. The monistic view simply asserts that dead is dead. Humans cease to live mentally, bodily, spiritually. There are no immortal remains; no disembodied eternal souls. The echoes of human lives remain in the memories of the living, to be sure. For a time. A lasting and reliable record of human lives exists in the in the memory of the biblical God. The eternal God remembers human lives in detail and accuracy. Biblically, humans are earthlings. They "return to the ground, for out of it you were taken; you are dust and to dust you shall return" (Gen 3:19). From this mortal vantage, the dead are really dead. They are not in a better place. They are not with beloved others who died before them. Family reunions occur *at* death, not *in* death. Dead is dead. Except, in Christian faith, for a biblical postscript (described subsequently).

A more popular, more consoling secular concept of death, also held uncritically by many Christians, conceives of death in dualistic terms. The body dies. But the soul—the human spiritual and mental self—survives and is conceived as immortal. The soul may also be understood as the real or most important self. The consoling or reassuring quality of this perspective reveals itself in death notices: Obituaries, if they mention religion, manifest optimism in regard to the departed, whose spirit moves upward and onward, to a better place and—it remains implied by the recitation of the departed's virtues—to a welcome verdict in the Last Judgment. This dualist understanding of human death is popular since it offers hope that the best part of us—our mental, spiritual selves—survive death. But such dualism of human mental-spiritual survival is problematic in a biblical context. Dust, no longer enlivened by the breath of God, returns to dust. Perhaps the notion of spiritual-mental survival arose from the influence of Greek Platonic dualism. The belief in Purgatory, where souls could atone for less than deadly sins and prepare for Judgment assumes a soul surviving physical death. But it seems that Purgatory is no longer a live concept. And the claim that human minds or souls survive death lacks biblical sources.

Individual life after death became conceivable and controversial in the time of Jesus. The conviction that God raised Jesus from the dead three days after his crucifixion gave disciples of Jesus hope that they, too, would be raised. Jesus became "the firstborn from the dead" (Col 1:18). That required adjustment of the idea of divine Judgment. Whereas Judgment had been conceived as a divine act in regard to a chosen people in the warnings of Israel's prophets, accountability to God now extends to individuals living and dead in a post-resurrection context.

CULTURAL INDIVIDUALISM AND GOD'S JUDGMENT OF NATIONS?

In individualistic modern cultures the concept of communal judgment has faded or even disappeared. There was an acknowledged sense of moral failure in Germany after the Second World War. The memory of the Holocaust—the mass destruction of European Jews and other minorities—has become a German national obligation. The American memory of slavery is an ongoing responsibility as well. The German expression in regard to the Holocaust has been described as "the inability to deal with its past." That may actually hold true for other nations as well. In earlier religious cultures one knew how to deal with national sins by naming, denouncing, and repenting specific sins. Modern secular times lack the contemporary voices of Israel's ancient prophets who warned nations of divine judgment over the plight of the poor and exploited. Contemporary national sins tend to remain unnamed, undenounced, unrepented. Along with the modern disappearance of the word "sin," national confessions of sins belong to the past. And that tends to prevent repentance, penance, forgiveness and closure.

A CHRISTIAN POSTSCRIPT TO DEATH

The difference between the secular dead-is-dead and the Christian version of the same concept is the postscript offered by God. The New Testament offers an epilogue to the dead-is-dead view. The human-divine story is to be continued. Human lives have an epilogue. At the end of historical time, God, who remembers the dead, will raise or resurrect them to new life, with both a new body and a new soul. *Soul* means the non-physical mortal and spiritual dimension of the self. Paul, the author of First Corinthians, declares (speculates) that the raised, renewed, restored human being will be imperishable and immortal (1 Cor 15:42–58). Since not all thus raised will be judged to be righteous or forgiven, some will not survive the Judgment well.

THE JUDGE

God's resurrection of Jesus, made a decisive difference for the identity of Jesus in relation to God (the Father). Dead being dead, Jesus *was raised* from the dead. The passive form here is vital, since being dead is beyond all thought and action. Being raised confirmed Jesus' identity as God's Messiah. And as the "first born of the dead" (Rev 1:5) he is said to be the Judge of the living and the dead. Jesus himself, however, before his resurrection seems to have regarded God, the Father, as the Judge of humankind. Since Jesus taught and acted in the name of God, that may hold to be true as well when it comes to Judging humankind.

Whether or not Jesus will be the Judge in the Great Judgment, his message focused on the coming rule of God. Get ready for God! God is near! Prepare yourself. Pray for it: "Your kingdom come. Your will be done on earth as it is in heaven" (Matt 10:6). Anticipating the ruling of God through transformed conduct, Jesus uses a pattern of "you have heard that it was said" (the traditional demands of biblical law) and "but I say to you" (Jesus' higher demands responding to God's character and nearness). The Sermon on the Mount (Matt 5–7) offers a wide range of Jesus' moral intensification of God's traditional law in anticipation of God's new ruling-in-fact. Jesus does not reject traditional laws, but seeks to fulfill them (Matt 5:17–20) and transforming them in a spirit of love. Such good works shine as lights "and give glory to your Father in heaven" (Matt 5:16).

Human moral judgment will itself be judged by Jesus/God in a future beyond time. Humankind individually, communally, inclusively and unavoidably—both the living and the resurrected dead—will be held to account. To be accountable implies that humans owe God sound answers in regard to what they did with "their" lives—the lives entrusted to them. Human lives belong to God. In contrast, in a secular culture in which lives are assumed to belong to the individual one has the right to do what one wants with that life (within reason and law). Biblically however, human lives belong to God who entrusts those lives to humans, who serve God as stewards. The double love commands provide the norms: loving God back and sharing that love with others.

CRITERIA FOR JUDGMENT

God, having created humankind for loving God back and for sharing God's love with each other, was disappointed early on by how humankind turned out (Gen 6:5–7). Though not in fact making an end of it all when it became clear that humans preferred to do their own thing, God made sure that it was clear what was expected of them. From the very beginnings of biblical religion, God insisted on moral norms for humankind, guiding human conduct with specific laws, commandments, warnings, insistence on justice and disciplinary acts. Ancient Israel's prophets warned an unrepentant people to turn (repent) and to become who they were meant to be—serving God as witness to the nations. Years of exile of the chosen people was God's judgment against them and was intended to restore them to their calling.

Judgment

The Judaic and Christian God does not just guide human conduct but loves and identifies with human beings. Feeding the hungry, offering water to the thirsty, welcoming strangers, clothing the naked, visiting the sick and imprisoned—God identifies with the persons in need of such help. God invites humankind to share God's identification with the least of humankind. When that does happen, God acknowledges that *as if it were done to God*! "Truly I tell you, just as you did it to one of the least of these who are members of my family, you did it to me" (Matt 25:40). This text touches on the very heart of God and of Christian ethics!

HELP WANTED!

Unfortunately, God's choices and priorities lack cultural, social and even personal appeal. Natural inclinations look toward oneself and one's own, directions different from where biblical traditions insist God to be pointing. Martin Luther warned that humans are curved in on themselves rather than outward toward God and others. Obeying and following God does not rely on natural inclinations. It requires help. The Christian church is a place of help, where worship can turn persons of faith into new and helpful directions. "So help me God" has other uses than verifying an oath. "Our soul waits for the LORD, he is our help and shield" (Ps 33:20).

If "the least of the members of God's family" have standing with God or God is standing with them, that requires cultural reality adjustments for those who expect to give an account to God of what they did with their lives. Jesus certainly insisted on moral preparation for the great Judgment to come. Neither Jesus nor God would be egalitarians when it comes to moral responsibilities. Helping the most in need takes precedent. That is parental logic: the child who is sick, handicapped, troubled comes first for family attention and care. The poor in spirit and the literally poor, the meek, the merciful, the pure in heart, the peacemakers, the wrongly maligned, the generous are the apple of God's eye.

SALVATION AS DOING OR BELIEVING?

There is a venerable misconception that being Christian is matter of believing more than (or even without) moral responses. The source of such conviction may well be the ancient Christian creeds: Apostle (120–250), Nicene (325) and Athanasian (sixth century) creeds. These creeds are dedicated to affirmations of divine Trinity, insisting on the identity of Jesus as God. The first sentences of the Athanasian Creed sets the theme: "Whoever wants to be saved should above all cling to the catholic faith. Whoever does not guard it whole and inviolable will doubtless perish eternally." In these three historical distillations of what counts when it comes to salvation is Christology, sincere belief in Jesus' divine status. Remarkably, these "faith summaries" omit any imperatives for actions that would witness to or express such faith. Here true belief saves the believer. Christian ethics seems lost in the search for the right theological affirmations.

Such one-sided insistence on right belief proves to be flawed and misleading for several reasons. For one, it assumes that the relationship between God and believers is one in which the human understanding of God must be attuned to the true nature of God and of Jesus. This insistence on knowing exactly who God is or Jesus is reminds one of magical incantations: one must get the words just right in order to achieve the intended effect. Yet in fact, one never has flawless knowledge about anyone, especially not of oneself. How much less can humans conceive the true nature or character of the holy God?

Moreover, the ancient creeds' theological focus makes the Christian confession into a head-thing. Getting the nature of God straight is essential to one's salvation. Yet biblically God does not command that humans understand God. The command is to love God and neighbor. And such love does not require theological sophistication or getting the nature of Jesus or God straight.

Perhaps it is also true that creedal insisting on the right conception of God or Jesus focuses on one's own faith. Rather than striving for a relationship with God in which one seeks God's presence, such creedal correctness seems to be so self-aware that it creates a mirror effect. One has to be ever so careful to get salvation truths just right. One eye on God, the other on one's own faith. No wonder that these ancient creeds had no eye left for Christian ethics.

Given Jesus' emphasis on renewed and intensified obedience to God's law, as in the Sermon on the Mount (Matt 5:1—7:27), it seems implausible that, in God's Judgment, confessing a creed would trump a life dedicated to helping "the least of these" who are members of God's family (Matt 25:40). God insists that help for those most in need take precedence over affirming true beliefs. That holds in the Letter of James and in Matthew's Gospel. The Letter of James: "So faith by itself, if it has no works, is dead" (Jas 2:17). And affirmatively, "be doers of the word and not merely hearers who deceive themselves" (Jas 1:22).

BELIEVING AS KEY TERM FOR CHRISTIANS?

Throughout these chapters "believers" has been used as a synonym for Christians and Jews. In a secular culture, that distinguishes the secular from the religious. But the term *believers* not only leads but may mislead when used as synonym for biblical faith. While *believers* takes on special meaning in a secular culture—as an exception to the general shift toward nonbelief—the term focuses on only one aspect of what it means to be Christian or Jew. The word *believers* can mislead by implying that believing is central or crucial to being a disciple of Jesus or of God. God may not be looking for believers but for *servants*. Or God may be searching for the merciful, given that mercy is one of God's key character traits. Again, God may hope for followers who help the least among us. Believing seems to be the only self-focused word here. It describes one feature of what it means to be Christian. The biblical commandment is to love God or, more accurately, to love God back. Loving God has bypassed believing in God way back. That holds for *serving* God as well.

Regular use of *believers* in these pages also may have misled the reader into searching for key truths to be believed. Certainly, Jesus intended to be believed when he preached his message of the near kingdom of God. But believing may not be as crucial as its advocates tend to assume. The *content* of what to believe tends to vary with age and maturity. Eventually believers may suspect certain changes over time with what they deemed essential to believe. In an analogical sense, this phenomenon resembles rereading old love letters written to one's spouse: Wincing, one no longer recognizes the lines as one's own and gratefully marvels that "she married me anyway!" The welcome recognition may be that the current self who wrote those awful lines long ago has left the old self behind. There may be a similar revision of what one takes to be essential Christian beliefs. And that is surely a good thing in that the relationship with God is alive. Being alive requires a tolerance for change and the hope that God's patience does not wear out when it comes to slow learners.

Another caution about *believing* is that the word focuses on humans. Revelation, in contrast, refers to God acting. It remains important not to confuse these words with each other. Believing seems self-reflective. Definitionally, that word does not reach out to others (except to God). Contrast the words "responsible" or "answerable." Those two words are inter-relational or communal. A biblically truer sense of the relationship between God and humans may be "God in search of humans." Giving humans credit for starting the God-human relationship is not a promising move. We may simply have been unaware of God when God initially reached out to us.

Assuming that everything important begins with humans is secular. To give that a respectable name, it is anthropocentric, even in religion. A truer sense of sequence when it comes to Christian faith is to begin with God. Christian ethics assumes God's saving and redemptive love. *Christian Ethics*, then, is the disciplined reflection of the meaning originating in or from God's self-disclosure. The working out of what is implied is extensive. Just as working out the meaning and implications of the wedding vow. Christian ethics is an intrinsic feature of that "working out."

And yet, who knows or who can set limits to the ways of God with humans? As best I know, faithful belief does not begin with affirmation of a creed, even if Christian instruction may begin there. Rather, Christian faith arises in experiencing the presence of the living God and responding to the holiness (the otherness) of God. Fitting analysis of the God-experience require time, reflection, personal and communal and God-focused language. "Experiencing the presence of God" is what "revelation" means. Being able to speak or write adequately about a God-encounter is quite another matter. In short, "believers" focuses on a human experience and therefore on humans. But the God-experience centers on God. As in the words of the psalmist: "O taste and see that the LORD is good" (Ps 34:8).

Jesus expects his disciples to believe his words. Here believing serves doing, acting, helping, serving. God seeks servants not mere believers. Jesus may have had the misunderstanding of faith as belief without its active expression in mind when he warned,

> Not everyone who says to me "Lord, Lord," will enter the kingdom of heaven, but only the one who does the will of my Father in heaven. On that day many will say to me, "Lord, Lord, did we not prophesy in your name, and cast out demons in your name, and many deeds of power in your name?" Then I will declare to them, "I never knew you; go away from me, you evildoers." (Matt 7:21–23)

The historical meaning of belief and salvation has undergone great controversy and played a key role in the disruption of the Roman Catholic Church and the separation of Protestants. Here "salvation" refers to the context of the Great Judgment. To be saved implies surviving God's Great Judgment. Differences over the criteria of divine Judgment separated Christians. The traditional Protestant version of being saved is that God's saving grace cannot be earned because Jesus' sacrifice on the Cross paid the price for human sin. Salvation can only be received gratis since God's grace cannot be earned. It is in grateful response to being forgiven that doing (helping, loving, restoring and the like) becomes fitting and right. Here believing in

God's saving act counts. Jesus speaking: "This is the work of God, that you believe in him whom he has sent" (John 6:29). "Those who believe in him [in the Son] are not condemned" (John 3:18). "But to all who received him, who believed in his name, he gave power to become children of God" (John 1:12). "And this is his commandment, that we should believe in the name of his Son Jesus Christ and love one another" (1 John 3:23). As best we know, such believing in Christ, linked with practiced love, would be redemptive in the Judgment.

Acts of love remain or unexpectedly become criteria for salvation. In effect, do this if you seek eternal life with God! Or, if one seeks a guiding moral principle for action, Jesus' new law seeks to *imitate God's character*: "Be perfect . . . as your heavenly Father is perfect" (Matt 5:48). If "perfect" proves too ambitious or daunting, Jesus' Sermon on the Mount (Matt 5–7) looks explicitly to doers of caring actions—without word about right beliefs. Jesus' directness in the Sermon insists on peacemaking, being salt of the earth and light of the world righteousness, non-resisters and enemy-lovers, debt-forgivers, God-servers and God-trusters, non-worriers, non-judgers, good-fruit bearers, hearers and doers of Jesus' words. Responsible doing, acting, living count when God is transforming the world! Reciting faithfully one of the traditional ancient creeds in total sincerity when being Judged seems remarkably irrelevant and misconceived.

THE MEANING OF LIFE: LOVE

What proves to be clearer and indisputable about God's Judgment, is that God, who loves human beings, makes human love indispensable in imitating God. The two greatest commandments include love for God and love for humans. Specifically important is loving humans who live at the margins of society or are mistreated. Humans live by being loved and loving, not by knowing much or perhaps even believing much. There is no divine imperative to be smart. But being loved by God and others and loving in response is literally what humans are made for! The command to love God does include "with all your mind" (Matt 22:37), but in that text mind serves love. Love is what counts. And love actively serves God and neighbor. Therein lies the *meaning of life!* Biblical traditions have never been secretive or mysterious on that score.

The reasonableness that humans should be judged in terms of how they lived made good sense to traditional biblical believers. Since human beings do not own their lives but are its stewards, they must give an account of their stewardship. Assumed here is the concept of God as Creator and

LORD who retains ownership of humans. That includes children. Begetting or having children does not make their parents into their owners, even if they claim their offspring as "ours" or "mine." Parents are entrusted with "their" children. Biblically, all humans are created by God and owe their lives to God.

By contrast, the *modern secular* notion is that each person owns his or her own life, has a right to such ownership, and is responsible primarily to him- or herself. Here standing or having worth is self-generated in the capacity to think and to choose, not derived or endowed. The ancient, and even medieval notion would foster a sense of dependence and gratitude, though overshadowed by the hardships of premodern life, such as deep poverty, plague, serfdom, and violence. A modern secular person may not even be aware of such traditional biblical concepts of God's ownership of human lives. Meeting God, if such be a description of God's Judgment, would be surprising in more ways than one. Human life is a trust not a case of human ownership.

CREEDAL REFERENCES TO THE GREAT OR LAST JUDGMENT

An ultimate or final divine Judgment is included in major Christian creeds. "[The Lord Jesus Christ] will come again to judge the living and the dead. At his coming all people shall rise bodily to give an account of their deeds. Those who have done good will enter eternal life, those who have done evil will enter eternal fire" (Athanasian Creed). The Nicene Creed speaks of the Lord Jesus Christ "who ascended into heaven . . . from thence he shall come again, with glory, to judge the quick and the dead." The Apostles' Creed is almost identical on this topic to the Nicene version.

The Athanasian Creed cited above insists that "Those who have done good will enter eternal life, those who have done evil will enter eternal fire." The Christians of the fifth century AD who created this creed were more focused on the trinitarian identity of Jesus than on a postmortem Judgment of human deeds. Indeed, as described earlier, these creeds remain silent about Christian ethics except for the warning cited above.

POST-DEATH SPECULATION

Mentioning Purgatory, a religious invention to create meaning and hope for the soul in the time between death and resurrection, may be the fitting

Judgment

occasion for acknowledging how little is known and knowable about anything beyond the fact that humans are mortal but hope for life after death. The biblical story initially envisioned human existence as mortal, as in the expression "from dust to dust" (Gen 3:19) and more explicitly later: human beings have no advantage over animals. "For the fate of humans and the fate of animals is the same; as one dies, so dies the other. They all have the same breath, and humans have no advantage over the animals; for all is vanity. All go to one place; all are from the dust, and all turn to dust again" (Eccl 3:19–20).

But in the time of Jesus, this ancient belief became questionable. And the conviction that God raised Jesus from the dead after his crucifixion established hope among Christians that disciples of Jesus would be raised as well. Jesus became "the firstborn from the dead" (Col 1:18). That in turn required adjustment of the concept of divine Judgment. What before had meant the judgment of a people with a divine mission, the people of Israel or the people of God, now extends to *individuals* who will be resurrected and will be included in divine post-mortem and post-resurrection Judgment.

In an individualistic modern and secular culture, the concept of communal judgment has faded. Modern times lack ancient prophets who warned nations of divine judgment resulting from communal indifference to the plight of the poor and exploited. Contemporary national sins tend to remain unnamed, undenounced, unrepented. "May God bless America" remains as the pious close of political rhetoric. The plea, "may God have mercy on America" remains unspoken and unheard. At most, one may hear of mistakes and regrets. National confessions belong to the past. And that closes the present to forgiveness. A history of slavery and of racism may be left behind but without confession, forgiveness and closure.

Secularized modern times not only dismiss a living Lord but avoid after-death speculations. That includes speculations over having to give an account of this life in a future beyond death. The modern imagination no longer envisions medieval images of all humans being weighed with heavenly scales and of the devil waiting nearby to snatch the souls of the damned. But a sense of what used to be called sins persists. And so does the need for making moral sense of one's life and the need for justice and forgiveness. For Christians, the hope for human resurrection remains linked with God's resurrection of Jesus. And humans' answer for the conduct of their lives to God remains a *present* responsibility.

APOCALYPTIC JUDGMENT AS IMMINENT

Turning again to the biblical past, apocalyptic Jewish writings first appeared circa 250 B.C. and continued well into the first centuries AD. Apocalypticism is the belief in the near advent of the apocalypse, the violent destruction of the world. Preceded by catastrophes, the ultimate destiny or end of the world as now known is near. Divine Judgment is part of this ultimate destiny of all human life, The inclusion of previous human lives will take place by God resurrecting the dead. The result of Judgment will be the salvation of the faithful and the eternal punishment of those condemned. In a post-Judgment transformed existence God will rule the world. And renewed and transformed human lives will finally become what they should have been all along.

Such anticipation of a cataclysmic transformation of the world not only reflects a rejection of this world as it has always existed, it abandons any hope of human endeavors to mend the world's flaws. Only God's intervention will offer hope for life as it was meant to be. Such hope can comfort and encourage the faithful in difficult times. It warned humankind of living in extraordinary and critical times. Indeed, theirs were the end times, dominated by evil and by suffering of the faithful. A new age and a new creation would follow in a new age. The technical term that describes such phenomena is *eschatology*: predictions about the ultimate outcome of human affairs. Apocalyptically, God has finally run out of patience with human evil and will intervene to set things right. The evil to be overcome includes supernatural forces and requires more than human power to vanquish. Key events of divine intervention will be the resurrection and judgment of the living and the dead and of reward and punishment in an eternal transformed future existence.

The Christian story began in such turbulent times. God sent God's Son to the chosen people with the same mission as that of Ancient Israel: To live in justice and mercy as a model to all nations. Unrecognized and opposed, Jesus proclaimed the ruling of God, healed and taught but was rejected and executed. The Christian witness insists that Jesus was raised from the dead! It was that divine attestation of restoring life after death that confirmed believers of Jesus' identity. And, by identifying with Jesus, the church saw itself as called to share his mission, to proclaim and to live Israel's ancient calling—in the name of Jesus. For eyes of Christian faith, Jesus as Son of God plays a vital role in this cataclysmic transformation. God's raising Jesus from the dead—"the firstborn of the dead"—signifies the beginning of an inclusive universal renewal. Jesus was expected to return soon to judge (Judge!) the living and the dead.

The Great Judgment implies that human moral judgment will itself be judged by God in a near future beyond ordinary time. Humankind individually, communally, inclusively and unavoidably—both the living and the resurrected dead—will be held to account. To be accountable implies that humans owe God answers in regard to what they did with "their" lives, the lives *entrusted* to them. God retains ownership of human lives. For Christians in modern times, that transforms the meaning of human life from self-ownership into stewardship. In God's Judgment, such stewardship owed to God would be measured by the ancient double love commands: love God back and share God's love with others.

EXAMPLES OF CHRISTIAN APOCALYPTIC TEXTS

Three samples of apocalyptic texts follow. In the first, humankind "will see 'the Son of Man coming on the clouds of heaven' with power and great glory. And he will send out his angels with a loud trumpet call, and they will gather his elect from the four winds, from one end of heaven to the other" (Matt 24:30–31).

From the New Testament book of Revelation:

> And I saw the dead, great and small standing before the throne, and books were opened. Also another book was opened, the book of life. And the dead were judged according to their works as recorded in the books. And the sea gave up the dead that were in it . . . and all were judged according to what they had done. (Rev 20:12–13)

The following chapter in the book of Revelation records the replacement of the old by a new heaven and earth.

> Then I saw a new heaven and a new earth; for the first heaven and the first earth had passed away, and the sea was no more. And I saw the holy city, the new Jerusalem, coming down out of heaven from God, prepared as a bride adorned for her husband. And I heard a loud voice from the throng saying, "See, the home of God is among mortals." (Rev 21:1–3)

Such are anticipated features of God's intention.

CHRISTIAN EXPECTATIONS AND ISRAEL'S PAST

Christian anticipation of divine intervention connects with Israel's ancient past. Divine Judgment arises out of ancient biblical roots. Biblical judgment originated from God's response to the failures of Adam and Eve. Their judgment deprived them of life in the Garden, of eternal life, and exposed humankind to life's hardships. After that, matters went from bad to worse in Genesis chapters 4 through 11.

> The LORD saw that the wickedness of humankind was great in the earth and that every inclination of the thoughts of their hearts was only evil continually. And the LORD was sorry that he had made humankind on the earth, and it grieved him to his heart. So the LORD said "I will blot out from the earth the human beings I have created." (Gen 6:5–7)

The great flood ensues. And yet, God tries again with Noah. The pattern of human moral failure, God's warning and intervening judgment and beginning again repeats itself historically—as in Israel's prophetic texts and in the story of the exile and return. Ancient Israel understood itself as a people chosen by God to be a blessing to humankind by witnessing to the love and justice of God in its life and conduct. This oddly chosen people—they were nobodies as nations go—was/is to serve God's efforts to teach humankind by example what humans were meant to be: children of God loving and serving God and each other as God's witness to all nations.

Despite repeated warnings and judgments, Israel's mission remained more aspirational than realized. The Christian story connects here: God sent God's Son to the chosen people with the same mission as for ancient Israel. Unrecognized and opposed, Jesus proclaimed the ruling of God, healed and taught but was rejected and executed. The Christian witness is that God raised Jesus from the dead! It was that divine attestation of restoring life from death that verified Jesus' identity for believers. And, by identifying with Jesus, the church saw itself as called to share his mission, to proclaim and to live Israel's ancient calling to become a blessing to the world—in the name of Jesus.

JUDGMENT DELAYED

Despite expectations, Judgment as the unique divine event was and remains delayed. While Jesus may have declared the advent of God, Christian hopes focus on Jesus returning as Lord and Judge. That second coming of Jesus or Parousia (arrival) was delayed but not relinquished. That event was thought to be imminent by early Christians. Jesus himself may have anticipated the end of time: "Truly I tell you, this generation will not pass away until all these things have taken place" (Matt 24:34). New Testament literature expects the divine advent through a transforming and near intervention of God.

When this second coming of Jesus delayed and delayed, such postponement called for explanation. For example, God counts time differently from humans:

> But do not ignore this one fact, beloved, that with the Lord one day is like a thousand years, and a thousand years are like one day. The Lord is not slow about his promise, as some think of slowness, but is patient with you, not wanting any to perish, but all to come to repentance. But the day of the Lord will come like a thief, and then the heavens will pass away with a loud noise, and the elements will be dissolved with fire, and the earth and everything that is done on it will be disclosed. (2 Pet 3:8–10)

The vision remains. Its understanding and intensity may vary over time. But in the confidence of believers, a promise of God outlasts time. Especially in difficult and trying times Christian communities hope and look for divine intervention, transformation and ultimate justice. Until that time, "in accordance with his promise, we wait for new heavens and a new earth, where righteousness is at home" (2 Pet 3:13). In times of great hardship and persecution, the Christian church remembers and reaffirms these apocalyptic hopes and expectations.

REWARDS?

An unexpected feature of moral instruction in the Sermon on the Mount is that Jesus does not just teach an intensified or radicalized ethics but that he repeatedly points out its rewards—five times in Matt 6! God will reward those who obeyed Jesus' radical teachings. Giving alms generously is storing up treasures in heaven (Matt 6:19–21). Apparently, Jesus was not troubled by the thought that looking for rewards may imply self-interest rather than genuine altruism or love of others. In other near-by texts Jesus does insist on serving God above all other priorities, including self-interest. "You cannot serve God and wealth" (Matt 6:24). "But strive first for the kingdom of God and his righteousness" (Matt 6:33) and the necessities of life will be provided as well.

Lest one concludes that striving for reward in doing the right thing inevitably assumes self-interest and prioritizes self, there is another rendition of the logic of rewards: In deeply caring human relationships, persons can become self-forgetful. A spouse, a parent, a child even, knowing what would please the beloved, may do something that extends beyond recognized or normal responsibilities, perhaps something extravagant. The motivation can be self-forgetful. The intent is expectation that this will make her/him smile. Pleasing God by caring for the needs of those whom God calls "members of his own family" (Matt 25:40) may be a self-forgetful generous act that might indeed make God smile. And that, just as in other genuinely loving relationships, is the reward. Its memory may well last beyond a lifetime. God's memory of it surely will last. This understanding of rewards may apply not only to the specific text in Matthew but may hold for Judgment as such.

PUNISHMENTS

Jesus the Savior will return as Jesus the Judge. As the counterpoint to the promise of rewards, God's Judgment threatens punishments. Jesus speaking as divine Judge: "Not everyone who says to me, 'Lord, Lord,' will enter the kingdom of heaven, but only the one who does the will of my Father in heaven" (Matt 7:21). And again Jesus: "everyone who hears these words and does not act on them will be like a foolish man who built his house on sand" (Matt 7:26). When tested, "great was its fall!" (Matt 7:27). That warning concludes the Sermon on the Mount. Could it be that though the house was in ruins its owner survived? A parable just a few verses earlier offers no hope of surviving: Fruit trees are judged by their fruit and "Every tree that does not bear good fruit is cut down and thrown into the fire" (Matt 7:19).

The Judgment focuses on Jesus, resurrected and transformed. This is the king, the Son of Man in his glory accompanied by angels, who pronounces Judgment on humankind. This Jesus, endorsed as the Son of God in his resurrection, then returning to humankind, holds humans accountable. His unique link with God has the effect that the judgment of Jesus is also the Judgment of God. The Judgment of Jesus/God originates in divine self-identification with the least, the least or the losers among humans. Here Jesus/God take sides. Such favoritism, again, reflects parental partiality for a child in need, sick, handicapped, in trouble. Whoever helps, aids, cares for such a child blesses the parents who identify with the child—in this case God identifying with the least among humans.

Theologically, God is the parent-a-step-removed. Jesus addresses God as Father. That Father is the God who made heaven and earth, created all living beings, formed humans into kin who reflect God's image. Responding to God's will—the purpose of Christian ethics—requires obeying that will, as in "your will be done on earth" (Matt 6:10). Those who actually do that are blessed as the righteous with eternal life. Good news! The "accursed," on the other hand, did none of that to the king or to the least with whom the king identifies. Their Judgment permits no excuse, destroys all hope, lacks all mercy: "You that are accursed, depart from me into eternal fire prepared for the devil and his angels" (Matt 25:41).

APOCALYPTIC WARNINGS

To pause over the closing sentence above, one may find that biblical text both startling and surprising: "accursed"? "eternal fire"? excruciating pain forever? Are these literally the words of Jesus and therefore the Judgment of God?

Nor are these apocalyptic texts unique:

> For it is indeed just of God to repay with affliction those who afflict you, and to give relief to the afflicted as well as to us, when the Lord Jesus is revealed from heaven with his mighty angels in flaming fire, inflicting vengeance on those who do not know God and on those who do not obey the gospel of our Lord Jesus. These will suffer punishment of eternal destruction, separated from the presence of the Lord and from the glory of his might. (2 Thess 1:6–9)

And a last damning text: after the inclusive Judgment of humankind according to what they had done, "Then Death and Hades were thrown into the lake of fire. This is the second death, the lake of fire; and anyone whose name was not found written in the book of life was thrown into the lake of fire" (Rev 20:14–15).

Associating such damning texts with Jesus, Son of God and Savior of humankind, can startle the reader. The Savior becomes the condemning Judge? Could these texts express early Christian resentments over their own mistreatment? Perhaps the "afflictions" of these early disciples have evoked a bitterness that spills over into their concept of God who will punish the mistreatment of early Christians?

The cited apocalyptic texts contradict key character qualities of the biblical God, presenting Jesus *as a hanging Judge*. To be sure, many biblical texts warn or declare divine judgment against human pride, injustice, indifference to the plight of the poor and oppressed. But such judgments usually reflected remedial intent. By contrast, the apocalyptic texts cited above, prove to be irremediably punitive. God has given up permanently on these sinners and extends their punishment into all eternity. This embittered God decrees eternal punitive justice. The God of love (1 John 4:8) becomes unrecognizable in those apocalyptic texts. The mission and calling of Jesus—"God did not send the Son into the world to condemn the world, but in order that the world might be saved through him" (John 3:17)—seems forgotten or abandoned.

Divine punitive justice replaces the merciful justice of God. Not only are sinners lost in the sense of being condemned to a second death, their suffering is to be prolonged, even eternal. Could the blessed who are invited to live with God forever—those who shared the kindness of God with their fellow humans—be content to know of the misery of those eternal losers? Could God the Father? Could the Lamb of God? That Judgment is described as final, beyond appeal and eternal. A helping and merciful God for sinners has no standing in this apocalyptic cosmos.

Such moral dualism affects Christology, the understanding of the mission and character of Jesus. The hope for the salvation of a sinful world is relinquished. Salvation is now restricted to saints. Analogously, the fate of the damned is also determined—without God and without hope. Such moral dualism offers an alternative, more threatening, and less redemptive version of divine Judgment. It seems incompatible with biblical theology that offers the good news of God's redemptive salvation to all humankind.

QUESTIONING APOCALYPTIC TEXTS

Apocalyptic texts focus on the future. One would think that one reason for doing that might be that the present disappoints or remains hopeless. The future must be better than the now! Biblical prophets predicted a future as a warning, however. It seems reasonable that one warns of the results of dangerous present practices. Israel's historical prophets anticipated cataclysmic outcomes of dangerous current conduct, as national disasters following idolatrous practices: bad practices, bad results. Apocalyptic texts display images more than texts as warnings. "You that are accursed, depart from me into eternal fire prepared for the devil and his angels" (Matt 25:41). Apocalyptic predictions tend to be bad news. They do offer warnings. But if they intend redemptive warnings, their constructive intent is difficult to discern. Apocalyptic self-assurance may be forgivable, even when not admitted or sought.

JUDGMENT AS REMEDIAL OR AS FINAL?

Foreboding apocalyptic passages predict a just and angry God who has run out of patience. The message of the final Judgment of all humankind is God putting humans on notice of a change in God's traditional approach to humankind. To be sure, Judgment was a familiar concept in Israel's past. Israel's historical prophets were sentinels who warned and threatened divine judgment and exile if the chosen nation violated its covenant calling to serve God as God's chosen people. Initially, God's judgment focuses on nations. In the context of New Testament, judgment extends to individuals as well. And if all humans are to be included in God's Judgment, the many who have died must be restored to life. The effect is God's Judgment universalized. Raising all and judging all constitute two major apocalyptic changes over earlier texts. Given this biblical advance notice, no one living should be surprised or forgetful of what awaits all humans. And may await them sooner rather than later.

God's Judgment, initiated by an inclusive universal resurrection, changes the meaning of death and therefore alters the meaning of life. All the dead shall be raised in order individually and communally to be judged for their moral conduct. That should correct a previously unavoidable injustice: the bad and the good died in a morally unbalanced world. The righteous may have died after a lifetime of poverty and deprivation. Others, who mistreated their fellow humans, may have died after a rich, long and satisfying life. Such existential imbalance of reward and punishment will be corrected by the universal resurrection-inclusive Great or Last Judgment. God's decree will set things right. One and all shall be held to account. Here is a final and inclusive justice after all! "Our" universe will ultimately make moral sense by balancing justice with deserved merit or punishment.

To begin with rewards, as argued above, rewards need not imply self-interest motives. When an act is not focused on the self but on another person, as in compassion for the suffering and needy, victims of injustices, poverty, or helplessness, the witness may simply become forgetful of him- or herself in coming to the aid of such persons. In fact, the Great Judgment text from Matt 25:31–46, discussed earlier in this chapter, may prove relevant here. Unnamed persons were singled out by Jesus for feeding the hungry, offering water to the thirsty, welcoming strangers, visiting prisoners, caring for the sick. Their surprise in being addressed as models means that they did not do it for rewards from God. The text remains mute about their motives. They just did it. No motives cited. And God took these helping acts personally. "Truly I tell you, just as you did it to one of the least of these who are members of my family, you did it to me" (Matt 25:40). Retrospectively and surprisingly—who knew?!—the memory of these caring acts, enhanced by Jesus' acclaim of them, become their rewards. In short, these are rewards that do not call for moral explanations but constitute blessings for whoever acted mercifully, for those who were helped and for those who witnessed and learned.

AN ALTERNATIVE TO APOCALYPTIC FEROCITY

Modern concepts of the nature and meaning of this world differ from biblical worldviews. What had been assumed biblically to be a divinely established order with power and wealth at the top and the poorest of the poor at the bottom now appears as institutional oppression of the poor. Biblical apocalyptic texts were written in pre-modern times. That implies that they assumed premodern convictions about political and social givens or facts. Specifically, early Christians assumed that their human world was hierarchically structured and divinely ordained, that they themselves belonged to the bottom rung of that hierarchy, and that the only remedy for their mistreatment was divine intervention.

In contrast, contemporary or modern Western concepts of political and social values are egalitarian. Human beings are equal in standing, and government should be of, by and for the people. That has the effect of making the present malleable conceptually and improvable practically. In terms of cultural secular assumptions, God drops out of the picture, and economic justice lies within human reach and responsibility. Christians may pray for divine help and blessing in responding to the needs of those least in human standing, but modern political assumptions now should make such aid conceptually humanly possible and imperative. The idea of such improvement of the human condition is a modern concept. That changes the nature of Christian ethics to offer prospects undreamed in biblical times. Such Justice that only God could create now becomes a moral imperative of distributive modern justice. While biblically "you always have the poor with you" (Matt 26:11; Mark 14:7) Western modernity considers that not a given but a moral challenge.

While the severity of apocalyptic texts—eternal damnation for the oppressors and endless enjoyment of the presence of God for the formerly exploited—may be hyperbole, desperate times called for desperate measures. But literally frightening the hell out of hearers or readers, misrepresents the patience and grace of God. Whatever the description of the New Testament's concept of divine Judgment, the nature of that judgment should be compatible with the character of the biblical God. Assuming that God's character reflects God's love and forgiveness in response to human indifference, failure and disappointment, then the cited dark apocalyptic passages (above) are not in fact describing God's decrees but may express resentment of early Christian authors over being unjustly treated by their contemporaries. Or hopeless passages may simply have been well meant hyperboles.

A MODEST VERSION OF PUNISHMENT?

The concept of punishment may well have become the neglected stepchild of Christian ethics. Punishments vary in intensity. Given the example from Matt 25:31–46 (the Great Judgment text), God, ascribing unmerited attention to people of no account, identifies with such losers! Who knew?! In the Judgment of Jesus or in God's eyes, the unconcerned or unmoved become aware of God's care for the least among humans. Those who did not notice the plight of those living on the margins now may see anew and differently. They recognize their own indifference and lack of compassion. Their punishment begins with their regret that they cannot undo the past. Even if they were to be forgiven—by those they neglected and by God whom they alienated by their indifference—their regret remains their punishment as long as memory lasts.

This unorthodox logic of reward and punishment may seem familiar. It should be familiar since everyday helpfulness as well as ordinary indifference recognized too late seem to be well-known experiences. In a constructive version, at some points in one's life one may become aware that the retrospective goodness of good acts lies in the joy of remembering, of having done that! And the pain of moral failings—when finally recognized—lies in the regret that one cannot undo the past or stop remembering. Even when—and perhaps especially when—one has been forgiven long ago.

Forgiving sins remains a key feature of God's character. And that divine character trait resists a God endorsing the apocalyptic recompense envisioned by firm but bitter disciples of Jesus. Theologically, the simplistic, dualistic apocalyptic judgment of saving the good and destroying the bad dismisses the need for and effectiveness of confession, repentance, and forgiveness. Thanking God proves more discerning than apocalyptically dividing saints and sinners into two domains—but rather regards a fallen humanity as universal and offers redemption to sinners.[3]

---

3. I express my gratitude to Professor Mark Allan Powell, professor of New Testament at Trinity Lutheran Seminary, for clarifying dimensions of biblical apocalypticism.

REVIEW

The task has been to reflect on the meaning of the biblical Great or Last Judgment. Human moral responsibility will be judged by God in a universal and inclusive Judgment. Such accountability applies to all human beings, past, present and future. That necessitates God's resurrecting the dead. Anticipating such Judgment should inform and transform human and especially Christian conduct. Much has been assumed in this chapter. Assumed has been that a resurrected person will remember his or her mortal life, that God affirms the life, teaching, and ministry of Jesus, and that the sacrifice of Jesus' life was to forgive and reconcile a sinful humankind with God and with each other. It was taken for granted or again assumed that the character of God—the pattern of divine action over time, all of time—would be consistent. The God of the past remains consistent with the God of a future and a future beyond time. Most important, it has been taken for granted that God loves God's children, humankind, considers them able to return God's love and to love each other, identifies with those who are the least among them as members of God's family and expects Christians to do the same.

Bibliography

"About the Death with Dignity Act." https://www.oregon.gov/oha/PH/PROVIDERPARTNERRESOURCES/EVALUATIONRESEARCH/DEATHWITHDIGNITYACT/Pages/index.aspx.

Anderson, Kenneth N., et al., eds. *Mosby's Medical, Nursing, and Allied Health Dictionary.* 4th ed. St. Louis, MO: Mosby-Year, 1994.

Bok, Sissela. *Lying: Moral Choice in Public and Private Life.* New York: Vintage, 1989.

Borowitz, Eugene B. *Renewing the Covenant: A Theology for the Postmodern Jew.* Philadelphia: The Jewish Publication Society, 1991.

Dorff, Elliot N. "A Methodology for Jewish Medical Ethics." In *Contemporary Jewish Ethics and Morality: A Reader,* edited by Elliot N. Dorff and Louis E. Newman, 161–76. Oxford: Oxford University Press, 1995.

Ellenson, David H. "How to Draw Guidance from a Heritage: Jewish Approaches to Moral Choices." In *Contemporary Jewish Ethics and Morality: A Reader,* edited by Elliot N. Dorff and Louis E. Newman, 129–39. Oxford: Oxford University Press, 1995.

The Episcopal Church. *The Book of Common Prayer.* New York: Church Publishing, 2016.

Falk, Ze'ev W. "Jurisprudence." *Contemporary Jewish Religious Thought: Original Essays on Critical Concepts, Movements, and Beliefs,* edited by Arthur A. Cohen, 512. New York: Scribner's, 1987.

Fletcher, Joseph. *Humanhood: Essays in Biomedical Ethics.* Buffalo, NY: Prometheus, 1979.

Gillon, Raanan. "Is There a 'New Ethics of Abortion?'" *Journal of Medical Ethics* 27 (2001) 5–9. http://dx.doi.org/10.1136/jme.27.suppl_2.ii5.

Hartman, David B. "Halakhah." In *Contemporary Jewish Religious Thought: Original Essays on Critical Concepts, Movements, and Beliefs,* edited by Arthur A. Cohen, 309–16. New York: Scribner's, 1987.

Hauerwas, Stanley. "Abortion, Theologically Understood (1991)." In *The Hauerwas Reader,* edited by John Berkman and Michael Cartwright, 603–21. Durham: Duke University Press, 2001.

———. "Christianity: It's Not a Religion, It's an Adventure." In *The Hauerwas Reader,* edited by John Berkman and Michael Cartwright, 522–35. Durham: Duke University Press. 2001.

Hick, John. *Faith and Knowledge.* New York: Cornell University Press, 1957.

Ignatieff, Michael. *The Rights Revolution.* CBC Massey Lectures. Toronto: Anansi, 2007.

Jersild, Paul. *Spirit Ethics: Scripture and the Moral Life*. Minneapolis, MN: Fortress, 2000.

Kant, Immanuel. "On a Supposed Right to Lie from Philanthropy." In *Immanuel Kant: Practical Philosophy*, translated by Mary J. Gregor, 611–15. New York: Cambridge University Press, 1996.

Lysaught, M. Therese. "Body." In *The Ethics of Sex and Genetics: Selections from the Five-Volume Macmillan Encyclopedia of Bioethics*, edited by Warren Thomas Reich. Rev. ed. New York: Simon & Schuster, 1998.

Maguire, Daniel C. *A Moral Creed for All Christians*. Minneapolis, MN: Fortress, 2005.

National Conference of Catholic Bishops. *Economic Justice for All: Pastoral Letter on Catholic Social Teaching and the U.S. Economy*. Washington, DC: US Catholic Conference, Inc. 1986.

Newman, Louis E. "Woodchoppers and Respirators: The Problem of Interpretation in Contemporary Jewish Ethics." In *Contemporary Jewish Ethics and Morality: A Reader*, edited by Elliot N. Dorff and Louis E. Newman, 140–60. Oxford: Oxford University Press, 1995.

Niebuhr, H. Richard, ed. *Faith on Earth: An Inquiry into the Structure of Human Faith*. New Haven: Yale University Press, 1989.

———. *Radical Monotheism and Western Culture*. New York: Harper, 1960.

Novak, David. *Covenantal Rights: A Study in Jewish Political Theory*. Princeton: Princeton University Press, 2000.

Paul, Richard, and Linda Elder. *Understanding the Foundations of Ethical Reasoning*. 2006.

Perry, Michael J. *The Idea of Human Rights: Four Inquiries*. New York: Oxford University Press, 1998.

Saliers, Don E. *Worship as Theology: Foretaste of Glory Divine*. Nashville: Abingdon, 1994.

Sedgwick, Timothy F. *The Christian Moral Life: Practices of Piety*. Grand Rapids: Eerdmans, 1999.

Shilling, Chris. *The Body and Social Theory*. Newbury Park, CA: SAGE, 1993.

Taylor, Charles. "Democracy, Inclusive and Exclusive." In *Meaning and Modernity: Religion. Polity and Self*, edited by Richard Madsen et al., 181–94. Berkeley: University of California Press, 2002.

Tennyson, Alfred Lord. "The Higher Pantheism." https://www.poetryfoundation.org/poems/45323/the-higher-pantheism.

Thompson, Della, ed. *The Concise Oxford Dictionary of Current English*. 9th ed. Oxford: Clarendon, 1995.

Thompson, Tommy G. "Benefits for the Unborn." *The Washington Post*, February 8, 2002, A30.

Thomson, Judith Jarvis. "A Defense of Abortion." In *Bioethics*, edited by John Harris, 25–26. Oxford Readings in Philosophy. New York: Oxford University Press, 2001.

Turner, Bryan S. *The Body and Society: Exploration in Social Theory*. 2nd ed. Thousand Oaks, CA: SAGE, 1996.

———. "The End(s) of Humanity: Vulnerability and the Metaphors of Membership." *Hedgehog Review* 3 (2001) 7–32.

"Universal Declaration of Human Rights." https://web.archive.org/web/20190105010706/http://www.un.org/en/universal-declaration-human-rights/index.html.

Williams, Simon J., and Gillian Bendelow. *The Lived Body: Sociological Themes, Embodied Issues*. New York: Routledge, 1998.

www.ingramcontent.com/pod-product-compliance
Lightning Source LLC
Chambersburg PA
CBHW050847230426
43667CB00012B/2182